The LEGAL ADVISOR for LIBRARIANS, EDUCATORS, & INFORMATION PROFESSIONALS

PROFESSIONAL LIABILITY ISSUES
FOR
LIBRARIANS
AND
INFORMATION PROFESSIONALS

Paul D. Healey

Neal-Schuman Publishers, Inc.

New York   London

The Legal Advisor for Librarians, Educators, & Information Professionals

No. 1—*The Complete Copyright Liability Handbook for Librarians and Educators,* by Tomas A. Lipinski

No. 2—*Professional Liability Issues for Librarians and Information Professionals,* by Paul D. Healey

Published by Neal-Schuman Publishers, Inc.
100 William St., Suite 2004
New York, NY 10038

Copyright © 2008 Neal-Schuman Publishers, Inc.

Printed and bound in the United States of America.

The paper used in this publication meets the minimum requirements of American National Standard for Information Sciences—Permanence of Paper for Printed Library Materials, ANSI Z39.48-1992.

PLEASE READ THIS

"This publication is designed to provide accurate and authoritative information in regard to the subject matter covered. It is sold with the understanding that the publisher is not engaged in rendering legal, accounting, or other professional service. If legal or other expert assistance is required, the services of a competent professional person should be sought." *From a Declaration of Principles adopted jointly by a Committee of the American Bar Association and a committee of Publishers.*

Library of Congress Cataloging-in-Publication Data

Healey, Paul D.
     Professional liability issues for librarians and information professionals / Paul D. Healey.
          p. cm. — (The legal advisor for librarians, educators, & information professionals ; no. 2)
     Includes bibliographical references and index.
     ISBN 978-1-55570-609-8 (alk. paper)
     1. Librarians—Malpractice—United States.   2. Library legislation—United States.
I. Title.

KF4316.H43 2008
344.73'092—dc22
                                       2008027609

▶Dedication

To Cory
Just for being the best son a father ever had

▶Contents

▶PART I
LIABILITY AND INFORMATION WORK

▶PART III
AVOIDING LIABILITY CLAIMS:
PROACTIVE APPROACHES AND TOOLS

▶ Series Editor's Foreword

As Charles Harmon, the editor at Neal-Schuman Publishers, Inc., and I were discussing ideas for book topics in *The Legal Advisor for Librarians, Educators, & Information Professionals* series, an obvious candidate was a title on librarian liability for torts and related harms. While the topic remains one of importance and concern for librarians there has been little written on the topic in recent years. The clear choice to write this book was Paul D. Healey. Paul's seminal 1995 article ("Chicken Little at the Reference Desk: The Myth of Librarian Liability," 87 *Law Library Journal* 515) is the benchmark of scholarship on the topic. The article is assigned reading in numerous library school courses, including my own Legal Issues for Library and Information Managers class that I teach regularly at the University of Wisconsin—Milwaukee (my home institution) and at the University of Illinois at Urbana-Champaign, where I summer as a visiting faculty member. My constant reference to the article over the years, as well as my many valued conversations with its author, convinced us that an updated and expanded treatment of these topics was long overdue in the literature.

The intersection of the law and libraries has become more pronounced over the last decade. From the USA PATRIOT Act and its reauthorization(s), CIPA, filtering, and First Amendment issues dealing with everything from meeting room allocation to barefoot patrons, to perennial concerns such as copyright and licensing, issues related to tort law and library collections and services continue to persist, not only as topics of abstract discussion in library school classrooms, but as practical issues in the field. This book, then, serves as a preparatory as well as a preemptory work. In the area of tort law related to information sources and services in libraries, questions constantly arise such as:

- ▶ "Can we really be sued for having an out-of-date reference book or for giving out incorrect or incomplete information?"
- ▶ "When does reference service related to legal or medical content cross the line into the unauthorized practice of a profession such as law or medicine?"
- ▶ "We received a letter from a publisher requesting that a copy of one of its books be removed because it contains defamatory or erroneous material—do we have to honor that request?"
- ▶ "Some of the Web sites our patrons access—we don't filter our Internet-accessible terminals—contain all sorts of potentially harmful information, such as how to concoct a 'date rape drug,' make a bomb from products found at the local hardware store, or other content that is pervasively harmful, such as hate speech of some sort. Are we liable if a patron used the library to access the content and then harmed someone with that information?"

As a library educator these past ten years I can attest to the reality that these and similar questions appear with increasing frequency on library-related blogs and lists, through participant questions at conferences, in-services or other training, and from future librarians in the classroom.

Paul Healey has done a masterful job of tackling the jumble of questions that emerge when considering liability (duty, fault, harm, etc.), immunity, and policy decisions inherent in the milieu of issues surrounding the library, librarians, and tort law. As with other books in the series the goal here is to offer practical opportunities grounded in sound legal scholarship. As a lawyer, librarian, and tenured faculty member, Healey is well-positioned to deliver on this goal.

Throughout the text there is a decided focus on organizing the presentation of legal concepts in specific contexts, such as type of information professional (librarian, broker, archivist, curator, etc.), library or entity (public, law, special, etc.), and professional function (reference service, acquisitions, etc.). The first several chapters speak directly to these basic ideas. Healey then talks about the "harm" that might arise through various forms of "errors" as well as other torts, applying legal analysis to assess the likely result under the law. Examples, case studies, and summary points throughout increase the usefulness of the text. Later chapters apply advanced concepts to specific contexts, such as law, medicine, information brokers, and archival and museum environments. The good news of immunity applicable in public employment settings is also discussed. This approach allows each reader to focus on matters directly related to his or her own professional setting. The book concludes on a functional note with a chapter advocating proactive approaches to avoid the legal entanglements discussed in the previous chapters from ever being triggered in your library setting. To further assist the reader the final three chapters cover training suggestions, policy development and implementation, and questions to help your institution conduct its own liability audit.

This book accomplishes two important goals of empowerment. First, it arms the reader with the basic legal concepts necessary to enable any librarian to undertake an independent assessment and conclusion regarding the possibility of professional liability. Secondly, and more important, readers will understand how to ensure that any threat of such liability remains in the remote confines of the hypothetical library school classroom or conference discussion.

This book is the second in this new series on a range of legal topics in libraries, from licensing to liability, from ADA (American with Disabilities Act) access and privacy to an array of protected speech issues, and more. While the number of legal titles published in the LIS area is proliferating, there are still numerous underdeveloped areas, resulting in an imbalance among topics. In addition, the titles are somewhat discordant in style. Furthermore, some still lack truly sound legal scholarship. By grounding practical discussions in expertly informed legal theory, this series seeks to inform future discussions of legal issues in LIS in a way that speaks equally powerfully to the legal and information-professional sides of the equation.

Practitioners in the library or information center in both the private and public sectors—including those serving schools, archives, manuscript and special collections, and, to a lesser extent, museum collections—should find this monograph and others in the series useful. This book, like others in the series, can be viewed as a "what" and as a "how" book: *what* is the law and *how* does it affect us, and *how* do we comply with it and use the law where we can to our advantage. Other administrators within your organization will find this book and others in the series useful as well, from chief information officers to network and computing managers to distance and other education coordinators and even general counsels. Like others in the series, this could also be used in support of library school-related curriculums, as well as serving as a textbook in library law- or possibly information policy- and ethics-related courses.

Each book in the series will follow a similar pattern: presentation of the law and its application through discussion of the law and examples specific to library (in its varied iterations), archive, or educational circumstances; case studies (Q&A or other format); bullet-point summaries concluding each substantive chapter; and compliance or practice tools, such as checklists, audits, model policy or other sample language, such as signage or notices where appropriate, etc. The goal of the series is to provide practical, readable information drawn from sound legal analysis on a variety of specific legal topics. Each title will be based on sound legal scholarship, written by leading experts in the field, and will offer practitioners a useful tool for compliance. As a result, this book accomplishes two additional goals. It serves a tool for creating a compliant environment within your library and its broader institutional context and, as a result, can help create a "law-aware" environment within your organization; thus, it functions as a risk-management device.

Future topics in the series include licensing, digital libraries, use of public library spaces, gifts, and privacy and confidentiality. The series editor and publisher are committed to including in the series only contributions of the highest quality, from contributors who have strong research foundations as well as experience in both law and libraries or related information settings. We hope that you enjoy our efforts and find them useful. We welcome your feedback as well as your ideas for new additions to the series.

Tomas A. Lipinski, JD, LLM, PhD
School of Information Studies
University of Wisconsin—Milwaukee

▶ Preface

When I left the practice of law to attend library school I thought I was leaving the legal world behind. I was amazed, then, at the number of legal issues that arose in my library school classes, and how often I was asked for legal advice or opinions related to the practice of librarianship. It is clear that legal issues, and particularly professional liability issues, are of great concern to librarians and other information professionals. Beginning in library school I began to do research and write on the topic, hoping to find answers to the questions my colleagues were so concerned about. This book is intended to bring those questions and answers together and to function as a clear, comprehensive guide to professional liability issues for librarians and information professionals.

One of the problems with writing in this area is the rampant confusion of topics and concepts that underlie the basic idea of professional liability. We tend to use terms like "liability," "malpractice," and "professional" in casual conversation, but in the legal world these terms have specific meanings and functions that are often not well understood by non-lawyers. Unfortunately, it is not uncommon to find articles in the library literature, written by non-lawyers who confuse or misunderstand legal concepts, and sometimes even give bad advice based on that misunderstanding. One of the primary aims of this book is to help non-lawyers understand the legal terms and issues underlying the concept of professional liability for information professionals. In addition, I hope to help you understand how these issues affect you as an information professional so that you can go about your work in the most effective way possible, and further to help those trying to formulate policy and procedures for information professionals.

We will be talking specifically about professional liability, and not about other legal issues faced by information professionals and libraries. We will not be talking about copyright, or liability for slips and falls in the library, or other legal issues like employment disputes or book challenges. Rather, the purpose of this book is to explore when and under what circumstances a librarian or information professional might personally face a liability claim for his or her professional activities.

In Part I, "Liability and Information Work," Chapters One and Two introduce readers to the concept of professional liability: Chapter One considers liability from the perspective of librarians and other information professionals, and Chapter Two considers the concept from a legal standpoint. Chapter Three looks at the ways in which liability can be expressed in concrete terms, through torts, contracts, and other legal instruments. Chapter Four looks at the obligations and protections specifically available to information professionals, and Chapter Five continues this theme by looking at potential sources of professional liability.

In Part II, "Liability Issues for Specific Segments of the LIS Professions," Chapter Six illuminates the discussion with a collection of case studies. Chapters Seven, Eight, and Nine delve specifically into liability issues affecting legal/medical librarians, information brokers, and archivists/curators, respectively.

In Part III, "Avoiding Liability Claims: Proactive Approaches and Tools," Chapter Ten begins by discussing proactive approaches to liability concerns. Chapters Eleven, Twelve, and Thirteen provide suggestions for developing training and policy-writing procedures, and for conducting a thorough liability audit of your institution. A glossary and index complete the book.

Though liability can be a fraught topic, there is some good news. At the time of this writing no librarian or information professional has been successfully sued and found liable for any normal professional activities. This does not mean that such a suit could never happen, but it does indicate that professional liability should be avoidable in the information professions. How and why it can be avoided is the point of this book.

This book is not intended to provide legal advice of any kind and should not be construed as doing so. If you feel that you have a professional liability problem you should seek the advice of competent legal counsel. Similarly, any policies or procedures about legal issues should be vetted by legal counsel to assure that they meet the legal requirements of your jurisdiction.

►Acknowledgments

First and foremost, many thanks to series editor Dr. Tomas Lipinski, who offered me the chance to write this book and provided so much help and advice along the way. Tom was an early and enthusiastic supporter of my somewhat contrarian views on librarian liability, and over the years has become both a mentor and a friend. During the course of writing this book Tom not only helped edit it but also separately served as a member of my doctoral dissertation committee—a combination of tasks far above and beyond the call of duty. In spite of such demands, he never lost his cheerful demeanor and helpful attitude. Thanks, Tom.

Many thanks also to the wonderful people at Neal-Schuman, particularly editors Paul Seeman and Elizabeth Lund. Their grace and professionalism in the face of missed deadlines and poor first drafts was much appreciated. If patience is a virtue, then the folks at Neal-Schuman are virtuous indeed.

Finally, on a personal level, a big thank you to my dear friend and colleague Dr. Timothy P. Hogan. While not involved in the substantive part of this project, Tim served as a sort of personal coach, exhorting me, calling me on my procrastination, and absorbing with grace my incessant whining about how hard it turned out to be to write a book. He kept me going when I would have given up and believed in me more than I believed in myself. Everyone needs a friend like Tim.

▶Part I

LIABILITY AND INFORMATION WORK

▶One

INTRODUCTION: LIABILITY AS AN ISSUE IN THE INFORMATION PROFESSIONS

1. ESSENTIAL BACKGROUND EXPLANATIONS

We live in a society where legal issues, particularly those of liability, play a large role. By almost any measure, Americans are a litigious bunch, and it sometimes seems that anyone can sue anyone over anything. In reality this is not true, but that does not necessarily stop some people from trying. In such a litigious society, the information professions have not been immune from concerns about professional liability. Some of these concerns are well grounded. Others are not.

The fact is that, as of this writing, no librarian or other information professional has been successfully sued for harm that occurred while providing information to their users or customers. Indeed, one of the recurring themes that you will find in this book is that a successful suit against an information professional for legitimate professional activities appears to be highly unlikely.

1.1 Why This Book?

This raises the question of why we even need such a book as the one you are now reading. There are several reasons why a book like this is important. The first is that a liability claim against an information professional is at least theoretically possible. The theoretical possibility of such a claim does not guarantee that it will ever happen, or be successful, but provides motivation to do what we can to avoid it.

Another reason for this book is that there has been a fair amount written on this topic in library journals and books, and some of that information is misleading. As will be discussed, much of this literature was written by non-lawyers who apparently didn't fully understand the issues they were discussing. While undoubtedly well-intentioned, such writing does more to confuse than illuminate.

1.1.1 Assessing Risk

A third reason is to provide some background and information that can be used to assess liability as a risk to you and your institution. This is problematic, because information professionals make important policy and resource decisions by balancing the needs and desires of their users with the perceived severity and likelihood of various risks. Services offered and resources expended on users are limited when those services are perceived to create a risk, or resources are needed to prevent a risk from resulting in damage to the institution. Liability is a legal risk that can lead to limiting services and diverting resources.

The problem lies, not in determining whether liability is a risk—it is, but in how the risk of liability is being assessed. Any risk can be assessed based on its likelihood and its severity. In other words, you can look at any given risk in terms of how likely it is to actually happen, and how much harm it might do if it did happen. A diagram of how such an analysis would work is given in the example below.

Analyzing risk in terms of likelihood and severity can be done by dividing risks into those that are likely and unlikely, and into those that are severe and not severe. Each risk can then be considered to fit into a category based on these two concepts. Thus, a risk can be likely and severe, likely and not severe, unlikely and severe, or unlikely and not severe. In the example below, several possible risks facing a library are arranged in their relative categories:

Risk assessment	Likely	Unlikely
Severe	Fire in the library	Meteor hits the library
Not severe	Running out of toilet paper	Water fountain broken

In the example, the possibility of a fire in the library is considered both relatively likely, and also potentially severe. For this reason substantial resources should be devoted toward protecting against fire. On the other hand, while having a meteor hit the library would undoubtedly cause severe damage, the likelihood of it happening is very small, and thus devoting excessive resources to this risk would be a waste of resources. In a similar vein, running out of toilet paper in one of the restrooms is fairly likely, but it is easily remedied, and its effects are not severe. The effect of having a water fountain break is also not severe, and it is also relatively unlikely. By looking at risk in this way we can make judgments about the nature and likelihood of risk, and make careful decisions about how to properly allocate library resources and provide services.

There is little doubt that the risk posed by potential liability is severe. Damages awarded to a prevailing plaintiff have the potential to be crippling, and defending any lawsuit, successful or not, can consume an enormous amount of resources. It is therefore not at all unreasonable to be concerned about the severity of the risk of liability. On the other hand, the likelihood of this risk is a wide-open question. Because such liability has never occurred so far, we don't have any good information on which to base an assessment of the likelihood of the risk.

Unfortunately, as we shall see in section 5.2 of this chapter, many who have written about the risk of liability for information professionals have treated it as highly likely. This would indicate that the risk of liability is both likely and severe, making both the limiting of services and the devoting of resources in order to avoid risk a reasonable course of action. For instance, refusing to answer certain kinds of questions at the reference desk, or paying for malpractice liability insurance, would both be reasonable responses to this risk. This is fine, if true. But if the risk of liability for information professionals is not likely, then services are being curtailed unnecessarily, and money is being wasted on unnecessary insurance.

It is vitally important that information professionals have the necessary information required to make informed decisions about the risk of professional liability. This, ultimately, is why this book is important, as it attempts to explain the issues surrounding professional liability for the information professions in a balanced and rational manner. In future chapters we will examine the concept of tort liability, which encompasses the issues of negligence and malpractice, and also look at such areas as contracts and compliance with laws and regulations.

We will also take a specific look at the issues facing each type of information professional, including librarians of all kinds, archivists, information brokers, and curators. We will start, however, by exploring some basic legal concepts that underlie the entire topic of professional liability.

1.2 Playing with Legal Theory

There is a caveat to be raised that applies to this entire book: Much of what will be discussed here involves legal theory. Legal theory is an elastic thing that can be bent and prodded into some amazing shapes. However, the fact that one can theorize something does not mean it can happen. In other words, being able to conceive of a situation where an information professional is held liable for some professional activity does not guarantee that this would actually happen.

On the other hand, the fact that something has never before happened in a court of law, or seems highly unlikely under legal theory, does not mean it is impossible. The law is always changing, and today's certainty can become tomorrow's open question—and vice versa. The best we can do right now is carefully analyze where things stand legally and try to reasonably project how those current positions will change or remain the same in the future.

1.3 Law Is Dependent on Time and Place

Law, by its very nature, is specific to time and place. A law is only enforceable within a particular geographic boundary, known as its jurisdiction. A state law is enforceable throughout the state in question, but not elsewhere. Federal laws apply across the entire country, but not in other countries.

The nature of state law makes it necessary that you familiarize yourself with the laws of your state, or seek competent legal advice about your situation. Every effort has been made to make this book as complete as possible, but there is no absolute guarantee that some precedent or law in a particular jurisdiction did not escape the author's attention.

In addition, law is constantly changing. New laws are enacted all the time, at both the federal and state levels. While laws, once in force, are good law until repealed or otherwise changed, such changes are also quite common. One of the challenges lawyers face is that of making sure that their understanding of the law on a particular topic is up to date. A clear implication of this for this book is that what may have been correct at the time this was written could have changed by the time you are reading it.

Because of this, this book can only serve as a guide to legal concepts. Nothing you read in this book should be considered legal advice. If you have a question about liability, or any other legal issue, you should consult an attorney who can advise you.

1.4 Statutes, Regulations, and Ordinances

Statutes, regulations, and ordinances are forms of law that govern much of our day to day life and can be a source of what we call liability to society. Much of the statutory and regulatory atmosphere of the information professions is beyond the scope of this book, but we can at least examine what these kinds of laws are and how they function.

Statutes are prescriptive laws enacted by a legislative body. State statutes are laws enacted by a state legislature, while federal statutes are enacted by Congress. Statutes can be passed on any subject so long as the content of the statute does not violate the federal or state constitution. This means that, for example, if legislators wanted to make the consumption of coffee illegal they could do so, as there is no protected right to coffee consumption in the constitution. Of course, legislators also have to stand for re-election on a regular basis, so that acts as a constraint on their activities. Legislation affects libraries in many ways, from such federal legislation as the Communications Decency Act, and the Digital Millennium Copyright Act to state legislation on such things as the privacy of circulation records.

Regulations are created by agencies of the executive branch of government. This occurs both at the federal and state level. Regulations are created when a statute, called enabling legislation, orders that regulations be created to carry out the specific aims of the enabling legislation. Regulations are pervasive in our society. Much of our interaction with government, from getting a driver's license to filling out our taxes, is largely performed under the aegis of regulations.

Although statutes and regulations do have a large effect on the operations of institutions in the information professions, there are almost no statutes that would impose personal liability on an information professional for normal professional activities.

Ordinances are laws enacted by local governments. Ordinances can share some or all of the qualities of legislation and regulations. Ordinances sometimes have an effect on libraries, but as strictly local law are far too geographically specific to be within the scope of this book. You may wish to get legal advice on any local ordinances that might affect the practice of your profession or the operation of your library or business.

1.5 Case Law and Common Law

In addition to legislation and regulations, our society is governed by common law, also known as case law. Case law is law that is made by the courts. Courts in America have the power to settle disputes and to interpret the laws and constitution of their jurisdiction. Many activities in society are not directly regulated by legislation or regulations. When a dispute arises concerning such activities, the courts will act to define the law that should apply. They will do this through appellate decisions that determine what the law should be in a given situation. This is case law.

Much of the subject matter of this book is subject to case law. This is particularly true of tort law and contract law. Both of these topics will be addressed at length in later chapters.

1.6 A Note on Terminology

It can be a challenge to talk about the issues described in this book, because many of the terms used have both casual, everyday meanings, and meanings that are legal terms of art. Every effort will be made to make clear in what sense a term is being used in this book, but a few particularly problematic terms are worth mentioning at the outset.

As is explained in section 1 of Chapter Four, the terms "profession" and "professional" are very slippery in their various shades of meaning. They can have a specific legal or sociological meaning, but also tend to be the best terms for a very generic description of a particular occupation, or of activity done at work. Unless indicated otherwise, the following meanings should be assumed:

- ▶ The phrase "information professions" should be taken to be a generic identifier for those occupations that include librarians, information brokers, curators, and archivists.
- ▶ Similarly, "information professional" will indicate a person who works in one of those occupations.
- ▶ "Professional activities" should be taken to mean actions taken while on the job and in the course of employment.

Indications of gender should also be considered to mean all genders, unless otherwise indicated.

2. WHAT IS LIABILITY?

At the outset it is important to ask what liability is, and what function it plays in our society. While the legal details of liability will be discussed in detail in Chapter Two, it is sufficient to say here that liability is the way that an individual can be held responsible by someone else for harm that they have caused. This is achieved by filing an action in a court of law that seeks to hold someone responsible. Liability really is not about blame. Its primary purpose, as a matter of public policy, is to provide compensation for harm on those occasions when some specific person or entity can legitimately be seen as responsible for the harm.[1] In addition, liability can be used to deter future harmful behavior,[2] and in a few restricted situations can be used to punish.[3]

In spite of how widespread lawsuits and liability seem to be in our society, there are still fairly strict standards that have to be met in order to successfully sue someone. These standards, also to be discussed in Chapter Two, mean that it is not true that anyone can sue anyone for anything. As a general rule, liability results when someone is harmed because someone else violated a duty they had to the person harmed. The duty can be something like the duty to follow traffic rules while driving, or the duty to make sure that conditions in your home are safe when you have guests. In the absence of such a duty, even the presence of real harm does not guarantee that someone will be found liable. This is true in the world of professional liability as well.

3. WHAT IS PROFESSIONAL LIABILITY?

It is important to understand what we are talking about when we discuss professional liability. The term covers a variety of legal predicaments. The most prominent, and most misunderstood, is tort liability for professional activities. Tort liability arises when someone violates a duty to another and harm results. Professional tort liability occurs when the harm happens because a professional acted in a way that did not live up to the standards of her profession. One of the most recognizable examples of professional tort liability is a medical malpractice claim. In such a situation, a patient alleges that she was harmed because the doctor treating her failed to follow established medical standards.

A malpractice claim against a librarian or information professional is a very common scenario in the library literature. Malpractice is a specific kind or professional liability, but not the only kind. There are other forms of professional liability as well. The discussion of how this concept relates to information professionals will make up the bulk of the material in this book. In addition to torts, professional liability is concerned with some other forms of legal actions. These can include contract claims, defamation and materials torts, and actions resulting from the violation of statutes and regulations. All such claims have in common that a professional finds themselves being held personally liable for actions taken as part of their work. All of these concepts will be explored in this book.

We should make clear what will not be covered in this book. There are two broad areas that we will not cover. The first is those actions for which you might be personally liable and are related to your work, but not specifically related to the practice of an information profession. An example of this kind of action would be a lawsuit based on a claim of racial discrimination. Such a claim may be work-related and seek personal liability, but it is not related to the practice of librarianship or an information profession. The second category is legal actions against your institution instead of against you as a professional. An example of this would be a lawsuit challenging a library's book selection policies, or a lawsuit based on a slip and fall in the library. Because these actions do not seek to hold someone personally liable for their actions as an information professional, they do not fall within our topic.

4. THE EFFECT OF LIABILITY ISSUES ON BEING AN INFORMATION PROFESSIONAL

Professional liability concerns itself with duty and harm, but refers specifically to liability arising out of the practice of a profession. This raises some interesting issues—issues that will be discussed at length in this book. One distinction worth raising here is that professional liability issues generally do not apply to employees. Employees who are performing duties within the scope of their employment are generally not personally liable when harm results. Professionals can be personally liable, often because they are not in fact employees. As we shall see, it can be very hard to define what a profession is, or who is a professional, and indeed some professionals can be employees and still be subject to professional liability. This will be discussed at length in Chapter Four.

Even if information professionals are professionals in the legal sense, and subject to the laws of professional liability, they are in an interesting position concerning claims of liability. Most professionals who have been faced with professional liability claims provide a service or product that, in essence, takes responsibility for their client's problem. Whether it be treating a disease or fixing a radiator, there is almost always a point where responsibility for solving the client's problem shifts from the client to the professional. It is not at all clear that this is what information professionals do.

Information professionals most often provide information that their users or customers request. In that sense it can be argued that they are solving a problem, but really only in a very limited way. Information professionals generally do not create the information they are supplying to their clients, and except in rare circumstances, they do not guarantee that they are supplying all the information available on the topic. They often do not attempt to judge the quality of the information they find, except in very broad terms. Further, information professionals almost never tell their clients how to use the information they've supplied, nor do they follow through to see if the client's problem was solved by the information.

This limited role that information professionals generally play in the larger problem for which the client is requesting information places them in a unique role, one that may serve to limit the exposure to professional liability risks. One way to look at this is to say that information professionals take a consulting role in dealing with their users, rather than taking responsibility for the user's need or problem.

5. THE STORY SO FAR: THE PRESENT STATE OF LIABILITY FOR INFORMATION PROFESSIONALS

The interesting thing about professional liability issues for information professionals is that there is a large amount of literature on the topic, but very little of the literature has been written by lawyers, or those with legal education or training, who are capable of applying sound legal analysis to the problem. In addition, there is no real legal precedent to guide us on most of the issues that are raised by the specter of liability. Unfortunately, because of the anxiety that the possibility of liability creates, much of the literature is alarmist in tone.[4] While it may seem safe to err on the side of caution, it is better to take a careful analytical view of the situation for appropriate guidance. Much of the information profession literature on liability has been lacking in this approach.

To read the literature in library and information science, one would think that professional liability for librarians and information professionals is, if not already an epidemic, then on the verge of being one. There are a large number of articles claiming that liability is either inevitable or highly likely.[5] These articles espouse a large number of theories, but many of them seem to be based on the pervasive lay person's feeling that anybody can sue anyone for anything, rather than any actual legal theory.

Running against this literature is the simple fact that, as of this writing, no librarian or other information professional has been successfully sued for harm that occurred while providing information to their clients. There are some cases relating to providing information in specific contexts, but their applicability to most information professionals is very limited.[6]

5.1 Searching for Cases

Because so much of the literature addresses the possibility of being sued for reference activities, one would assume that such suits are common. As a result, a first logical step in exploring the nature of professional liability for information professionals is to search for legal cases in which librarians and other information professionals have been sued for their professional activities. This is important for a number of reasons. First it indicates to some extent whether such suits are actually being brought. Second, and more important, any existing cases would show how the law is being applied in such situations. In other words, published cases indicate whether the courts are finding information professionals liable, and under what theories of law. Such cases would be important and informative whether or not they resulted in actual liability for the professional involved.

Within the library science literature, other authors have done searches, to a greater or lesser extent, to see if legal cases exist in which libraries or librarians have been sued for professional activities at the reference desk.[7] None of those authors have reported finding such a case. Although a few authors claim to be referencing a real situation when telling stories about liability actions, none who do so give any details, and their stories cannot be verified. Apart from these few anecdotal offerings, none of the writers discussing the possibility of liability seems to be drawing on actual cases of liability claims.

In order to determine whether any cases exist, a search was conducted by the author on both the Westlaw and LexisNexis legal databases. Both LexisNexis and Westlaw cover all reported state and federal appellate court decisions. A number of searches were run on both LexisNexis and Westlaw that varied in their intent to be specific or broad. The full text of all cases in each database was searched. In addition, a search was performed on the Westlaw Key Number digest system. This system groups case law by topic and allows for more targeted use of search terms. Search precision was elusive given the type of search terms used, and while every search turned up at least some cases, none proved relevant to this topic.[8]

Searches were done using search terms which combined variants of "library" and "librarian," "information," "liability" and "liable," "law," "injury," "negligence," "tort," and "malpractice." All searches utilized the native Boolean search language for the particular service being searched. In addition to online sources, two legal encyclopedias[9] and several established treatises on tort law[10] were also consulted.

The results of all these searches were the same. No reported cases were found in which an information professional has been held personally liable for professional activities. This result is in line with that of other writers on the topic.

There is one caveat to the results of this search. The LexisNexis and Westlaw databases contain appellate cases, but only have a small number of trial court decisions.[11] Because appellate decisions are used as precedent, it is generally only appellate decisions that end up in legal reporters and decision databases. The problem with the American case reporter system is that a lack of reported appellate cases does not necessarily mean that such suits have not been filed, or even litigated and won by one of the parties. There are a number of possible reasons for a potentially significant claim or suit not being published in case reporters. For example, the reporter system would not include suits which were appealed but not designated by the court for publication, suits that were litigated but not appealed,[12] suits that were filed but settled prior to litigation, and claims that were settled before a suit was filed.

While this creates the theoretical potential for extant claims in which information professionals were found liable or admitted liability, in reality it is unlikely that such cases would exist without our being aware of them. As a practical matter, it is likely that any actual suit against a library would have been reported heavily in library news organs and written about in journals related to the information professions. For example, *American Libraries*, the official monthly magazine of the American Library Association, devotes a significant portion of each issue to news from and about libraries across the nation, down to the level of book challenges and controversial firings. This is also generally true for *Library Journal* and other library news organs. It is only logical that any full-blown claim against an information professional for malpractice or negligence would have been reported in such a forum. No such actual news accounts were found in the literature.

In addition, while it is certainly no guarantee that claims have not arisen and been settled without litigation, it is a fact that lawyers have an affirmative duty to protect the interests of their clients. In a case of the type envisioned here, where there is no established case law and where there are significant public policy issues at stake, to capitulate to the demands of a plaintiff whose claim is based on untested legal theory would be irresponsible. Precisely because of the interests at stake, it is unlikely that any information professional represented by competent counsel would settle a claim of negligence or malpractice, and would almost certainly proceed to trial unless the claim was dropped. Once tried, any outcome adverse to the information professional would almost certainly be appealed, and any appellate decision reported. Thus, we can be relatively certain that if any information professional had been found liable, or even if such issues had not been tried and appealed, the case would be reported either in case law or in the literature.

5.2 The Literature

The first article in the library literature to raise the specter of liability for activities at the reference desk appears to be a short piece by Allan Angoff that appeared in *American Libraries* in 1976.[13] The article tells of a hypothetical claim against a library for providing a patron with a book that had inadequate information on building a patio. The patio subsequently collapsed, and the patron was said to be pursuing legal action against the library. There is no conclusion or advice, and the story is apparently intended as a morality tale about the potential legal pitfalls of reference service. The item was printed as if it were a straight news story, except for a note from the editors at the bottom of the page explaining that the item was not about an actual incident.

Angoff's fake news item may have become something of an urban legend in the literature. Another later article cites an unidentified news report of a 1970s Connecticut situation (the Angoff mock news story was set in New Jersey) in which "[a] library was sued because it provided a book containing inaccurate information on a construction project that resulted in injury to the plaintiff."[14] This article goes on to say that the suit was later dropped. Because the source of the news article is not cited, it is impossible to determine whether this was a genuine conflict or a misinterpretation of Mr. Angoff's fable. If this is a separate, actual incident, it is the only one reflected in the literature, but the lack of source documentation in the article makes it impossible to check.[15]

Another article, written for information brokers, takes a similar anecdotal approach.[16] The article starts with the following provocative introduction:

> Malpractice lawsuits can happen to you! It can happen to independent information professionals, like information brokers or consultants, and it can happen to librarians working in traditional settings. I know, because it happened to a friend of mine already.

The author then recounts a tale of an unnamed librarian friend who was being threatened with a lawsuit for not effectively searching for patents. Unfortunately we get no further details, including any outcome to the matter, and the entire story looks suspiciously like a legerdemain intended to set up the thrust of the article. It is worth mentioning, however, that patent searching is a specialized activity that that average librarian or information broker is really not trained to do. As such, patent searching is probably beyond the scope of normal and reasonable activities for an information professional.

A more important question to ask in the face of claims of potential lawsuits is what theory or theories are being put forward in the literature that would indicate thàt liability is possible. This is where some of the literature, much of it written by non-lawyers, raises some questionable and even troubling claims. As an example, one article says that patrons know that they have the right to sue because of actions taken on the basis of inaccurate information provided by librarians.[17] The rise of "consumerism" is also cited, under the reasoning that patrons are more conscious of value and of being cheated or wronged.[18] Another author states affirmatively that because patrons accept what a reference librarian tells them as fact, the patron will sue if the information leads to harm.[19] These are all bold claims, but none are backed up by any reasonable legal theory.

As for why the flood of litigation has not yet hit, some authors have suggested insufficient anger at inaccurate information,[20] although this explanation would appear to directly contradict the theory, put forth by the same authors, that such suits would be based on consumerism. Nasri says librarians have not been sued for malpractice because they are not seen as lucrative targets, or in his terms "not collectible."[21] Interestingly, he cites teachers as an example of professionals who he claims are now getting sued,[22] but does not see any problem with collectibility in their case, although as a group teachers are not significantly better paid than librarians.[23] Generally, collectibility is not an issue when there is the potential for an institutional codefendant, and it strains credibility that this factor is significantly suppressing the number of suits against librarians.

The standards applied in the literature in order to find liability are also diverse. Dunn raises the possibility of libraries being held to a strict liability standard of negligence because they have, as she puts it, "a contractual sort of agreement in which the patron, in seeking information, is tacitly agreeing to accept as available for him to choose to use, the information provided by the library/librarian."[24] She goes on to say that the library "by inference 'says' that the information is accurate."[25] As will be discussed, strict liability has nothing to do with libraries or information professionals, nor is there any basis for interactions at a reference desk being contractual in nature.

By very loosely defining the term "profession" and then by globally attaching the concept of malpractice to any professional activity that is in error, Nasri comes to the conclusion that malpractice suits against librarians are a real possibility.[26] Unfortunately, he presents no legal theory to back up this chain of assumptions. Nasri's main contention in support of potential liability is a syllogism: Professionals can be sued for malpractice, librarians are professionals, therefore librarians can be sued for malpractice. Nasri also claims that the "person who provides the information is liable for the harm caused by it."[27] This is an extremely broad and powerful assertion, and one for which he again cites no legal authority. In fact, this assertion is directly contradicted by the Restatement of the Law of Torts,[28] and by prominent experts in tort law.[29]

Not all of the literature is without legal foundation. John Gray has written an excellent response to the Nasri article. He points out that the relationship between reference librarians and patrons is not contractual.[30] He goes on to say that in order for a reference librarian to be found liable, a patron would have to show that it was reasonable to rely on the librarian as an expert in the particular subject area on which information was sought.[31] This is accurate, and will be discussed at length in later chapters.

The only exception to this, in Gray's view, is when bodily injury results, but he says that the reliance by the patron on the information would have to be reasonable under the circumstances, the librarian would have to have understood that this reliance was taking place, and the librarian would have to be shown to have ignored reasonable care in ascertaining the accuracy of the information.[32]

Martha Dragich has taken both Angoff and Nasri to task on the issue of liability.[33] She points out correctly that, in the Angoff situation, the patron's claim is against the creator of the work (i.e., the author and publisher of the book on building decks) and not the library. If the standard that Angoff posits were to exist, each librarian would need to be able to verify every fact in her collection—an obvious impossibility. In one of the only applicable cases on the subject of the provision of faulty information (dealing with a claim of libel against a video rental store based on information in a rented tape), the California Court of Appeals said that "one who merely plays a secondary role in disseminating information published by another, as in the case of libraries" cannot be held liable unless it knew or had reason to know the information was false.[34] Dragich also points out that malpractice involves the breach of a professional duty that causes actual harm to a client. This is not the same, as Nasri would have it, as guaranteeing a satisfactory result in every transaction. We will explore why this is so in Chapter Three.

In addition to the lack of a viable legal theory for most possible claims against information professionals, the library literature largely overlooks the possible defenses against such an action. These can include a lack of duty of care between the information professional and the user or customer, and a lack of reasonable reliance on the part of the claimant. In addition, until recently none of the literature had raised the possibility of tort immunity for librarians or information professionals employed by public institutions. All of these possibilities will be discussed in this book.

Do not worry if this all leaves you a bit confused. The point of this book is to tease out and explain the various potential legal theories for professional liability for information professionals. In Chapter Two we will look at relevant aspects of liability, including how it functions in our legal system, how it is enforced, how it functions on a personal and institutional level, and how the concept of tort immunity works. Chapter Three will provide an in-depth discussion of tort and contract law, including the nature of torts and negligence, defense to tort claims, contract law, and other legal issues.

With a grounding of the basics of liability and law in hand, we will move on in Chapter Four to look at information professionals and liability and will discuss the whole thorny issue of delineating who is a professional, and what being a professional means in terms of liability, as well as looking at the issue of duty of care as it relates to the information professions. In Chapter Five we will explore specific potential sources of liability for the information professions, focusing on the concepts of harm and error.

From there we move on to look at liability issues from the specific viewpoint of the separate strands of the information professions. Chapter Six looks at liability issues for librarians, while Chapter Seven focuses specifically on the liability problems related to law and medical librarianship. Chapter Eight discusses the liability issues facing information brokers, while Chapter Nine does the same for curators and archivists.

Finally, Chapter Ten will sum up with general advice for avoiding liability, and Chapters Eleven, Twelve, and Thirteen will provide suggestions for training, developing policy, and library audits.

Before we get to all that, we should pause and take a moment to define who exactly these information professionals are that we keep mentioning. The rest of this chapter will do just that.

6. THE INFORMATION PROFESSIONS

This section of the chapter defines, at least for the purposes of this book, who information professionals are and where they work. We will then look at the activities that information professionals engage in and the clientele they engage with, to begin to identify areas that may have legal implications. Subsequent chapters will bring this all together in the context of individual areas of the profession.

Before we do so, a note is in order. The term "information professional" is used throughout this book as a way of identifying the various groups defined below. In doing so, the term is being used in a casual or informal way. The term "professional" can be a loaded one in legal settings (as we will see in Chapter Four) and can have a specific legal meaning. "Information professional" is used in this book as a generic identifier, and is not intended to convey any strictly legal meaning.

6.1 Who We Are

In order to focus our discussion, it is important to understand who we are talking about under the broad rubric of information professionals. For our purposes, information professionals include librarians, information brokers, archivists, and museum curators.

6.1.1 Librarians

Librarians are those who organize, manage, and provide information to users of a particular institution or entity. Most commonly, librarians work in public or academic libraries, in schools, or in companies, firms, or other organizations. While the range of tasks that librarians perform are far too numerous for a single definition, it can be said that librarians collect and maintain information appropriate for their users, and they usually assist users in finding the information they need. Librarians constitute the largest group of information professionals.

Some people make the distinction that in order to be called a librarian one must hold a master's degree in library and information science. There is controversy about this idea, and many people without a master's degree work in libraries and perform the same tasks as credentialed librarians, including rendering reference assistance to users. From a legal perspective this distinction is not important,[35] and in this book the term "librarian" will apply to anyone providing library services.

In terms of liability, the most common scenarios presented in the library literature contemplate some sort of interaction with a library user, such as a reference error. It is conceivable, though, that other areas of library work could have similar risks. We will be considering the issue of liability as it applies to librarians of all kinds. Broadly speaking, this includes public services and technical services librarians in public libraries; school libraries; academic libraries, whether public or private; and librarians in special libraries.

6.1.2 Information Brokers

Information brokers are those who search for and supply information to clients for a fee. A key aspect of this line of work is that the service provided is done for a fee that is paid by the client. As we shall see, this direct, commercial relationship has a large effect on liability issues.

A further issue for many information brokers is self-employment. Many information brokers are self-employed, and as such would not have the protection of employment status when facing a liability claim. For this reason, personal liability is a very real possibility for this branch of the information professions.

6.1.3 Archivists

According to the Society of American Archivists, the primary task of the archivist is to establish and maintain control, both physical and intellectual, over records of enduring value.[36] This work encompasses collecting, storing, preserving and disseminating archival records.

6.1.4 Museum Curators

Curators direct the acquisition, storage, and exhibition of collections, including negotiating and authorizing the purchase, sale, exchange, or loan of collections. They are also responsible for authenticating, evaluating, and categorizing the specimens in a collection.[37]

6.2 Information Professionals and Their Work

Within the context of the individual branches of the information professions, this book will focus on the actual professional activities of information professionals and how those activities are affected by liability. The following sections define this information work, and do so in three broad categories. First, we will look at the users of the services of information professionals, defining who they are and how they relate to the information professional and the institution, and delineate the various issues that arise with different types of users. Second, we will look at the public services aspect of the information professions, and examine the activities involved in directly serving users. Finally, we will look at technical services, and those tasks and activities that are centered on acquiring, organizing, and accessing information.

6.2.1 Relations with the World: Patrons, Users, Clients, and Customers

All of the conceptions of possible liability involving information professionals identify the potential claimant as someone who uses the services of the professional. This is logical for a number of reasons. For one thing, as will be explained in a later chapter, employers cannot sue employees (although they can discipline them or terminate their employment). This book also does not discuss criminal actions by the government to enforce laws. Criminal activity on the part of an information professional would have to be seen as outside the normal appropriate scope of that person's duties as an information professional.

As a result, we are concerned with liability that would arise from our interactions with those we serve: customers, clients, users, patrons, or any other class of persons who receive the services of information professionals. Our relationship with these people can take several forms, depending on the situation.

For purposes of clarity, in this book the term "user" will be used for most people who receive information services. This term can be considered synonymous to "patron" or "client." The only exception to this will be in the case of people who are paying a specific fee directly to the information professional for information or an information service. In that case they will be referred to as "customers."

6.2.1.1 Casual and Public Users

For librarians and other information professionals who work in institutions open to the public, many of the people they serve will be members of the public, or what can be called casual users. Such users have certain qualities in common. Their relationship with the institution is casual in the sense that they are normally not paying a direct fee for access to the institutions or its services.[38] Thus, a member of the public can usually ask a question at the reference desk of a public library without paying a fee, or even needing to prove that they live in the community the library serves. The same would be true for reading a book or magazine in the library's reading room. Checking out materials would normally require a library card, which may in turn require being a resident of the community, but even that would normally be free of a specific fee for that service.

As discussed later in this book, the gratuitous nature of such information services has an important effect on the possibility of liability. As we will see in Chapter Three, gratuitous services are generally granted a much lower standard of care when harm occurs.

6.2.1.2 Institutional Users

Institutional users are those whose relationship with the information professional is the result of their formal relationship with the institution that employs the information professional. This relationship to the institution provides access to the library or information professional, and determines the level and types of services available to the user. The two most prominent types of organizations with institutional users are academic institutions and corporations or firms.

At an academic library institutional users would include the faculty, staff, and students of the academic institution, which could be a school, college, or university. These users have the ability to use the library or the services of the information professional by virtue of their relationship to the institution. The institution may limit or delineate what services are available to particular users based on their relationship. For example, a college library may be willing to obtain materials via inter-library loan for a faculty member, but refuse to do so for an undergraduate student.

Note that institutions such as universities may have casual users as well as institutional users. In the case of a public university, members of the public may be allowed to use the library. These users will still be casual users, however, because they have no relationship to the institution. As such they may be able to have access to the collection while in the library, and may be able to use reference services, but might not be able to get circulation privileges.

The users of corporate and special libraries are almost exclusively employees of the corporation or institution that houses the library. Access to information services is based on this employment relationship. Because in corporate and special libraries users and information professionals are both employees, liability issues are dominated by the implications of that relationship. This will be discussed at length in later chapters.

In rare instances a special library might be open to institutional or casual users. For instance, the library of a professional association might be open to members of the association, and not just employees. In this case such non-employee users would be considered institutional. Similarly, some special libraries might be open to the public, but those users would be considered casual users of the library.

6.2.1.3 Paying Customers

Paying customers are those who are paying a specific fee for information or information services. This is something different from those who indirectly pay for a library or information service by paying taxes or paying tuition. In this case, the transaction between a customer and an information professional is much more like a retail sale; the customer pays a fee for specific information or services. The most common example of this is the services provided by an information broker, who finds and supplies information to customers for a fee. As we shall see, a direct fee for an information service can have an effect on liability issues.

6.2.1.4 Donors

Donors are not users in the normal sense, but can be an important constituency for a library or museum. Donors provide money or materials for use in a museum or library. In the case of money donations, the funds received can be unrestricted, meaning they can be used for any purpose, or restricted, in which the funds must be used for the purpose for which they were donated. Examples of restricted funds include a donation to a building fund, in which case the money can only be used to build a new building, or funds donated for the acquisition of a certain kind of material.

Another very important form of donation is in-kind donations. In-kind donations are donations of specific objects or items for use by the institution. Here again the intentions of the donor are paramount. Some items are donated without restrictions. In such a case the item can be retained, or used in any way the institution sees fit, and can also be sold or otherwise disposed of. In many cases, however, in-kind donations are given with the intent that they be retained and used by the institution. The strings attached to such a donation can create headaches for an institution, and such donations should be handled with care. In some cases it is better to decline a donation, and risk offending a donor, than to accept an in-kind donation the does not fit the institution's objectives or creates other burdens.

6.2.2 Information Work: Public Services

Public services is a broad term that we will use to refer to information services that interact directly with users or customers. Reference services, information brokering, circulation, and displays and exhibitions all come under the rubric of public services.

6.2.2.1 Reference, Information Provision, Information Brokering

The most common example of public services work in the information professions is the direct provision of information at the request of users or customers. In libraries, this takes the form of reference services. Reference covers a broad swath of activities, from providing quick facts and ready reference, to complex research services. In each case the librarian or information professional uses professional judgment to find and supply information that meets the needs of a user. Information brokering is similar, except that the context is that of a customer paying a fee for the information.

6.2.2.2 Circulation

Circulation policies allow library users to check out and use materials away from the library. Many library circulation departments also handle shelving and other stacks related issues. Although circulation is part of public services, most liability issues that arise relate to circulation policies and confidentiality of circulation records. These issues do not involve personal liability. Confidentiality of circulation records are governed by statute, and are beyond the scope of this book.

6.2.2.3 Display and Exhibition

Institutions that collect and display items of interest, particularly museums, must deal with a number of issues related to such display. Sometimes items are donated or sold on the condition that there will be restrictions on how, where, when, or under what circumstances such items can be displayed. Even without such restrictions, under certain circumstances display of some items might violate someone's right to privacy or give rise to a claim of defamation.

6.2.3 Information Work: Technical Services

Technical services include information work that does not directly interact with users. It includes selecting and acquiring materials, cataloging and organizing materials in the collection, archiving and preserving, and curating.

6.2.3.1 Selection and Acquisition of Materials

Selection and acquisition of materials is a core library function. Libraries must strive to achieve maximum impact with limited funds. This requires intelligently selecting materials that are appropriate for the collection, and managing the process of acquiring those materials. Although not a source of personal liability, selection decisions are common sources of controversy. Book challenges are a fact of life for public libraries because of the diverse range of opinions and beliefs in any community. In academic settings, faculty and other stakeholders can demand materials that exceed the funds available for acquisition, leading to political battles over the collection.

6.2.3.2 Cataloging and Organizing

Cataloging is the process of identifying materials by topic and arranging them within the collection. Cataloging is complicated and difficult, but it is not a source of personal liability.

6.2.4 Archiving

Archiving is the process of collecting and preserving materials enduring value. As with museums, donations or acquisitions can commonly be made with conditions, including how much of the materials are to be preserved, and how access to the material is to be allowed. This can create a complex landscape for the archivist. As with libraries, archivists may find themselves being offered items that do not fit the mission of the archives, that do not have the value that the donor believes they do, or that are so burdened with restrictions that they are not worth the trouble of adding to the collection. In addition, such issues as provenance and good title, private information in the collection, and copyright can create liability issues for archivists and curators.

6.2.5 Information Brokering

Information brokering is the process of selling information and information services. Typically used by businesses, information brokers will conduct research on request, producing information for use by the customer. The customer will pay a fee for this service. Information brokers handle a wide variety of tasks, from exhaustive studies of a topic to competitive intelligence.

6.2.6 Curating

Curating is the process of selecting items for display in a museum or exhibit, and of caring for items that are part of a collection. Curators generally must know much about the items in the collection and their context in the world of such items. Curators are often called upon to assess the value of items, both monetarily and culturally, and to create displays that advance the understanding of those viewing the exhibit.

7. IMPORTANT POINTS ABOUT THIS BOOK

▶ The purpose of this book is to inform, not advise. Nothing in this book should be considered legal advice. Consult an attorney for guidance on your particular situation.

▶ When discussing professional liability we are concerned with the possibility of personal liability for professional actions. Institutional liability is not covered in this book.

▶ This books attempts to analyze the risks of professional liability using established legal theory. Because no actual professional liability claims have been litigated against information professionals, the results of the analysis are necessarily speculative.

8. HOW TO USE THIS BOOK

This book is intended as a general guide on liability issues for information professionals. It will give you a basic idea of how the law works, and point to liability issues for the information professions as a whole, and for specific branches of the professions. Here are some suggestions about using this book:

▶ Chapters One through Five provide the basic background required to understand and analyze the legal issues faced by all information professionals. Most, if not all, readers of this book would benefit from reading those chapters.

▶ Chapters Six through Nine each relate to a specific branch of the information professions. While each of these chapters might provide information or be of interest to all readers, if you work in a specific branch of the profession, you should be able to glean the most relevant information for your situation by reading only those chapters that relate directly to your work.

▶ Chapter Seven relates specifically to law and medical librarianship, but is intended for any librarian or information professional who deals with legal or medical information requests, even just occasionally.

▶ Chapters Ten through Thirteen provide proactive ideas for avoiding liability and have sections relating to each of the information professions. They should be of interest to all readers.

▶ The information in this book is intended to help you understand liability issues, and begin to plan how you will control potential liability in your professional activities. It is only intended to be, and can only be, a broad and basic beginning to your knowledge on this topic.

▶ **If you have questions about potential liability for your professional activities, or on any other legal topic, you should seek legal advice from a licensed attorney in your area. Nothing in this book should be considered legal advice. The purpose of this book is to inform and educate, and nothing in it should be relied on without consulting competent legal counsel.**

ENDNOTES

[1] Dan B. Dobbs, *The Law of Torts* § 1 (2001 & Supp. 2004).

[2] *Id.*

[3] *Id.*

[4] See, e.g., Allan Angoff, *Library Malpractice Suit: Could It Happen To You?* 7 American Libraries 489 (1976); Susan Dunn, *Society, Information Needs, Library Services and Liability,* 26 Iowa Lib. Q. 18 (1989); Carol Ebbinghouse, *Disclaiming Liability,* 8 Searcher 3 66–71 (March 2000); William Z. Nasri, *Malpractice Liability: Myth or Reality?* 1 J. Lib. Admin. 4 (1980).

[5] As an example, all of the articles cited in the previous note ascribe to this theory.

[6] There are two examples of successful suits over supplied information, but neither involved a librarian or information professional. One was a suit against a publisher, the other was a suit against a video store. Some authors have reasoned by analogy to apply these cases to librarians and information professionals.

[7] *E.g.,* Dunn, *supra* note 4; John A. Gray, *Personal Malpractice Liability of Reference Librarians and Information Brokers,* 9 J. Lib. Admin. 74 (1988); Gerome Leone, *Malpractice Liability of a Law Librarian?* 73 Law Lib. J. 45 (1980); Thomas Steele, *Liability of Librarians for Negligence,* 26 Public Librarian 8 (1987).

[8] Often the cases returned related to prisoner conflicts over access to a law library, or a library was party to a suit involving such things as employment discrimination, conflicts over building repairs, or lease problems.

[9] Corpus Juris Secondum and American Jurisprudence 2nd.

[10] Dobbs, *supra* note 1; Fowler W. Harper, et al., *The Law of Torts* (2nd ed. 1986); William R. Prosser, *Law of Torts* (4th ed. 1971).

[11] Under current judicial rules, only cases which are so designated by a court are published, and only published cases have value as precedent. Thus, the case reporter system, which is what the relevant portions of LexisNexis and Westlaw consist of, contains only those cases that can serve as precedent for other cases in the relevant jurisdiction. Most, but not all, reported cases are appellate cases, meaning they are the decision of an appellate court. It is this decision, and not the original trial court findings, which is used as precedent. Increasingly, unreported cases are also included on LexisNexis and Westlaw, and were thus searched along with the published cases.

[12] Some federal district court cases and some trial court decisions in certain states are reported. This is the exception rather than the rule, but to the extent it happens it strengthens the reliability of the search.

[13] Angoff, *supra* note 4.

[14] Steele, *supra* note 7.

[15] Such a case did not turn up in the research done for this book, but if the case was dismissed before trial it is not likely to have been published in any legal case reporter. That said, it also does not appear anywhere else in the library literature.

[16] Ebbinghouse, *supra* note 4.

[17] Dunn, *supra* note 4.

[18] Nazri, *supra* note 4; Dunn, *supra* note 4.

[19] Nasri, *supra* note 4, at 3. Nasri also sees the possibility of personal liability for library directors and trustees under the legal doctrine of respondeat superior. He fails to understand that this doctrine, which can make an employer liable for the misdeeds of an employee, applies at the institutional level. A director or trustee would not be personally liable unless they were personally involved in the incident which was the subject of the claim.

[20] Dunn, *supra* note 4, at 20; Nasri, supra note 4, at 4.

[21] Nasri, *supra* note 4, at 4.

[22] *Id.*

[23] Median annual earnings of kindergarten, elementary, middle, and secondary school teachers ranged from $43,580 to $48,690 in May 2006. As of May 2006 nonsupervisory librarians of all kinds taken together earned an average of $49,060. *Occupational Outlook Handbook, available at* http://www.bls.gov/oco/ (last visited June 29, 2008).

[24] Dunn, *supra* note 4, at 20 n.4.

[25] *Id.,* at 20.

[26] Nasri, *supra* note 4, at 5.

[27] *Id.*

[28] *Restatement (Second) of the Law of Torts,* 552A (1977). Restatements are publications by the American Law Institute (ALI). ALI is composed of prominent legal scholars, practitioners, and judges, whose task is to summarize and state the law in all jurisdictions.

[29] See, e.g., Dobbs, *supra* note 1, at 472; Harper, *supra* note 10, at 7.7; Prosser, *supra* note 10, at 105.

[30] Gray, *supra* note 7, at 74.

[31] *Id.*

[32] *Id.,* at 77.

[33] Martha J. Dragich, *Information Malpractice: Some Thoughts on the Potential Liability of Information Professionals,* 8 Info. Tech. & Lib. 265 (1989).

[34] *Osmond v. EWAP, Inc.,* 153 Cal. App. 3d 842 (1984).

[35] The one situation in which credentials could become important is in the debate on whether or not librarians are professionals. This topic is discussed at length in Chapter 4.

[36] *Available at* http://www.archivists.org/prof-education/arprof.asp (last visited June 29, 2008).

[37] *Occupational Outlook Handbook, available at* http://www.bls.gov/oco/ocos065.htm (last visited June 29, 2008).

[38] Taxpayers can argue that they pay for the services of a tax-supported library. The word "fee," however, connotes a direct payment for a specific service or product. Paying taxes is not the sort of direct payment that is encompassed by the concept of paying a fee.

►Two

UNDERSTANDING LIABILITY

IN THIS CHAPTER

We take a look at basic legal concepts necessary for a thorough understanding of professional liability issues. These include:
► An explanation of the concepts of public and private law
► The concept of liability to society and liability to others
► The difference between civil and criminal actions
► The different roles of federal and state law
► Pursuit of remedies when liability occurs
► The concept of immunity

1. WHAT IS LAW?

No society could function without a system of laws with which to regulate affairs and interactions. Law, by its very nature, has the ability to compel each of us to conform our behavior to certain standards or rules, and to punish us in various ways when our behavior strays from those standards. A basic part of this concept is liability. Liability is defined as "[t]he quality or state of being legally obligated or accountable; legal responsibility to another or to society, enforceable by civil remedy or criminal punishment".[1] The essential elements of the concept of liability include our obligations to others, and the ability of society to enforce those obligations.

Liability takes a number of forms in our society, and is part of a complex body of what is known as public and private law. Public law is law in which the government acts in the interest of society. The most common form of public law is a criminal prosecution, in which the state prosecutes someone who has broken the law, doing so in the interest of society. Private law consists of legally enforceable obligations between individual private parties. These private parties may be individuals, groups, corporations, or even the government, but in each case they are a party to some sort of agreement or obligation that can be enforced at law.

Example: Public Law

One night two vandals break into a public library. While in the library they spray-paint profanity on the walls, break several computers, and pull many books off the shelves. The police arrive and arrest them. The vandals are charged with a crime, prosecuted by the state, convicted, and sentenced to pay a fine and serve a jail term. The library has no involvement in the prosecution, and does not receive any part of the fine, which goes to the state. This is an example of public law, in which the wrongdoer is prosecuted by, and answers to, society. Although the library was the victim, it is not a party to the criminal action.

Example: Private Law

As a result of the vandalism, the library must pay to replace the broken computers and repaint the damaged walls. The library must also pay overtime to several employees to reshelve all the books that were pulled off the shelves. The library decides to sue the two vandals to recover the money it cost to do the repairs. This is an example of private law, in which someone can use the courts to get damages for harm that was caused by another. The lawsuit is solely between the library and the two vandals. The government and society are not a party to this action.

When discussing professional liability we will be dealing with private law. While it is possible that information professionals could run afoul of some government regulation or law during the course of their work, we are mostly concerned with being held liable by another person or entity. For example, when a reference librarian is worried that she will be sued for giving out incorrect information, or an information broker is concerned that he has not found all the information his client needs and that he might face liability as a result, in both of these situations the concern is that someone will pursue liability as a matter of private law.

1.1 Liability vs. Guilt and Civil vs. Criminal

The public and private forms of liability tend to operate in two separate legal systems: the criminal and the civil. The criminal legal system handles those issues that involve liability to society. A person found liable in the criminal system is termed guilty. The system in which people can pursue claims of liability directly against another person is called the civil law system. In that system someone who is found to have violated a duty is called liable.

While only the government can pursue a criminal action, not all government enforcement is criminal in nature. There are instances in which the government might proceed against a private party as a civil litigant. In this case, the government is a party trying to resolve a dispute with another party.

In civil, or private, law the most common cases arise either under contract law or tort law. Contract law is the law of agreements between parties. Parties to a contract are legally obligated to carry out the terms of the agreement, and failure to do so can be enforced in court. Tort law is the much broader area of law in which a party can seek redress for various types of wrongs or harm. Tort law covers everything from seeking damages for injuries suffered in a car accident, to suing a doctor for malpractice, to pursuing a claim of slander or libel, and much more.

1.2 The Role of Federal and State Law

In America we must deal with both federal and state law. The federal government makes laws in areas that are delineated in the U.S. Constitution. Although a full description of the purview of federal law is far beyond our scope, suffice it to say that federal law applies to areas specifically listed in the constitution, such as copyright or bankruptcy; the protection of individual rights under the U.S.

Federal Law

Bill has been copying music CDs using a library computer and using peer-to-peer software to distribute the music to others over the Internet. A record distributor discovers that John has been copying and distributing music they own the rights to. They sue Bill for copyright infringement. Since copyright is specifically mentioned in the U.S. Constitution,[2] copyright is a matter of federal law,[3] and the action against John would take place in a federal court.

State Law

The library, in the hope of preventing further CD copying on library computers, signs a contract with a local computer store to provide software and monitoring services that would detect copyright violations. The store requires partial payment in advance from the library, but after receiving the payment does not do the work or provide any software. The library decides to sue the store over the breach of the contract, seeking the return of the advance payment. Contract law is a state law matter and is governed by state statutory and common law,[4] so this action would take place in a state court.

Constitution, including claims of discrimination; and instances where the federal government as an entity has an interest in an issue.

All other areas are matters of state law. These include those areas that affect professional liability, including the law of contracts and torts. State law can be, and often is, different from state to state. This makes any discussion of professional liability much more complicated. If, for example, the Illinois Supreme Court were to decide that reference librarians can be sued when they give out information that contains errors, this would affect librarians in Illinois but not librarians in other states. In order for librarians in Iowa or Florida to be subject to this precedent, it would first have to be adopted by the courts in their states. Such adoption is not automatic, or in any way a foregone conclusion.

2. LIABILITY TO SOCIETY

Often when people think of the force of law, they are thinking of the ability of government to force us to comply with laws and to punish us for transgressions. This form of liability is to society, and the person answers to the state directly. For example, someone who vandalizes library property might be charged with criminal damage to property and is liable to the state for that crime. The vandal may have other liabilities to the victim (see below), but in paying for his crime he answers to the state. Violations of written laws or regulations are almost all situations in which the violator is liable to society. The key idea is that the government, in acting against the accused, is representing the interests of society as a whole.

2.1 Criminal, Civil, and Regulatory Liability

The most common situation in which one thinks of being liable to society would be for violating a criminal law. Criminal laws are intended to proscribe activities that, in essence, harm society when they take place, and require society itself to pursue liability for the offender. Such actions include many activities seen as generally wrong, ranging from murder and theft to drug possession and even speeding. As mentioned, criminal liability does not preclude a victim from pursuing civil liability for the same act, but the criminal action takes place between the accused and society.

Civil liability occurs between two private entities or persons. A common example of civil liability is litigation over a car accident. After the accident, one of the parties files a lawsuit claiming that the other party was responsible for the accident and therefore for the damages that occurred as a result. The litigation occurs between the two parties, and the state is not involved, other than providing the court system as the forum for deciding the dispute. Civil actions can result in monetary damages and certain forms of injunctive relief, but not imprisonment. Prison or jail sentences are only possible in criminal law.

Regulatory liability occurs when a person or entity violates a governmental regulation. In certain circumstances the government, in its role of serving the interests of the people, can pursue liability in civil court and as a regulatory body. Government agencies create and enforce regulations in the areas of their concern, and have the ability to enforce those regulations in court. For example, your state's Department of Environmental Quality might have regulations against storing large numbers of tires on private property without a permit. If your neighbor has stored many tires in his back yard, the DEQ could enforce their regulations by taking your neighbor to court. This would be a civil action for regulatory enforcement, as opposed to a criminal action, and the intended outcome would be to force your neighbor to clean up his yard, and perhaps pay a fine.

3. LIABILITY TO OTHERS

Our society also has a system of law that provides for direct liability of one person to another. This form of liability occurs when a person fails to follow an established duty of some kind and is liable to another person who was harmed by that failure. The most common examples of this are torts and contracts. Each of these forms of liability will be examined at length in this book.

It is important to understand that while the violation of a law and resulting liability are intertwined, they are not the same thing. As an example, let us assume that, while driving, you fail to stop at a stop sign. The fact that you failed to stop at the stop sign is a violation of traffic laws, and you can be punished for this violation—say, by receiving a citation and a fine—regardless of whether any harm resulted from your actions. If you caused an accident by running the stop sign, any people who suffered harm in the accident can sue you for their damages, based on your failure to fulfill your duty to stop at a stop sign. Note that they can do this, regardless of whether you were ever cited or punished by the state for violating the traffic laws. Even if you were not cited, if the plaintiffs can establish that you failed to stop at the stop sign, and that this resulted in their harm, they have established that you violated a duty and that you are therefore liable.

3.1 Contract: Undertaken Duties

Contracts are agreements that are legally enforceable. Because of their legally enforceable nature, a contract carries with it the risk of liability when its terms are violated or not fulfilled. In order for a contract to be legally enforceable, the agreement it contains must have certain qualities. The most important of these is that the agreement is voluntary. As a result, the duties implied by a contract are undertaken duties. This means that they are voluntarily assumed, as opposed to those duties imposed on us by society. Contract law, and the potential for liability that it creates, will be discussed in more detail in Chapter Three.

3.2 Tort: Relational or Imposed Duties

Tort law relates to our duties to others, and the ability of private parties to seek compensation when they incur harm because those duties are not fulfilled. Unfortunately, some of the basic concepts of tort law in America are widely misunderstood. It will serve us well to define some basic terms and explore basic tort law concepts before we begin to describe how they affect information professionals.

A tort is often defined as a civil wrong. A tort occurs when someone fails in a duty to another and harm occurs as a result. A common example of this is a car accident. When someone fails in his duty to obey the rules of traffic, and in doing so causes an accident, he has committed a tort for which he can be found liable. The most commonly known torts in America are personal injury and property damage claims. These arise from car accidents, slips and falls, and other situations where property is damaged or injury occurs because others failed in their duty to conduct themselves in a safe manner or keep a safe premises.

While personal injury and property damage torts are best known, there are many other forms of tort, and these will be discussed in Chapter Three. The main point to understand about torts right now is that the duty is imposed rather than by agreement. When you decide to drive your car you undertake the duty to do so safely, and risk liability if you do not, whether or not you agree to. The duty is inherent in the act. Similarly, if you invite guests to your house, you have a duty to keep the surroundings reasonably safe for them. If you fail to do so, you may be liable for any injuries to them that result because you failed in your duty to keep the premises safe. These imposed duties are also relational, as they arise out of your relationship to the other party; for example, as a driver your relationship to other drivers on the road, or as a host to your guests.

4. PURSUIT OF REMEDIES FOR LIABILITY

When harm occurs for which someone is liable, society provides specific mechanisms for pursuing remedies for the harm. The appropriate remedies for civil liability will be determined by the court, but can include monetary compensation, and various forms of injunctive relief. The appropriate mechanism for pursuing a remedy is determined by the nature of the harm and the relationship of the parties.

4.1 Pursuit of Remedies by the Victim

With most tort or contract claims it is up to the person harmed to pursue the claim. This is done by filing a lawsuit in court alleging the harm that the defendant has caused and requesting damages. There are significant obligations on the claimant in making this happen. It is up to the claimant to be aware of the harm and gather the necessary facts on which to base the claim. She must find an attorney who will take the case on her behalf. Once retained, it is very common for the attorney to negotiate with the defendant in an attempt to settle the case without bringing suit. This is often a successful procedure, but if it is not, the plaintiff must act by filing a lawsuit.

In most jurisdictions plaintiffs must file their action within a certain period of time, commonly referred to as the statute of limitations, or they lose the right to pursue the claim. Statutes of limitations vary from state to state, and can also be different for different types of claims. As an example, in Illinois, a lawsuit over a personal injury claim must be initiated with two years after the injury,[5] and a defamation claim must be initiated within one year,[6] while a suit over a contract claim can be initiated any time within ten years after the harm occurred.[7]

Once the suit is filed and the defendant notified of the case through a procedure called service of process, then both parties must meet certain requirements of the court. One of these requirements is that of producing evidence for review by the other side, called discovery. Discovery takes a number of forms, and can include the examination of documents and physical evidence, as well as questioning potential witnesses.

Witnesses can be questioned in person, or by being required to answer written questions. The process of questioning witnesses in person is called a deposition. In a deposition, the plaintiff, the defendant, and any witnesses may be questioned under oath by attorneys for both parties. Written questions are referred to as interrogatories. They are presented to the witness to be answered, and the witness must attest that the answers are truthful and complete.

Throughout the process of discovery, negotiations for a settlement will often continue. The vast majority of lawsuits are settled before trial.[8] If not, the plaintiff is entitled to a court trial, which will be heard and decided either by a judge or by a jury, at the defendant's option. At the conclusion of the trial, the judge or jury will decide either in favor of the plaintiff or the defendant, and, if the judgment is for the plaintiff, will determine the amount of damages to be paid by the defendant. Once this judgment has been entered, the plaintiff will have the right to collect it. If the defendant refuses to pay all or part of the judgment, the plaintiff can use the power of the court to seize property belonging to the plaintiff in order to satisfy the judgment.

4.2 Pursuit of Remedies by the State

Contrast this civil action with the procedures when the state is responsible for pursuing a case. The most common examples of such situations are criminal cases and regulatory enforcement actions. In a criminal case, the victim is not responsible for pursuing the case or bringing an action, beyond reporting the crime if no one else has done so. The police will investigate the alleged crime. Once the police determine a crime has taken place, they will then turn the matter over to prosecutors, who will pursue criminal charges against the defendant on behalf of the state. Often in a criminal case the victim is merely a witness and has no other role. The state prosecutes the defendant and enforces the judgment if a conviction is obtained. Once convicted, the defendant may be incarcerated, or forced to pay fines. If fines are ordered, the money paid goes to the state, and not to the victim.[9]

4.3 Pursuit of Remedies by Employers and Institutions

Pursuit of remedies by employers or institutions is not part of the formal legal system of liability, but it should be mentioned as an enforcement mechanism when discussing professional liability. Whether or not an information professional's activities can ever rise to the level of legal liability, employers can effectively create liability through discipline or loss of employment. This is especially true if the employer feels that actual legal liability is a possibility. Employers are fully within their rights to discipline employees who make mistakes or do not meet standards, whether those are the standards the employer has for the job, or those it perceives to be the standards of the profession. Unlike the civil or criminal liability systems, there are no standards of proof or necessity of harm for an employer to act against an employee.

5. INSTITUTIONAL LIABILITY

Often, when harm occurs within the premises of an institution or as the result of the actions of an employee, it is the institution itself that will be held liable. This is partly because of the doctrine of respondeat superior, a legal term that means that employers are responsible for the actions of their employees. This concept will be addressed below, and at length in Chapter Four.

5.1 Claims Against the Institution but Not the Professional

A number of common types of tort claims that do not specifically involve the actions of an employee can be made against an institution. These actions are beyond the scope of this book but will be briefly outlined here to add to your understanding of tort law.

5.1.1 Premises Liability

Premises liability is liability that arises because of conditions within the physical location (or premises) of a given entity or institution. Although premises liability can take many forms, the most common are injuries that result from unsafe conditions that lead to harm. Common examples are broken steps or slippery floors that cause people to fall, improperly stored items that fall and injure someone, or poor lighting around a building that causes people to trip and fall. Premises liability is an issue for any business or institution that is open to the public, and is in no way unique to libraries, museums, or the information professions in general.

Note that the claimant in a premises liability case will be someone from outside the institution, such as a customer, patron, or visitor. Employees cannot sue their employers for injuries on the job. Instead, employees can seek recourse for injuries through the workers' compensation system.[10] This system was statutorily created with the specific intention of preventing employees from suing their employers for injuries on the job.

5.1.2 Institutional Policies and Actions

Institutions can also be sued for actions or policies that cause harm. Once again, it would not be an individual employee being sued, but the institution itself. For example, a library user who has been forced to leave the library because of body odor problems might bring suit asking for the policy to be changed. Similarly, a group denied access to the library's meeting room might claim that the policy is discriminatory.

5.1.3 Discrimination and Other Claims

A claim of discrimination would generally be brought against the institution as a whole, even if the claimed discriminatory behavior occurred at the hands of a particular employee. Discrimination claims are governed by federal law and often by state law as well; they must be pursued in accordance with those laws. Discrimination law is another area that is beyond the scope of this book.

5.2 Claims Against Both the Institution and the Professional

It is entirely possible for claim to be made both against an institution and a professional at the same time. For example, a patient who is injured during surgery could very likely sue both the doctor who performed the surgery, and the hospital where the surgery took place. The question of whether this is proper depends on the status of the professional involved and the nature of the act that is claimed to have led to harm. This will be discussed in detail in Chapter Four.

5.2.1 Employer Liability for Employee's Actions (Respondeat Superior)

It is a settled doctrine of tort law that an employer is responsible for the errors of an employee, as long as the employee's actions occurred in the course of his duties. This doctrine, sometimes referred to by the Latin term "respondeat superior," the superior must respond, also means that employees are generally shielded from personal liability for harm that occurs on the job. Thus if a janitor in a public library spills water on the floor while cleaning, and a library user slips in the water and is injured, the janitor will not be personally liable for the harm, because cleaning is part of his normal duties as janitor.

There are some limits to this concept. One is that the activities that led to the harm must be part of the person's assigned duties, sometimes called the scope of employment. If the library janitor is pursuing a side occupation by using his workspace to repair electronic devices for members of the public, and does so without the knowledge of his employer, he would be personally liable for any claims that arise out of that activity because it is beyond the scope of his employment.

The doctrine of respondeat superior comes into question when a professional is involved. For the professions that have faced professional liability claims, especially licensed professions such as law and medicine, employment status does not shield the professional from a tort claim. This is discussed in more detail in Chapter Four.

5.2.2 Res Ipsa Loquitur Claims

Sometimes harm can occur in a situation where it is impossible for the person harmed to determine the specific circumstances under which harm occurred. Under the doctrine of Res Ipsa Loquitur, the plaintiff can pursue a claim against the defendant without needing to first show specifically how the harm occurred.

"Res ipsa loquitur" is a Latin phrase meaning "the thing speaks for itself." In tort law, it is a doctrine that comes into play when the plaintiff's injury and the immediate events surrounding it can by themselves show negligence, even though the plaintiff is unable to prove any specific act that was unreasonably dangerous.[11] As such it serves as circumstantial proof of negligence. The idea is

---

Example: Res Ipsa Loquitur

A classic example of a res ipsa loquitur situation occurred in California in 1944 in the case of Ybarra v. Spangard.[12] In this case, the plaintiff emerged from anesthesia after an appendectomy with an unexplained and disabling injury to his shoulder. He sued the doctors and nurses involved in the operation on the theory that the injury must have happened during surgery. The trial court dismissed the action, saying that without a better idea of who did what during the operation and what exactly happened to the plaintiff's shoulder, there was no sustainable claim to be pursued. The California Supreme Court overruled the trial court decision based on the doctrine of res ipsa loquitur. In its decision, the Supreme Court said that "where a plaintiff receives unusual injuries while unconscious and in the course of medical treatment, all those defendants who had any control over his body or the instrumentalities which might have caused the injuries may properly be called upon to meet the inference of negligence by giving an explanation of their conduct."[13]

that if the conditions are such that it is more likely than not that the harm occurred as a result of negligence by the defendant, the defendant can be found liable, even if the plaintiff lacks the means to prove exactly where the harm occurred.

5.2.3 Joint and Several Liability

Joint and several liability means that all of the defendants in a lawsuit are responsible for their share of the damages, at the same time that any one or more of the defendants can be responsible for the entire damages. This means that if a group of defendants is found liable and a judgment for damages is won, the plaintiff can pursue all of the defendants for payment, or can seek the entire judgment from any one or more defendants. This allows the plaintiff to collect the damages from any of the defendants who have the ability to pay without regard to that defendant's actual share of the damages. In turn, a defendant who ends up paying more than his share will generally have the right to seek compensation from nonpaying defendants. This is called a right of contribution and indemnity.

Example: Joint and Several Liability

On a winter night a library user falls and injures herself on ice in the library parking lot. The library has contracted with a private snow removal company to clear the parking lot of ice. The injured person sues both the library and the snow removal company for her damages. At trial, the jury finds that the library was 30 percent responsible for the plaintiff's injuries, and the snow clearing company was 70 percent responsible. The plaintiff is awarded $100,000 in damages, with 30 percent to be paid by the library, and 70 percent to be paid by the snow removal company.

After the trial the library pays the plaintiff $30,000, or 30 percent of the total award, thereby satisfying their part of the damages. When the plaintiff tries to collect the remaining 70 percent from the snow removal company, they find that it only has $30,000 dollars available to pay its part of the judgment. Under joint and several liability the plaintiff can choose to get the remaining $40,000 of damages from the library, even though the library has already paid its share of the award. Once the library has paid the additional amount, it will have the right to try to collect the extra $40,000 it paid from the snow removal company under its right of contribution and indemnity.

6. TORT IMMUNITY

In certain circumstances someone could commit a tort—that is, fail in a duty that causes harm to another—and still be free of liability, for the simple reason that she cannot be held liable, regardless of her fault. This concept, referred to generally as immunity, is conferred upon certain groups as a matter of public policy, or in some cases by statute. In civil matters, most commonly immunity is extended to government officials and employees acting in their official capacities.

The presence of an immunity means simply that the intended defendant cannot be sued. This is true regardless of fault, or of any other issue present in the claim. To quote one source: "An immunity is a defense to tort liability which is conferred upon an entire group or class of persons or entities under circumstances where considerations of public policy are thought to require special protection for the person, activity or entity in question at the expense of those injured by its tortious act. Historically, tort litigation against units of government, public officers, and charities, and between spouses, parents and children, has been limited or prohibited on this basis."[14]

The two kinds of immunity of interest to us here are governmental immunity and statutory immunity. Governmental immunity protects officials and employees of governmental bodies in the performance of their duties. Statutory immunity is conferred by statute on any person who qualifies for immunity under the terms of the statute.

6.1 Governmental Immunity

Governmental immunity is the doctrine that forbids lawsuits against the government. Currently in American law, unless there is a specific law allowing a party to sue the government for a particular claim, the government is immune and cannot be sued.[15] The function of immunity is not to decide the issue in favor of the government defendant, but to bar the suit from being filed in the first place. For information professionals, it is possible that immunity could be a bar to a tort claim for those information professionals who are employees of governmental organizations. This could include librarians employed by public libraries, court or governmental libraries, or academic libraries at state-run universities. It could also apply to archivists working for government archives, employees of government-run museums, or any information professional who is an employee of a governmental body.

As a general rule, it has always been fairly difficult to sue a public employee. This concept has been firmly embedded in British, and later American, common law since at least the thirteenth century.[16] This protection, intended to allow for the unimpeded functioning of government, applies only to actions that occur within the scope of employment. Intentional misconduct or malicious actions are excluded.[17] This blanket ban on suing the government has softened in recent years as the federal government and most states have enacted tort claims acts that allow some lawsuits against the government when damages occur at the hands of government employees. As an example, the Federal Tort Claims Act allows the federal government to be sued for negligent or wrongful acts by federal employees that result in property damage, personal injury, death, and some other harms.[18]

State governments have passed similar laws, limiting immunity for public officials at the state and municipal levels. The coverage of these statutes varies widely.[19] These acts generally make certain procedural requirements for a suit to proceed,[20] and may also require the state to indemnify employees for any damages or costs.[21] This means that a public employee who causes harm can still be sued, but the government must pay to defend the suit, and also pay any damages. The effect is similar to having liability insurance. A member of the public can sue, and can win monetary damages, but the public employee will not face personal responsibility for the costs of the suit or the damages.[22]

This immunity for government employees would appear on the surface to provide protection for any information professional who is also a government employee. The issue is unfortunately a bit more complicated than it appears. The immunity available for government employees is for actions and decisions that are referred to as discretionary in nature.[23] What constitutes a discretionary action has not been clearly defined, but generally relates to decisions and actions that involve some choice, decision-making, application of expertise, or other intentional activity on the part of the employee. Immunity is not available for actions that are considered ministerial.[24] Ministerial actions are those that are not discretionary, meaning that they can only be done one way, and without the exercise of judgment or expertise required for discretionary governmental functions.[25] Examples of ministerial functions have included driving a car, posting signs, and moving furniture, while examples of discretionary functions have included evaluating reports and deciding upon parole release.[26]

The issue of immunity, and the nature of discretionary actions that are immune, has been further complicated by the presence and evolution of several different judicial standards for discretion in the federal and state courts. The particular standard that would apply to a publicly employed information professional faced with a liability claim would depend on the standard adopted by his state. However, at least one writer in the library literature feels that librarian activities are generally discretionary in nature under current standards.[27] While there is limited case law on the topic, there have been cases in which a public librarian has been held to be immune from suit when deciding not to add a particular book to the collection,[28] and when deciding what materials to include in a law library collection.[29]

The conclusion that the actions of librarians are probably discretionary for purposes of immunity comes with the caveat that it seems possible that direct requests for specific information, that is, requests that do not require judgment or professional acumen, could be seen as ministerial, and thus not be subject to immunity. Even if specific information requests are seen as ministerial, and thus not subject to governmental immunity under normal doctrine, a state can define immunity by statute in such a way that even ministerial functions should be covered.

For instance, in Illinois public employees are specifically immune by statute from claims arising from the provision of information, including library materials. The statute states that a "local public entity is not liable for injury caused by any action of its employees that is libelous or slanderous or for the provision of information either orally, in writing, by computer or any other electronic transmission, or in a book or other form of library material."[30] Though this provision has never been tested, it would appear to protect publicly employed librarians in Illinois from any claims arising from providing information.

The general immunity doctrine does not apply, meaning the government can be sued, for certain types of claims, such as civil rights violations.[31] There is also no immunity when the suit seeks injunctive relief, such as a change in a library's policies, rather than money damages.[32] Immunity can also be absolute or qualified. Absolute immunity is complete exemption from civil liability; it is generally granted to public officials with legislative or judicial roles. Qualified immunity, usually provided to public employees, provides immunity from suit so long as the employee's activities do not violate a statute or the constitution.[33]

This topic is both complex and extremely variable from jurisdiction to jurisdiction. As such, it is not possible to give more than a general discussion of the topic here. That said, information professionals employed by governmental bodies would be advised to explore the possibility of immunity from suit for their professional actions based on the particular laws of the jurisdiction in which they work.[34]

6.2 Statutory Immunity

While governments can use statutes to limit governmental immunity, and provide members of the public with rights to sue the government that they wouldn't otherwise have, statutes can also grant immunity to those who would otherwise not have it. Statutory immunity is immunity that is created by a statute, and applies to any person or entity who qualifies for the protection of immunity as defined by the statute. There are a number of such statutes at the state and federal levels. For instance, the Volunteer Protection Act is a federal act that protects volunteers from suits over damages that result when they are doing volunteer work and acting in good faith.[35] Many states have similar laws.[36] One grant of statutory immunity that is of particular importance to libraries is section 230 of the Communications Decency Act.[37]

6.2.1 Immunity under 47 USC 230

While some parts of the Communications Decency Act have been struck down as unconstitutional, section 230 is still in force. The section grants immunity under what is referred to as a "good Samaritan" provision to libraries and Internet service providers in two ways. First, it says that such entities are not to be treated as publishers, and therefore potentially liable, for any offensive or illegal material encountered by a user that was originated by someone else.[38] This means that a library cannot be held responsible if a user uses library computers to view or download offensive or pornographic materials.

This provision has been tested and upheld in the Livermore case in California.[39] In that case, a mother sued the public library for harm incurred by her son when he downloaded pornographic images at the public library. The court found that the library did not create or develop the materials, and because of that was immune from civil liability under section 230.

The second protection provided by section 230 is to make libraries and other entities immune from suit for restricting access to objectionable material.[40] This section has had mixed results in protecting libraries from suit. While it appears to offer immunity from a claim for money damages based on harm caused by filtering of library computers, it does not protect a library from suit for injunctive relief or from a First Amendment claim. In the Loudon case,[41] a county library was sued for placing Internet filters on its computers. The court in Loudon found that section 230 protected the library from suits for monetary damages but not for an action for injunctive relief.[42]

7. QUESTIONS AND ANSWERS

1. What is the difference between public and private law?
Public law refers to law that enforces the interests of society as a whole. Thus, something like prosecuting a criminal is public law. Private law concerns legally enforceable relations between two private individuals or entities. A lawsuit to enforce the terms of a contract or to get damages for a car accident would be examples of private law.

2. How does liability to society differ from liability to others?
The difference is closely related to the public law and private law distinction. When someone violates a public law, such as by committing a crime, his liability is to society. In the case of a crime, he will be prosecuted by the state and will pay any fines to the state as well. Liability to others occurs when someone violates a duty and causes harm to another person. The claim for damages will be pursued by the aggrieved party, rather than the state, and any damages awarded will go to the other party.

3. What is the difference between federal and state law?
Federal law is law made by the federal government, and covers areas of federal concern, such as copyright and bankruptcy. State law is made by the states, and covers all other areas, such as tort law and contract law.

4. What is the difference between contract law and tort law?
Contract law involves legally binding agreements that are voluntarily made between two or more parties. When a violation occurs, it involves the failure of one of the parties to the agreement to live up to its terms. Tort law involves the violation of a duty imposed by society. If a failure to uphold the duty results in harm to another, that person can seek damages for harm.

5. How are remedies pursued in legal actions?
If the legal action involves public law, then remedies are pursued by the state, and can involve fines, imprisonment, or injunctive relief. If the action is a civil law action, such as a tort or contract claim, remedies must be pursued by the party that incurred the harm. Remedies in civil actions can include money damages and injunctive relief.

6. What is immunity?
Immunity is a legal doctrine that protects a particular person or entity from being sued, regardless of fault. Traditionally the government, including public officials and employees, has been immune from suit when it causes harm. This immunity has been limited with the adoption of federal and state tort claims acts that allow suits against the government for some types of harm.

8. IMPORTANT POINTS TO REMEMBER

▶ Liability can be to society or to another person, depending on the situation.
▶ Liability can result from unintentional wrongful acts, acts that are intentionally wrong, and failing to act when a duty to do so exists.
▶ It is possible and even likely that publicly employed information professionals would be immune from tort claims so long as their actions are discretionary in nature.

ENDNOTES

[1] *Black's Law Dictionary* 932 (8th ed. 2004).

[2] U.S. Const., art. I, § 8, cl. 8.

[3] 17 U.S.C. § 101 et seq.

[4] Robert A. Hillman, *Principles of Contract Law*, 12 (2004).

[5] 735 ILCS 5/13–202.

[6] 735 ILCS 5/13–201.

[7] 735 ILCS 5/13–205.

[8] According to the Bureau of Justice Statistics, "Of the 98,786 tort cases that were terminated in U.S. district courts during fiscal years 2002 and 2003, 1,647 or 2% were decided by a bench or jury trial." The remainder were settled or dismissed. Available at http://www.ojp.usdoj.gov/bjs/civil.htm (last visited June 29, 2008).

[9] Sometimes the court will order a criminal defendant to pay compensation to the crime victim for the harm caused by the crime. Though still part of the criminal action, compensation does go directly to the victim.

[10] Workers' compensation is a complex area of the law, encompassing both federal and state law. For a good overview, see the Cornell Law School Legal Information Institute page on workers' compensation, *available at* http://www.law.cornell.edu/wex/index. php/Workers_compensation (last visited June 29, 2008). The U.S. Department of Labor Web site has information on workers' compensation, including listings of all state workers' compensation laws, *available at* http://www.dol.gov/esa/owcp_org.htm (last visited June 29, 2008).

[11] Dan B. Dobbs, *The Law of Torts* § 154 (2001 & Supp. 2004).

[12] *Ybarra v. Spangard*, 25 Cal.2d 486, 154 P.2d 687 (1944).

[13] *Id.*, at 494.

[14] Edward J. Kionka, *Torts in a Nutshell* 341 (2d ed. 1992).

[15] Mary Minow & Tomas A. Lipinski, *The Library's Legal Answer Book*, 2 (2003).

[16] Louis L. Jaffe, *Suits Against Governments and Officers: Sovereign Immunity*, 77 Harv. L. Rev. 1 (1963).

[17] John Cannan, *Are Public Librarians Immune from Suit? Muddying the Already Murky Waters of Law Librarian Liability*, 99 Law Lib. J. 7, at 12 (2007).

[18] 28 U.S.C. § 1346(b), § 1402(b), §2401(b), and § § 2761–2680 (2006).

[19] Minow, *supra* note 15, at 3.

[20] Cannan, *supra* note 17.

[21] Dobbs, *supra* note 11, § 273.

[22] *Id.*

[23] Dobbs, *supra* note 11, at § 273.

[24] *Id.*

[25] *Id.*

[26] *Chamberlin v. Mathis*, 729 P.2d 905, 910 (Ariz. 1986).

[27] Cannan, *supra* note 15, at 16.

[28] *Via v. City of Richmond*, 543 F. Supp 382, (E.D. Va. 1982).

[29] *Knisley v. United States*, 817 F. Supp. 680 (S.D. Ohio 1993).

[30] 745 ILCS 10/2–107.

[31] Minow, *supra* note 15, at 5.

[32] *Id.*

[33] Minow, *supra* note 15, at 6.

[34] For a good general discussion of immunity issues as they relate to libraries, see Minow, *supra* note 15, at 1–11. For a comprehensive look at immunity law at the state level, see Jon L. Craig, ed., *Civil Actions Against State and Local Governments, Its Divisions, Agencies and Officers* (2002). For federal tort immunity see Jon L. Craig, ed., *Civil Actions Against the United States, Its Agencies, Officers, and Employees* (2002).

[35] 42 U.S.C. § 14501 et seq. (2006).

[36] Minow, *supra* note 15, at 7.

[37] 47 U.S.C. § 230 (2006).

[38] 47 U.S.C. § 230(c)(1).

[39] *Kathleen R. v. City of Livermore*, 87 Cal. App. 4th 684 (2001).

[40] 47 U.S.C. § 230(c)(2)(A).

[41] *Mainstream Loudon v. Loudon County Library*, 2 F. Supp. 2d 783 (E.D. Va. 1998).

[42] *Mainstream Loudon*, 2 F. Supp. 2d, at 790.

►Three

TORTS, CONTRACTS, AND OTHER LEGAL ISSUES

IN THIS CHAPTER

In this chapter we will look at specific types of legal issues that can arise for information professionals. These include:
- ► Torts in general
- ► Negligence concepts, including malpractice
- ► Defamation and materials torts
- ► Defenses to tort claims
- ► Contracts
- ► Other legal issues, including confidentiality and fees

Having looked in Chapter Two at what constitutes legal liability in our society, we turn now to specific forms of liability that may have some impact on information professionals. The most prominent of these, and the most likely to be of concern to most information professionals, is the law of torts. In this chapter we will look at how tort law works, and what kinds of situations are subject to tort liability. Following that we will look at contract law and also at such concepts as defamation and confidentiality.

1. TORTS

As we have seen in the previous chapter, most professional liability is a form of civil liability, and falls under the rubric of tort law. Tort law provides individuals with the ability to seek redress and compensation through the courts when they have been harmed by someone who has failed in a duty toward them. A tort, then, is defined as a civil wrong, other than a breach of contract, for which the court will provide a remedy in the form of an action for damages.[1]

Tort law provides three theories under which actions by the defendant can lead to liability to the plaintiff. Only one of these, negligence, is really relevant to the activities of information professionals, but it is a good idea to understand the others, at least in order to differentiate them. These three theories of recovery are intentional misconduct, strict liability, and negligence.[2]

1.1 Intentional Misconduct

Intentional misconduct is the deliberate, intentional infliction of harm on another, and is almost always actionable.[3] An example of intentional misconduct in the library context would be a reference librarian who intentionally gives false or misleading information while intending to create harm. One assumes that this scenario would be rare. In any event, the crux of the complaint is the intentional nature of the act. Because our concern here is with actions by information professionals that are done in good faith as a part of professional duties, the concept of intentional tort is not relevant to this analysis.

> **Intentional Misconduct**
>
> Joe becomes angry at Jill and throws a book at her, hitting her on the head and injuring her. Joe's act constitutes the intentional tort of battery. Jill can sue Joe for battery and recover damages for her injuries.

1.2 Strict Liability

Strict liability is "liability that does not depend on actual negligence or intent to harm, but that is based on the breach of an absolute duty to make something safe."[4] In essence, strict liability is liability without fault, and the defendant is subject to liability for conduct that is neither negligent nor an intentional tort.[5] Strict liability reflects the public policy that some activities are inherently dangerous and can only be controlled by holding those who engage in them strictly liable for damages that result from their actions.[6] As such, strict liability is intended for situations where the defendant's activity is unusual and abnormal in the community, and where the danger which it threatens to others is unduly great.[7] Examples of such activities include product liability and the handling of ultra-hazardous materials.[8] The actions of information professionals of all types are generally not unusual, abnormal, or unduly dangerous and do not fit the mold of strict liability situations.

It is interesting to note that some writers in the library literature have cited strict liability as a possible form of liability for librarians.[9] The reasoning seems to be that librarians deal with books and information, both of which are products, and since some products can sometimes be subject to strict liability standards, it would follow that librarians can be subject to strict liability. This argument fails on any number of levels, including that librarians are not the manufacturers of the products they are using; that books, as products, are not abnormally dangerous; and that librarians' activities are not unusual and abnormal in the community. In addition, strict liability has only rarely been applied to published or printed materials, although it has occurred in a few instances.

Strict Liability

In 1975, Willard Wahlund, an experienced commercial pilot who worked for Braniff Airlines, was flying a private plane and experienced trouble with his navigation system. Wahlund attempted to make an unscheduled landing at a small West Virginia airport. To find the airport he used navigation charts supplied to him by Braniff and published by the Jeppeson publishing company. There was an error on the chart concerning the airport at which Wahlund was trying to land, and as a result of the error, the plane crashed, killing Wahlund and his passenger.[10]

At trial, the publishing company was found strictly liable for the error on the chart. On appeal, the appellate court stated, "We believe that the trial court did not err in classifying appellant's charts as products. The charts, as produced by Jeppesen and supplied to Wahlund by Braniff, reached Wahlund without any individual tailoring or substantial change in contents—they were simply mass-produced. The comments to § 402A, [of the Restatement (Second) of Torts], envision strict liability against sellers of such items in these circumstances. By publishing and selling the charts, Jeppesen undertook a special responsibility, as seller, to insure that consumers will not be injured by the use of the charts. . . . This special responsibility lies upon Jeppesen in its role as designer, seller, and manufacturer."[11]

Information professionals do provide a service, and attempts to hold persons rendering a service of some kind to a strict liability standard have been tried in some limited cases, but have had no success. The courts do not appear to have any interest in applying strict liability standards to service situations.[12] The idea that information professionals might be subject to strict liability for their normal professional activities appears to have no legal merit.

2. NEGLIGENCE

The vast majority of tort claims are based on negligence. Negligence is defined as a tort claim based on the negligent activities of some party that result in harm to another.[13] Were information professionals to be subject to a claim of professional liability, such a claim would almost certainly arise under a claim of negligence.

This has not happened to date. As a result, in the legal literature theories of negligence liability for information providers have not been widely addressed, and the major tort treatises do not address the topic at all.[14]

2.1 Negligence Elements

The concept of negligence would seem to imply that any act that leads to the harm of another is actionable. In fact, four elements must exist, and be proved, in a successful negligence claim. Those elements are:

1. the presence of a duty of care recognized by law;
2. a failure to meet the duty of care;
3. a reasonable or close causal connection between the violation of the duty and the resulting harm (referred to as "proximate cause");
4. actual loss or harm to the interests of another.[15]

In order to succeed, a plaintiff must prove all four elements separately.[16] In other words, a successful claim would need to show that there was a duty of care, that the defendant failed to meet the duty, that this failure was the proximate cause of the plaintiff's harm, and that the plaintiff did indeed suffer harm of a type which will be compensated by the court.[17] If any one or more of the elements are not satisfied, the claim will fail.[18] In order to make this clear, the concepts of duty of care, proximate cause, and harm should be examined separately.

2.2 Duty of Care

Duty is defined as a relationship that imposes a legal obligation on one person for the benefit of another.[19] In negligence cases duty of care is a legally recognized obligation to conform to a particular standard of conduct toward another.[20] Generally, the first two elements of a negligence claim, duty of care and the failure of that duty, taken together constitute actual negligence. In other words, negligence results from the presence of a duty and the failure to conform to that duty. This, combined with the additional elements of proximate cause and harm to the plaintiff, is required in order for negligence to result in liability.

The relationships under which a duty of care arises can be formal or implied, but they must exist in some form that is recognized at law. A library that is open to the public has a legal duty to make sure that the property is reasonably safe. If this is not done, and a user is injured, the library has failed in its duty and is negligent. Similarly any driver on the road has assumed the duty of obeying all traffic rules, and failing to follow those rules could lead to a negligence claim if an accident results. On the other hand, someone without a legally recognized duty cannot be held liable even if preventable harm results.[21] For example, a pedestrian who

Elements of a Negligence Claim

An 18-month-old toddler was allowed by her mother to wander in a public library in New York. While wandering, the child fell and struck her head on a fixed metal shelf divider on a library bookshelf. The mother sued, alleging that the library was negligent in placing a divider with sharp unprotected edges in a section of the library designated for children. The case was dismissed by the trial court because the mother failed to show all of the elements of negligence.

The mother appealed, but the appellate court agreed with the trial court. It pointed out that the library had a duty to maintain safe premises, but that the shelf was in normal condition, and that it was not reasonable to expect someone to fall against in the way that the toddler did. Because of this the plaintiff had failed to show a violation of the duty, and thus did not show that the library's failure in their duty was the proximate cause of the toddler's injuries.[22]

witnesses another person about to be harmed because they have fallen in the middle of the street has no legally recognized duty to that person, and therefore cannot be held liable for failing to act.

2.2.1 Misfeasance, Malfeasance, and Nonfeasance

Negligence can take the form of a number of different types of actions, or failures to act, that lead to liability. Lawyers have specific terms that are used to describe these actions. Three of the most common are referred to as misfeasance, malfeasance, and nonfeasance.

Misfeasance describes the most common circumstances under which negligence liability occurs. Most negligence liability is based on affirmative conduct that is improper or unreasonable.[23] It can also be described as a "lawful act performed in a wrongful manner"[24] In layperson's terms, misfeasance occurs when you do something wrong, even when by mistake or without intending to. If you become distracted while driving and change lanes without looking to see if the next lane is clear, and in so doing collide with another vehicle, you are at fault because you failed to yield to traffic in the next lane as required. This is true in spite of the fact that you did not intend to cause an accident. This is misfeasance.

Malfeasance is to cause harm through an intentionally bad act.[25] Thus if you intentionally drove through an intersection without stopping at the stop sign, perhaps hoping to beat the other traffic through the intersection, your actions are intentionally wrong and are thus malfeasance. Note that it is not necessary that you intended the harm that resulted from your actions, but only that you intended to do the wrong thing that resulted in the harm.

The distinction between misfeasance and malfeasance is largely one of intent. In many cases it can be unclear which is involved, but sometimes the difference is crucial. For instance, if while driving you collide with another vehicle because you made a mistake, your misfeasance would lead to liability for the damage you caused. On the other hand, if you hit the other vehicle intentionally (malfeasance) you would not only be potentially civilly liable, but could also face criminal liability as well.

As a practical matter, another consequence of intentional bad acts can be the invalidation of insurance coverage. Most people have insurance on their car and their home, and one of the protections such policies provide is coverage for civil liability for car accidents, accidents in the home, and even such things as claims of libel and slander. However, most insurance policies exclude coverage for intentional acts that result in harm. Thus, if a driver intentionally collides with another vehicle, that driver's insurance company might be within its rights to refuse to cover the damages that result. With liability issues, intentions can make a difference.

Nonfeasance is a failure to act to prevent harm when you are required to do so.[26] The key issue with nonfeasance is the failure to act in the presence of a known duty. This limits the application of the concept, because in many cases there is no such duty. While most people would agree that they should render aid to others when they have the chance to, and this may well be desirable for society as a whole, there is generally no legal obligation to act to help another, unless you have a very specific type of relationship with that person that requires you to act.

As a general rule, a person has no duty to act to prevent harm to another, even if there would be no harm or inconvenience to that person in doing so.[27] For nonfeasance to lead to liability requires not only that the defendant foresee injury to the plaintiff and have an opportunity to prevent the injury, but that a special relationship exists between the plaintiff and the defendant. It is this special relationship that creates the duty on which liability will be based.[28]

No Duty to Act in Aid of Another

Mr. Yania, a man involved in the coal strip-mining business, visited another coal miner, Mr. Bigan, at his mine site. While there, Bigan apparently began to taunt Yania, as a result of which Yania jumped into a water-filled trench in the strip mine and drowned. Bigan did nothing to attempt to help Yania as he was drowning.

Yania's widow sued, claiming, among other things, that assistance should have been rendered Yania by Bigan. On this point the trial denied her claim, and the appellate courts agreed. As the appellate court put it, "[t]he mere fact that Bigan saw Yania in a position of peril in the water imposed upon him no legal, although a moral, obligation or duty to go to his rescue unless Bigan was legally responsible, in whole or in part, for placing Yania in the perilous position."[29] Since Yania was considered to have been a competent adult, the fact that he may have jumped into the water in response to Bigan's taunts was immaterial. Yania was responsible for entering the water, and Bigan had no obligation to render assistance to him.

Not only is there no general obligation to help others but, out of concern that potential tort liability would prevent people from assisting others, laws have been developed to specifically protect those who volunteer to act in aid of another.[30] These so-called "Good Samaritan" statutes have been enacted in all 50 states.[31]

The special relationships in which nonfeasance can lead to liability have been specifically created by the courts. These relationships include those between innkeeper and guest,[32] common carrier (such as a bus, train, or airline) and passenger,[33] employer and employee,[34] landowners and someone they invite onto their land,[35] parent and child,[36] and ship captain and sailor.[37] In addition, any situation in which someone promises to aid a particular group of people—for example, as a condition of employment—can create a duty to act.[38] This would apply to such groups as private security guards and lifeguards. As a general rule, there is no duty to act to help others except in these special cases.

The difference between misfeasance and nonfeasance can be subtle, and at times may amount to a distinction without a difference. According to a prominent text on tort law, "there arose very early a difference, still deeply rooted in the law of negligence, between 'misfeasance' and 'nonfeasance'—that is to say, between active misconduct working positive injury to others and passive inaction or a failure to take steps to protect them from harm."[39] The important point here is that failing to act when a duty to do so exists can lead to liability just as much as an active violation of a duty or obligation when a special relationship exists.

Distinguishing Misfeasance, Malfeasance, and Nonfeasance

1. Dave is talking on his cell phone while driving and, distracted by his conversation, does not notice that the traffic light ahead of him has turned red. He enters the intersection and collides with another vehicle. He did not intend to disobey the traffic signal. Dave unintentionally committed an act that violated a duty he had and caused harm. Dave has engaged in misfeasance.

2. Theresa is driving and is late for an appointment. She decides to run a stop sign in order to get ahead of other traffic, assuming that the other cars approaching the intersection will stop at their respective stop signs and thus, by default, let her through first. She knows this is wrong. One of the other cars proceeds, and Theresa's car collides with it. Theresa has intentionally violated her duty, causing harm, and has engaged in malfeasance.

3. Jeff has a swimming pool in his backyard. Jeff's role as a landowner requires him to act to protect the safety of guests at his home, including swimmers in his pool. The daughter of some visiting friends enters the deep area of the pool but cannot swim and begins to call out in distress. Jeff sees the girl but does nothing to help her, and the girl drowns. As the landowner, Jeff has an obligation to act to protect any invited guests on his property. Jeff has engaged in nonfeasance because he failed to act to aid the girl.

The result of all this is that liability can result from unintentional wrongful acts that violate a duty of care, acts that are intentionally wrong, and failing to act when a duty to do so exists. You might well ask how one knows when a duty exists. This is an excellent question, one that can only really be answered in the context of a particular activity. That said, it is worth mentioning that duties can arise from many sources, including the laws and regulations of our society, from basic property rights, and from the standards of a given profession.

2.3 Proximate Cause

Proximate cause is the concept that there is some reasonable connection between the failure of the defendant to conform to a duty of care and the harm suffered by the plaintiff.[40] The reasonableness of this connection is of paramount importance.[41] While the issue of causation is often simple, there are many cases where the harm results from a chain of circumstances, such that the responsible party is harder to determine. This topic can be quite complex in practice, and a thorough examination is beyond the scope of this book. For our purposes it is sufficient to understand that the negligent act—that is, the violation of a duty—must have been a reasonably direct cause of the plaintiff's harm in order for liability to ensue.

> **Proximate Cause**
>
> Jerry throws a ball that breaks Jenny's window. The ball hits her in the chest, and glass from the window cuts her arm, resulting in injuries requiring medical attention. Jerry's act of throwing the ball is the proximate cause of Jenny's injuries.
>
> Jerry rolls his ball down a hill, where Bill picks the ball up and then attempts to throw it back to Jerry. By mistake, Bill throws it through Jenny's window, injuring her. Jerry's act of rolling the ball down the hill may have started the chain of events that led to Jenny's harm, but his act alone would not have injured her. Jerry's act of rolling the ball is not the proximate cause of Jenny's injuries.

In the case of using information that leads to harm, an essential aspect of proximate cause would be the reasonableness of relying on the supplied information. That the creator of an information source might be liable for faulty information is fairly clear.[42] However, when the claim is against the disseminator of the information, the issue is less clear. By making a claim against an information professional, the plaintiff is not just saying that the information was somehow inadequate, but also that the information professional knew or should have known this was the case but supplied it anyway, and further, that it was reasonable to rely on the information professional without any further analysis or judgment.

The reasonableness of such reliance is a proximate cause issue, but also reflects the presence or absence of a duty of care. If, for example, there is a duty of care for librarians at working at a reference desk, it becomes reasonable for patrons to rely on the information supplied without any further analysis or judgment, and the act of supplying inaccurate or inappropriate information can be seen as a proximate cause of the plaintiff's harm. On the other hand, if there is no such duty, and the librarian is not making guarantees about the information supplied, then it is not reasonable for patrons to look to the librarian as the proximate cause of their harm. This, it would seem, is precisely where the legitimate controversy rests about this issue for information professionals, as well as most of the apparent misunderstanding of this area of law in the library literature.

Most of the literature that discusses this issue focuses on what activities constitute negligence on the part of librarians.[43] As we have seen, this is only part of the issue. The real question in litigation would not be whether the librarian was negligent in her activities, but whether those activities had a reasonable causal connection to the plaintiff's harm. Such a causal connection would require a duty of care.

This highlights the crucial fact that the potential for professional liability for information professionals hinges on the nature of their relationships with their clients. For this reason separate chapters of this book will deal with the specific circumstances of various branches of the information professions.

2.4 Harm

Liability to others depends entirely on the concept of harm. Without harm the idea of civil liability is meaningless, because without harm there is nothing for which to make amends. For instance, if you drive through a stop sign without stopping but no accident occurs, there can be no liability to other drivers because there was no harm. Again, you might still be liable to society for the crime of failing to obey the stop sign, but that is a different matter. With liability to society, any act that violates a law is said to inherently harm society, because in order for society to function, it is necessary that laws be followed. Therefore criminal liability can occur simply because the law was broken. But without actual harm to another there can be no civil liability. Harm in civil liability can take various forms, but the two forms most relevant to our discussion are personal harm and economic loss.

2.4.1 Personal Harm

Personal harm occurs when someone is physically or emotionally hurt. Emotional harm is much harder to define or identify than physical harm, but is nonetheless an important part of the concept of personal harm. The list of those things that constitute personal harm can seem endless, but all involve some sort of physical or emotional damage. Physical personal harm can include physical injuries of all kinds, as well as pain and suffering resulting from injuries, and permanent impairments. Emotional harm involves damage to emotional health, whether from an actual injury or from the trauma of the event that led to the harm. It can also include loss of enjoyment of life, loss of companionship, and other emotional injuries.

Obviously, there is a large gray area when discussing certain kinds of harm. If someone loses a limb in a car accident, the nature of the injury and the effect the injury has on the person's life is readily apparent, or easily ascertainable. In cases of pain and suffering, or certain forms of emotional harm, ascertaining the actual harm suffered is much more difficult. In such cases it will often be up to a jury to weigh all the facts and decide if harm occurred, and if so, to what extent.

2.4.2 Economic Loss

Economic loss, as the term implies, involves any harm that costs the victim money, either in outright expense, or the loss of the present or future value of something. Thus, in a car accident, the actual damage to a vehicle, which costs money to repair, is an economic loss, as are medical bills for any injuries. In addition, such things as the loss of future earnings because a crippling injury will keep the victim from working are also economic losses.

Economic Loss

1. Bert is driving on the highway when another car crosses the center line and collides with his vehicle. As a result of the accident Bert loses his left leg. During the course of being treated Bert suffers much pain. He also becomes depressed. As a result of losing his leg he can no longer engage in many activities he used to enjoy regularly, including dancing and rock climbing. These are all examples of personal harm for which he can be compensated.

2. Bert's injuries require extensive hospitalization and medical care, all of which costs many thousands of dollars. Bert also loses wages because of his inability to work while recovering from his injuries. Finally, the loss of his leg means that he will be unable to work in the future, and so he has lost future income as well. These are all examples of economic losses.

2.4.3 Compensation for Harm

Once we establish that harm has occurred, and that someone is properly liable for that harm, how do we compensate the victims? The history of how harm has been compensated since ancient times makes for interesting reading.[44] Ancient rules of retaliatory justice, blood money, and other forms of compensation have evolved to the point that, at least in the United States, compensation for civil liability is entirely monetary in nature.

Monetary compensation for economic loss is a fairly straightforward proposition. In the case of a car accident, the liable defendant would be required to pay for the repair of the other vehicles involved in the collision, the medical bills for those who were injured, and perhaps any lost wages due to the accident. Such damages are generally fairly easy to compute. It is important to understand that civil damages are only intended to compensate those harmed, not to enrich them. While in some very rare cases a defendant might be ordered to pay punitive damages, which are not direct compensation, this is highly unusual and restricted to certain specific situations.

Computing damages can be more problematic in the case of less tangible harm. For instance, in a case where someone was injured, it is not uncommon to see claims for compensation for pain and suffering. How to value such suffering monetarily can be very difficult. Similar issues arise for claims of loss of companionship or loss of enjoyment of life.

2.5 Malpractice

The term "malpractice" is commonly used in the library literature when referring to information professional negligence and liability for information professionals. Malpractice is a form of negligence that is usually applied to professionals in relation to their professional duties.[45] In malpractice, the duty of care that is owed reflects the standards of competence and due care of the profession involved.[46] The legal issue involved is the extent to which professional standards are translated into legal principles.[47] Malpractice is not limited to certain professions,[48] but it is interesting to note that most of the professions for which malpractice is an active issue have in common the fact that the professional in question does not just assist the client, but actually assumes responsibility for dealing with the client's problem or situation. This assumption of responsibility—for example, by treating an illness, dealing with a legal problem, or taking care of financial affairs—would logically tend to create a duty of care because of the potential for identifiable harm to the client at the hands of the professional. The concept of profession as it relates to the information professions will be discussed in detail in Chapter Four.

With malpractice, as with other forms of negligence, liability results not just from negligence, in the form of the failure of a professional duty, but also from a reasonable causal connection between that failure and the plaintiff's harm. Many interactions with a professional have an unsatisfactory or even harmful outcome. But losses at the hands of a professional (whether involving money, legal interests, or even a life) do not, in and of themselves, indicate malpractice. Rather, liability for malpractice requires that the harm be reasonably caused by professional activities that fail to uphold the profession's standards and duty of care.

To put it simply, in a malpractice claim the duty of care arises from the standards of the profession involved and from the professional relationship between the parties. Negligence is determined by comparing the facts of the case to the standards of the profession involved. This presupposes two important concepts: first, that the professional relationship involved is such that a duty of care could ever exist between the professional and the person harmed, and second, that the profession involved has ascertainable standards that can be used to determine if a duty of care has been violated.

While there is no definitive list of professions subject to malpractice claims, in many professions, the professionals' relationships with their clients do not give rise to a duty of care such that a malpractice claim is even applicable. The answer to whether a malpractice claim is possible for a given profession requires a careful analysis of the basic nature of the profession and its relationship with clients. The information professions provide an especially difficult case in which to determine if malpractice liability is possible. For many information professionals it is not at all clear that it is. This issue will be discussed at length in the next chapter.

2.6 Negligent Misrepresentation

Negligent misrepresentation is an important tort to consider when discussing information professionals. Because this tort relates directly to providing information, it can logically be seen as a possible source of liability for information professionals. That said, none of the major sources on tort law specifically discuss librarians or information professionals in the context of this tort.[49]

Negligent misrepresentation is related to other misrepresentation torts, but comes into play when the activity that led to harm arose out of negligence, rather than intentional misrepresentation or deceit.[50] According to the Restatement, negligent misrepresentation occurs in the following situation:

> One who, in the course of his business, profession or employment, or in any other transaction in which he has a pecuniary interest, supplies false information for the guidance of others in their business transactions, is subject to liability for pecuniary loss caused to them by their justifiable reliance upon the information, if he fails to exercise reasonable care or competence in obtaining or communicating the information.[51]

While on its face this language would appear to apply directly to information professionals, in actual examination the issue is more complicated. In the comments accompanying this section of the Restatement, there are requirements that would place this tort outside the realm of most information professionals. For example, the comments state that holding the supplier of information to a duty of care would only be appropriate when the supplier was "manifestly aware of the use to which the information was to be put, and intended to supply it for that purpose."[52] While this might be true for information brokers, it is unlikely to be true for librarians.

The rule also requires that the information supplier have a pecuniary interest in the transaction. How this would relate to most information professionals is unclear. On one hand the comments say that simply being employed by the entity providing this information is sufficient to find pecuniary interest.[53] On the other hand, the comment also says that one who gives information gratuitously does not have a pecuniary interest in the transaction.[54] It is possible that the gratuitous nature of most reference interactions would not be seen as providing a pecuniary interest, although this has not been tested in court. Information brokers, on the other hand, would almost certainly be seen as having a pecuniary interest in their transactions.

The Restatement also says that negligence can only occur if the person supplying the information fails to exercise the care or competence of a reasonable person in obtaining or supplying the information.[55] This raises the thorny issue of what duty of care actually can be discerned for any of the information professions. This topic will be discussed at length in Chapter Four. Suffice it to say here that it may be very hard to determine exactly what duty of care, if any, exists in the information professions.

A final issue is that the Restatement requires that the person relying on the information be justified in doing so.[56] It is once again difficult to say with any certainty that someone seeking important information would be justified in relying solely on a librarian without doing some independent verification or checking concerning the information. This is a more likely possibility for information brokers.

While negligent misrepresentation is the closest we come in established tort law to a tort that fits the activities of information professionals, it is still not at all clear that the tort does, in fact, fit. For the tort to apply, the information professional would have to be seen as having a pecuniary interest in the transaction, to have failed to uphold an undetermined duty of care, and to have done so under circumstances in which the person harmed could justifiably rely on the information. With the exception of the activities of information brokers, this seems to be a hard set of requirements to meet for the activities of most information professionals.

3. MATERIALS TORTS: DEFAMATION

Another potential form of tort that might be of concern to information professionals is a materials tort. This tort revolves not around the actions or intent of information professionals, but of the content of the information in their collections or that they supply to others. The most common tort in this category is defamation.

Defamation is the act of injuring the reputation and good name of another by communicating a false and defamatory statement to others.[57] The tort of defamation includes both libel, which is written defamatory remarks, and slander, which refers to oral remarks. In both cases, a crucial issue is whether the defamatory remarks were "published." "Publication" is a legal term of art here, and means that the remarks were somehow transmitted to third parties, whether orally or in written form.[58] A publisher of defamatory remarks is responsible for all harms proximately caused, including foreseeable repetition by others. In addition, one who repeats the remarks is also a publisher and subject to liability.[59]

The potential liability for repeaters of defamatory information creates a risk for libraries and information professionals. The question is whether one who merely distributes information, such as a library, can be liable for defamation. In general, American courts have determined that repeaters of defamatory material must do so intentionally or negligently in order to be liable for defamation.[60] This means they must supply the defamatory material with intent to defame, or supply it even though they know the material is defamatory.

Mere transmitters—that is, those who distribute defamatory material, but do not know that it is defamatory—are not subject to such liability. Such transmitters have been considered to include libraries.[61] This position has been adopted by the Restatement (Second) of the Law of Torts, which says, "one who only delivers or transmits defamatory matter published by a third person is subject to liability if, but only if, he knows or has reason to know of its defamatory character."[62]

The rationale for this is that a mere transmitter does not create a new instance of publication, but simply distributes the original publication. This is known as the single publication rule, and has been found to apply to libraries.[63] While the single publication rule appears to protect libraries, and by extension, other information professionals, the protection is not assured once there is notice that defamation has occurred.

Defamation

A public library acquires a history of the civil rights struggle in the library's state, published by the state historical society. Unbeknownst to the library staff, the book contains defamatory statements about a prominent local citizen. The citizen borrows the book from the library and reads it, discovering the defamatory remarks.

Q: Can the defamed person sue the library for defamation because it had the book in its collection?

A: No. Under the single publication rule, the library is not liable for defamation unless it had notice of the defamatory content.

Q: If the publisher notifies the library of the defamatory content in the book, can the library then be held liable for defamation?

A: Yes. Once the library has knowledge of the defamatory content of the book, it can be held liable for defamation if it continues to allow the work to be distributed or circulated.

4. TORT LIABILITY FOR COMMERCIAL PUBLISHERS

In our discussion of materials torts (section 3) we used the terms "publish" and "publication" as legal terms of art, in a way that had nothing to do, necessarily, with being in the business of publishing. This section deals with publishers in that more prosaic and common sense: as businesses that create and distribute books and information of all kinds on a mass scale. Because information professionals deal extensively with publications of all kind, it is worth our while to take a look at what liabilities publishers face, particularly for publishing information that is inaccurate or otherwise wrong.

A famous, if fictional, mock news story written by Allan Angoff and published in *American Libraries*, tells of a claim against a library for providing a patron with a book that had inadequate information on building a patio.[64] Angoff's concern was whether the library could be liable in such a situation, but what about the publisher of the book? If a publisher publishes faulty information that leads to harm, can the publisher be held liable?

As a general rule—but not at all a complete answer—the courts have largely shielded publishers from tort liability in order to protect robust free speech and publishing.[65] This has happened in several areas of tort, including with intentional torts, in situations where harm resulted from someone using a publication in some way, and in situations where information in a publication was wrong.

In intentional torts, generally where someone is claiming to have been defamed, the U.S. Supreme Court has established two different standards for liability: one for public figures and another for private individuals. In both cases, the tort requires publication of a factually wrong statement; truth is an absolute defense for such a claim.[66] Generally, public figures can only recover damages when an untrue statement is published knowingly and with actual malice.[67] Private figures can recover if a false harmful statement is published through mere negligence.[68] These standards apply when a published statement amounts to defamation.

For publications and statements that someone uses or relies on, the standards are generally much stricter. For instance, the so called "speech-act" doctrine says that publications are protected as free speech if they advocate lawlessness in the abstract, but that this does not extend to speech or writing that becomes an integral part of a criminal act.[69] Similarly, music lyrics that advocated suicide were determined to be protected when it was alleged that a teenager committed suicide in response to them.[70] In this case, the court found that the teenager's response to the lyrics was not reasonable.

None of these cases address the issue of information that is inaccurate or wrong. Such a situation would appear to raise issues that are more like those raised by a faulty product than those of free speech. Here again, though, the courts have leaned toward protecting publishers from liability. For instance, the Supreme

Court of Hawaii declined to hold a publisher liable when a book it had published recommended a beach that turned out to have dangerous surf.[71] The court held that the publisher had no duty to investigate the beach or warn readers. It said that it would be too onerous to publishers to lay a duty of "scrutinizing and even testing" all information in their publications.[72] This standard would appear to protect publishers even if they publish information that is materially inaccurate or wrong.

These cases look at publisher liability through the lens of a standard tort claim. In doing so, they have found that the publisher had no duty, as in the beach case, or that reliance was not reasonable, as in the suicide case. But we have already seen in section 1.2 of this chapter that certain forms of publications, such as aeronautical charts, can be considered products, such that strict liability can be invoked. You will recall that in strict liability, issues of duty and reasonableness do not arise, because strict liability is liability without fault. In other words, the analysis is not about negligence, but about faults in a product.

Where is the line that divides applying regular negligence analysis to a publication from treating it as a product subject to strict liability? The answer is not clear. However, the aeronautical charts example discussed in section 1.2 may be an anomaly. In another seemingly egregious case, the court declined to see a publication as a product subject to strict liability. In that case, the publisher of an encyclopedia of mushrooms was sued when several users became ill and needed liver transplants after getting inaccurate information in the encyclopedia.[73] The court refused to extend strict liability concepts to the ideas and expressions in the book, and instead said that the tangible part of the book, the paper and binding, were the only parts of it that could considered a product for purposes of strict liability.[74] The court feared that doing otherwise would inhibit free expression and that the specter of strict liability would prevent authors from writing on any topic that could result in harm.[75]

While this line of cases doesn't fully resolve the issues, it seems clear that, even in the event a publication contains inaccurate information, there is a strong likelihood that the publisher will be protected from liability.

5. DEFENSES TO TORT CLAIMS

In addition to the requirement that a plaintiff prove all of the elements of negligence in a tort claim, there are also defenses against such a claim that can be used by defendants. These defenses include contributory negligence and assumption of risk.

5.1 Contributory Negligence

Contributory negligence would appear to be the most likely defense against a claim of negligence based on the use of information supplied by an information professional. Contributory negligence is defined as "conduct on the part of the plaintiff which falls below the standard to which he should conform for his own protection, and which is a legally contributing cause co-operating with the negligence of the defendant in bringing about the plaintiff's harm."[76] This highlights, for liability purposes, the difference between professional activities in which a professional takes responsibility for a client's problem, and those in which the professional merely supplies information or materials that the client uses as he sees fit. In short, it speaks to the reasonableness of trying to hold the professional responsible for the harm that resulted.

In a situation such as that proposed by Angoff,[77] where a book was claimed to contain faulty information, the library could easily and logically assert that the claimant contributed to his own harm. The library did not build the deck, nor did it direct him how to do so. It gave him information that he requested, and that he was responsible for using appropriately. There is no way to tell if the damage resulted from bad information, as claimed, or because the claimant lacked the skill and knowledge to build his deck.

5.2 Assumption of Risk

Another potential defense for information professionals, again related to the tenuous relationship between information services and the resulting harm, is assumption of risk. In its simplest form, assumption of risk means the plaintiff has entered voluntarily into some relation with the defendant that he knows to involve risk, and so is regarded as tacitly or impliedly agreeing to relieve the defendant of responsibility, and to take his own chances.[78]

5.3 Other Responses to a Tort Claim

In addition to these affirmative defenses, there are other objections that can be raised in response to a tort claim. These would include challenging each of the elements of the tort claim, including lack of duty, lack of proximate cause, and, potentially, lack of harm.

5.3.1 Lack of Duty

A first, and perhaps most important, objection to a negligence claim against an information professional would be to challenge the existence of a duty of care. Since no such duty of care has yet been recognized at law for information professionals, the plaintiff would have to show how a duty had come into existence. The mere allegation that harm occurred (as in the Angoff situation) is not enough. The plaintiff must show that a legally recognizable duty existed and that the information professional failed in that duty. In litigation, the defendant can object to the claim by what is referred to as a demurrer, a motion in which it is alleged that the plaintiff has failed to state a claim upon which relief can be granted.

It should be noted that one would only argue that there had been no failure of a duty if a duty actually existed. Unless there is an established duty of care, arguing about the failure of the duty is a moot point.

5.3.2 Lack of Proximate Cause

Assuming that some sort of duty of care has been established or successfully alleged, the next objection would be to the proximate cause of the failure of the duty to the plaintiff's harm. In order to satisfy the requirements of proximate cause, the information professional's actions would have to have led directly to the harm. In most cases, people take the information that they get from information professionals and evaluate it for themselves, then use it for their own purposes. It would be very hard under most circumstances to place the work of the information professional as the proximate cause of the harm.

5.3.3 Lack of Harm

One of the scenarios mentioned regularly in the library literature is the possibility that librarians would be sued simply because the information they provide is wrong. These scenarios seem to imply that simply making a mistake automatically leads to harm. However, without resulting harm, there is no basis for such a claim. The plaintiff would have to show that the wrong information led to a definite, compensable harm. This harm would have to also be caused by of a violation of a duty recognized at law. The fact that a piece of information given out by an information professional turned out to be in some way wrong does not, by itself, lead to harm.

6. THE RIGHTS OF PRIVACY AND PUBLICITY

In America we have some limited rights to privacy. Violation of a person's right to privacy can lead to liability, as can violation of what is called the right of publicity. These issues can come up for information professionals in a number of contexts. First, an action such as revealing someone's circulation records could conceivably violate their right to privacy, and lead to a liability claim. Also, displaying certain items from the collection of a library, archive, or museum could either violate the right to privacy, or the right of publicity. Understanding these rights is important for most information professionals.

6.1 Right of Privacy

Although many people assume that we all have a basic right of privacy, the law in this area is actually quite complex. The U.S. Supreme Court has identified an implied right to privacy in the U.S. Constitution, but it is not explicitly listed in the text, and its derivation and use remain controversial.[79] The bulk of privacy law in America is state law, and can be either legislative or common law in form.[80] As a result, the right of privacy varies from state to state.[81] In some states privacy rights are protected by statute, and some states have adopted all or part of a common law tort of invasion of privacy. The Restatement (Second) of the Law of Torts has adopted the tort of invasion of privacy as part of its text.[82]

In spite of the variability of this area of law, there are a few basic concepts that can be addressed generally as they relate to information professionals. There are generally four grounds for a claim that privacy rights have been violated. They are: intrusion into seclusion, public disclosure of private facts, false light, and appropriation.

6.1.1 Intrusion into Seclusion

Intrusion into seclusion involves activity that pries or intrudes into an area in which a person is entitled to privacy.[83] The act of intrusion must be such that it would be offensive to a reasonable person. As an example, spying on someone in the privacy of their home and then revealing graphic details of their sexual activities would be an example of intrusion into seclusion. People have a reasonable expectation of privacy in their homes, and spying on someone and revealing what was found would be offensive to a reasonable person. It is important to note, however, that liability for intrusion into seclusion rests with the person or entity who has performed the intrusion. A museum, archive, or library that possesses the fruits of the intrusion would not be liable, unless the insitution or its personnel had participated in the act of intrusion itself.[84]

Intrusion into seclusion can be claimed by anyone who is affected, regardless of whether the claimant is a private person or a celebrity. Although some aspects of a celebrity's activities are considered public in ways that they would not be for a private person, intrusion into seclusion involves intrusive acts that would offend a reasonable person, and celebrities are as protected by the law as anyone else.

6.1.2 Public Disclosure of Private Facts

Public disclosure of private facts involves disclosure of embarrassing private facts in a manner that would be objectionable to the average person.[85] It is not enough to simply disclose the private facts. In order to be liable, a person or institution must actively publicize or promote the private information.[86] For this reason, if a library, museum or archive possesses embarrassing private information about an individual, the mere fact of possessing the information would not, in itself, be actionable. Indeed, it is entirely possible that the institution could make the information available to the public—for example, by making files available to researchers—without incurring liability. On the other hand, if the information is made part of a display or exhibit, or otherwise publicized or promoted by the institution, liability is possible.

6.1.3 False Light

False light is similar to public disclosure of private facts in that it requires a highly public disclosure of private information, but it also requires that the public disclosure mislead the public by placing someone in a false light.[87] Thus, false light requires that the publicized information either be false in itself, or be information that creates a false implication. As an example, if a library created a display about a prominent local person, and by using false information and innuendo created the implication that the person was an abuser of illegal drugs, the subject of the display would have a claim under false light. Keep in mind, however, that the cause of action for a false light tort varies in its requirements from state to state, and some states have refused to adopt it as a tort.[88]

6.1.4 Appropriation

Appropriation is the use of a person's likeness or name without a person's permission, in order to create profit.[89] It is similar to the right of publicity, discussed below, but is a separate tort. Thus, if a museum or archive were to take a picture of a member of the public and then, without permission, use that person's likeness in advertising and other promotional materials, the institution could be liable for appropriation. An important distinction between appropriation and the right of publicity is that a claim of appropriation can be made by any person whose likeness or name is used for profit without their permission. Unlike with the right of publicity, it is not necessary that the person already be profiting from their name or likeness in order for them to have a claim.

6.2 Right of Publicity

Right of publicity essentially protects the right of celebrities or famous people to profit from their identity. The right of publicity creates an enforceable property right in one's name, likeness, or other personal attributes, and prevents the unauthorized commercial use of the attributes.[90] The right is specifically intended for people who derive economic benefit from their name, likeness, or other personal attributes. Personal attributes can be any identifying skill or feature that is uniquely associated with the person, such as voice quality or special physical ability.[91] As such it prevents others from unjustly enriching themselves by using a famous person's name or likeness without permission. It differs from the tort of appropriation in that it is only available to those who already benefit economically from their identity. In addition, its function is to protect a celebrity's public image, as opposed to protecting them from violations of their privacy rights.[92]

Violation of the right of publicity requires unauthorized use of the name, likeness, or attribute, along with commercial harm. Thus, the unauthorized use must detract from the economic benefit the originator enjoys from use of the name, likeness, or attribute.[93] In many states, the right of publicity extends to the celebrity's estate, and thus can continue after death. This means that items in a collection that depict a deceased celebrity might still be subject to the right of publicity.

7. CONTRACTS

Achieving an understanding of the basics of contract law is very useful in understanding liability concepts. Once again, for purposes of exploring professional liability issues, we must make a distinction between contracts that are personal obligations—and could therefore lead to personal liability—and contracts signed on behalf of an employer. This is because in the latter case, any liability will inure to the organization and not the professional. Contracts are a common thing in the work world, but information professionals who are employees of institutions are unlikely to encounter situations in which they must sign work-related contracts as personal obligations. On the other hand, for self-employed information professionals, especially information brokers, signing a contract as a personal obligation might well be routine.

7.1 What Is a Contract?

Contracts are specific, intentional agreements between two parties.[94] Contracts must be voluntarily undertaken and agreed to, and must reflect a common understanding between the parties as to the nature of the agreement, often referred to as a "meeting of the minds." The majority of interactions between most information professionals and their clients are not contractual in nature. One exception to this would be information brokers, who may have a contractual relationship with their clients. This will be discussed at length in the chapter on information brokers.

With a contract, liability occurs if a party to the contract fails to live up to the terms of the agreement. This failure is referred to as a breach, and can be remedied by suing the breaching party. If the contract is legal and viable, the court will enforce the terms of the contract, or provide for damages.

7.2 Key Contract Concepts

A contract requires an offer and acceptance of the terms of agreement.[95] an exchange of value,[96] competency on the part of all parties, and legality of terms.[97] Offer and acceptance means that one of the parties makes an offer of the terms of the agreement to the other. The other must then formally accept the offer in order for the contract to go into effect. This process can involve various forms of negotiation, through a process called counteroffering.

All of the parties to a contract must be competent, meaning that they must be legally capable of entering into an agreement. Most adults are legally competent. Legal incompetence can occur because someone is underage, under civil commitment for mental health reasons, or is the ward of a guardianship. In order for a contract to be legally enforceable, it must also involve terms that are legal. Thus a contract that would require a party to engage in an illegal act, or contains terms that are unduly onerous on a particular party will not be legally enforceable, even if both parties agreed to the terms.

Contracts may be informal in some ways, but they must be intentional and involve a meeting of the minds.[98] It is not true that all contracts must be in writing,

---

Contracts

A manager at a local manufacturing company asks an information broker to find information on companies in the state that are capable of producing a particular part that the manufacturer needs. The manufacturer needs the information on or before a certain date. The information broker says that she will search for the information and supply what she finds by the required date for a fee of $1000, to be paid upon receipt of the information.

Q: Is there a contract?

A: Yes. In spite of the fact that nothing about the agreement is in writing, there is an agreement (meeting of the minds) with definite terms that includes an offer (to find information by a certain date) acceptance of the offer, and consideration (the payment of the fee). Such an agreement is a valid contract that can be enforced in a court of law.

Q: If the information broker fails to provide the information by the required date, has there been a breach of the contract?

A: Yes. If the information broker did not supply the information on time, then she has failed to meet one of the expressed terms of the contract, and so has breached it.

Q: If the manufacturer later requests further information by the same date, and the information broker declines to provide the extra requested information, would the manufacturer breach the contract by refusing to pay all or part of the fee because the extra information was not supplied?

A: Yes. Although contracts can be modified after they are entered into, doing so requires the explicit agreement of all the parties. Since the information broker did not agree to the change, the contract was not modified, and the manufacturer must pay the agreed fee.

although most are, and a written contract is generally a good idea. The important thing is that there was a meeting of the minds. This term means not only that there was an agreement but that all of the parties had the same idea of what the contract was about.

8. OTHER LEGAL ISSUES

Apart from contract and tort law, a number of other issues create the potential for liability for information professionals.

8.1 Confidentiality

The concept of confidentiality is an important part of the ethics of librarianship.[99] Confidentiality can be protected by law, encompassing the concepts of confidentiality, or preserving the secrets of another, and privilege, or the right not to be compelled to disclose those secrets while under oath.[100] The extent of a privilege is determined by state statute, and generally (but not always), those professions that are required to maintain confidentiality are also granted some sort of legal privilege concerning the confidential information.[101]

Confidentiality requirements and legal privilege can arise from statutory or common law, and are common for such professions as medicine, law, and psychology. In the case of the information professions, apart from library circulation records, there are few laws protecting confidentiality.[102] The main obligation to protect exchanges involving information professionals derives from ethics, not law. There is also no legal privilege to communications between librarian and patron, and no legal sanction for violation of confidentiality.[103] This distinction is important, not just because it forecloses a potential basis for a cause of action, but because it also lowers the expectations of patrons in their dealings with information professionals.

8.2 Fees

Liability for a profession can clearly be created or raised by charging a direct fee for the service rendered. When a fee is charged for a service, liability can be created based on the inherent possibility of economic loss to the plaintiff as a direct result of the transaction. Charging a fee also creates a presumption that a contractual agreement was made.[104] The few court cases that address liability in the area of information provision (although not specifically libraries) have required that a contractual or fiduciary relationship, such as previously described between an information broker and a client, or that some sort of special relationship exist.[105]

9. IMPORTANT POINTS TO REMEMBER

▶ Most tort actions are based on negligence, which is when the failure to uphold a duty leads to harm.

▶ The elements of a negligence action are the presence of a duty, failure of the duty, proximate cause, meaning that the failure of the duty directly resulted in harm, and harm.

▶ Key questions for information professionals include whether a duty of care exists in their interactions with users and customers, and whether the failure of any such duty could reasonably be the proximate cause of any harm.

▶ Negligent misrepresentation is the tort that comes closest to the scenarios in which information professionals work, but its applicability is not at all clear.

▶ Contracts are legally binding agreements to take some action in return for some form of remuneration or reward, called consideration.

▶ A legally binding contract requires an offer, acceptance of the offer, definite terms, and a meeting of the minds.

▶ Contracts do not have to be in writing. Oral contracts are valid, provided they have the other necessary elements of a contract.

ENDNOTES

[1] Dan B. Dobbs, *The Law of Torts*, § 1 at 1 (2001).

[2] *Id.*, § 1 at 2–3.

[3] *Id.*; Restatement (Second) of the Law of Torts, § 13 (1965).

[4] *Black's Law Dictionary* 8th ed. (2004).

[5] Dobbs, *supra* note 1, § 342 at 941.

[6] Restatement, *supra* note 3, § 519.

[7] Dobbs, *supra* note 1, § 346 at 950.

[8] Restatement, *supra* note 3, § 520.

[9] See, e.g. Susan Dunn, Society, *Information Needs, Library Services and Liability*, 26 Iowa Lib. Q. 18 (1989).

[10] *Saloomey v. Jeppesen & Co.* 707 F.2d 671 (2nd. Cir, 1983).

[11] *Id.*, at 677.

[12] E.C. Cowley, Annotation, *Application of Rule of Strict Liability in Tort to Person Rendering Services*, 29 Am. Law Rep. 3d 1425 (1970, Supp. 2006).

[13] Dobbs, *supra* note 1, § 110.

[14] Jerome Huet, *Liability of Information Providers: Recent Developments in French Law Contrasted with Louisiana Civil Law of Liability and United States Common Law of Torts*, 5 Tul. Eur. & Civ. L. F. 103 (1990).

[15] Dobbs, *supra* note 1, § 114.

[16] *Id.*

[17] *Id.*, § 115.

[18] Dobbs, *supra* note 1, § 114.

[19] Restatement, *supra* note 3, 4 at 7.

[20] Dobbs, *supra* note 1, § 114.

[21] David A. Hyman, *Rescue without Law: An Empirical Perspective On the Duty to Rescue*, 84 Tex.L. Rev. 653, 655 (2005–2006).

[22] *Dabnis v. West Islip Public Library*, 846 N.Y.S.2d 331 (N.Y. App. Div. 2007).

[23] William P. Statsky, *Essentials of Torts* (1994).

[24] *Black's Law Dictionary* 1021 (8th ed. 2004).

[25] *Black's Law Dictionary* 977 (8th ed. 2004).

[26] *Black's Law Dictionary* 1080 (8th ed. 2004).

[27] Dan B. Dobbs, *The Law of Torts* § 314, at 853 (2001); Hyman, *supra* note 21 at 655; Statsky, *supra* note 23, at 35.

[28] Statsky, *supra* note 23, at 36.

[29] *Yania v. Bigan*, 397 Pa. 316, 155 A.2d 343 (1959).

[30] Danny R. Veilleux, *Annotation, Construction and Application of "Good Samaritan" Statutes*, 68 ALR4th, 294 (1989).

[31] *Id.*, at 300.

[32] Restatement, *supra* note 3, § 314A(2).

[33] Restatement, *supra* note 3, § 314A(1).

[34] Restatement, *supra* note 3, § 314B.

[35] Restatement, *supra* note 3, § 314A(3).

[36] Dobbs, *supra* note 1, § 317.

[37] Statsky, *supra* note 23, at 37.

[38] Restatement, *supra* note 3, § 323.

[39] W. Page Keeton et al., *Prosser and Keeton on the Law of Torts* § 56, at 374 (5th ed. 1984).

[40] Dobbs, *supra* note 1, 180.

[41] *Id.*

[42] Indeed, producers of faulty information might even find themselves being held to a strict liability standard in the event of harm, under the theory that information, in this context, is a product. See *Brocklesby v. United States*, 767 F.2d. 1288 (1985); Blodwen Tarter, *Information Liability: New Interpretations for the Electronic Age*, 11 Computer L. Rev. & Tech. L.J. 495 (1992).

[43] See, *e.g.*, Teresa Pritchard-Schoon & Michelle Quigley, *The Information Specialist: A Malpractice Risk Analysis* 13 Online 57 (1989).

[44] F. Parisi, *The Genesis of Liability in Ancient Law*, 3 Am. L. & Econ. Rev. 82 (2001).

[45] Irving J. Sloan, *Professional Malpractice* 7 (1992).

[46] *Id.*

[47] *Id.*, at 5.

[48] *Id.*, 1–6.

[49] See, Restatement, *supra* note 3, § 552; Dobbs, *supra* note 1, § 472.

[50] Edward J. Kionka, *Torts*, 471 (4th ed. 2005).

[51] Restatement, *supra* note 3, § 552(1).

[52] *Id.*, § 552, comment a.

[53] *Id.*, comment d.

[54] *Id.*, comment c.

[55] Restatement, *supra* note 3, § 552, comment e.

[56] Restatement, *supra* note 3, § 552(1).

[57] Kionka, *supra* note 50, at 435.

[58] Dobbs, *supra* note 1, § 402, at 1121.

[59] *Id.*, at 1123.

[60] *Id.*, at 1122.

[61] Rodney A. Smolla, *Law of Defamation*, § 4:92 (2d ed. 2006).

[62] Restatement, *supra* note 3, § 581 (1977).

[63] Andrea G. Nadel, *What Constitutes "Single Publication" Within Meaning of Single Publication Rule Affecting Action for Libel and Slander, Violation of Privacy, or Similar Torts*, 41 A.L.R.4th 541 (1985).

[64] Allan Angoff, *Library Malpractice Suit: Could It Happen to You?* 7 Am. Libr. 489 (1976).

[65] A. Bruce Strauch, *The Tort Liability of Publishers*, Acquisitions Librarian 26, at 155 (2001).

[66] *Id.*, at 167.

[67] *New York Times Co. v. Sullivan*, 376 U.S. 254, 280 (1964).

[68] *Gertz v. Robert Welch, Inc.*, 418 U.S. (1974).

[69] *Rice v. Paladin Enterprises*, 128 F.3d 233 (4thCir. 1997). See Strauch, *supra* note 65, at 162–163.

[70] *McCollum v. CBS, Inc.*, 249 Cal. Rptr. 2d 187 (Cal. Ct. App. 1988).

[71] *Birmingham v. Fodor's Travel Publications, Inc.*, 833 P. 2d 70 (Haw. 1992).

[72] 833 P.2d at 79.

[73] *Winter v. G.P. Putnam Sons*, 938 F.2d 1033 (10th Cir. 1991).

[74] *Id.*, at 1034.

[75] *Id.*

[76] Restatement, *supra* note 3, at § 463.

[77] Angoff, *supra* note 64.

[78] Restatement, *supra* note 3, § 496C (1977).

[79] John E. Nowak & Ronald D. Rotunda, *Constitutional Law*, § 11.7 (5th ed., 1995).

[80] Dobbs, *supra* note 1, § 1197.

[81] Tomas A. Lipinski, *Tort Theory in Library, Museum and Archival Collections, Materials, Exhibits, and Displays: Rights of Privacy and Publicity in Personal Information and Person*, in *Libraries, Museums, and Archives: Legal Issues and Ethical Challenges in the New Information Era*, 47, 48 (Tomas A. Lipinski, ed. 2002).

[82] Restatement, *supra* note 3, at § 652A to 652I.

[83] *Id.*

[84] *Id.*

[85] Lipinski, *supra* note 81, at 49.

[86] *Id.*

[87] Lipinski, *supra* note 81, at 50.

[88] *Id.*

[89] Lipinski, *supra* note 81, at 51.

[90] Lipinski, *supra* note 81, at 52.

[91] *Id.*

[92] *Id.*, at 53.

[93] Lipinski, *supra* note 81, at 52.

[94] John Calamari & Joseph Perillo, *The Law of Contracts*, 26 (3d ed. 1987).

[95] *Id.*, at 73.

[96] *Id.*, at 183.

[97] John A. Gray, *Personal Malpractice Liability of Reference Librarians and Information Brokers*, 9 J. Lib. Admin. 74 (1988).

[98] Calamari & Perillo, *supra* note 94, at 26.

[99] RASD, *Guidelines for Medical, Legal, and Business Responses at General Reference Desks*, § 2.3.

[100] See, *e.g.*, Robert I. Karon, *Privilege and Confidentiality: Confusing Principles*, 23 Tax Adviser 406 (1992); Fred C. Zacharias, *Privilege and Confidentiality in California*, 28 U.C. Davis L. Rev. 367 (1995); Gary W. Paquin, *Confidentiality and Privilege: the Status of Social Workers in Ohio*, 19 Ohio N.U. L. Rev. 199 (1994).

[101] Karon, *supra* note 100.

[102] Rosemary Del Vecchio, *Privacy and Accountability at the Reference Desk*, 38 Reference Libr. 137 (1988).

[103] Mark Stover, *Confidentiality and Privacy in Reference Service*. 27 RQ 242 (1987).

[104] Anne P. Mintz, *Information Practice and Malpractice: Do We Need Malpractice Insurance?* 9 Online 20 (1984); Tarter, *supra* note 42, at 492.

[105] Huet, *supra* note 14, at 105. In light of this, the concept of being paid directly for the service may be one of the crucial differences between librarians and information brokers in their potential for incurring liability. Tarter, *supra* note 42, at 492.

▶Four

INFORMATION PROFESSIONALS AND LIABILITY

IN THIS CHAPTER

▶ Why the concept of "profession" is important in liability issues
▶ What is a profession
▶ Whether the information professions meet the definition of a profession
▶ The concepts of fiduciary and consultant
▶ Employment status and personal liability
▶ Standards and duties of care for the information professions

This book addresses the possibility of personal liability for informational professionals from activities that occur during the normal course of their work. The personal nature of the potential liability is a crucial distinction. Liability for institutions is an entirely different matter, and this book does not attempt to address those issues.[1]

A crucial issue for liability is to determine, if possible, what duty of care exists for information professionals in their work. Determining a duty of care would allow us to understand those points at which the failure of that duty could be the proximate cause of harm. This, in turn, would point to standards for liability, whether it be personal liability for the information professional, or liability for the institution because of an employee's acts.

Even if a duty of care can be found, it does not automatically follow that the information professional involved would be personally liable. If she were considered an employee, and not a member of a profession subject to personal liability, liability for her acts would lie with the institution. On the other hand, some professionals can be subject to personal liability for their actions regardless of their employment status. The question is whether information professionals fall within that group.

The possibility of individual liability for information professionals must necessarily start with three critical aspects of the person's professional and employment status. The first is whether an information professional is truly a professional in the sense required for legal liability to ensue, independent of employment status. The second issue is whether a given information professional would be considered an employee for purposes of liability, and thus not be personally liable for work-related activities. The third issue is the effect of self-employment on potential liability.

1. STANDARDS AND DUTIES OF CARE FOR THE INFORMATION PROFESSIONS

Regardless of whether information professionals should be considered professionals in the legal sense, it is entirely possible that their work activities could give rise to a duty of care toward their users. A duty of care by itself does mean that personal liability will be possible for the information professional, only that someone harmed would have a cause of action against someone. As an example, the library janitor may have a duty of care to mop up any spilled water in library hallways. If he fails to do so, and if someone is injured from a slip in the water, that person will have a cause of action. In this case, even though the janitor had the duty to prevent the harm, it is the institution that would be sued. The janitor is protected from personal liability by his status as an employee.

The main question in analyzing duty of care is whether the activities of the information professions are such that a duty of care can be derived. Without such a duty of care, liability is simply not possible. However, a duty of care can arise simply out of the activities and actions of the parties involved. If we look at professional activities, we can look for those that indicate the presence of a duty.

1.1 What Standards of Care Arise from the Activities of the Information Professions?

It might be helpful to look at the idea of a duty of care for the information professions from a different angle. Instead of looking at those things that clearly militate against the possibility of liability, perhaps we should examine whether such a standard could somehow be created, were someone determined to do so. This, in turn, raises the issues of reasonable reliance and proximate cause.

1.1.1 Reasonable Reliance

It is well established in both tort and contract law that liability relies on reasonable expectations.[2] At what point would it be reasonable for someone to rely on an information professional to the extent that, should harm occur, the information professional should be held liable for the harm? This is the essential question underlying the issue of reasonable reliance. In other situations reasonable reliance is clear. With many professions, the professionals clearly take responsibility for problems, and if they do not live up to the standards of their profession, they can be seen as being responsible for the resulting harm.

As an example, consider a patient who goes to a doctor because he is experiencing abdominal pain. He relies on the doctor to use standard professional skill to diagnose and treat his problem. This does not mean that the doctor is responsible for creating a good outcome for the patient. If the patient turns out to have terminal cancer and dies, the doctor will not be held liable, so long as she acted with all reasonable medical skill to treat the patient. A poor outcome does not by itself indicate malpractice. If, on the other hand, the doctor dismisses the patient's pain as indigestion without investigating further, then she can be held liable because her actions were not up to the standards of the medical profession, and harm resulted. In both situations, it was reasonable for the patient to rely on the doctor to treat her condition. Reliance is also reasonable with other occupations that involve assuming responsibility for the needs or problems of a client.

For information professionals the concept of reasonable reliance is not so clear. An information broker may contractually agree to find all of the information a client needs and to verify its accuracy and completeness. In such a case, it would appear reasonable that the client rely on the information provided as accurate and complete. This is not to say definitively that information brokers satisfy the requirements of reasonable reliance, but that an argument can be made for it, depending on the specific facts of the case. Indeed, in this case the expectation arises not out of a general standard or duty of care, but out of the terms of the specific agreement between the parties.

The situation for a reference librarian in a public library seems much less likely. Public librarians are generally dealing with casual users who approach the reference desk with specific requests. The idea that a reference librarian knows so much about the library user's situation, and is such an expert on every topic she is asked about, that it would be reasonable for the user to rely on the reference service as a complete and definitive answer to the information he needs is a bit of a stretch. Reference librarians may be experts on finding information, but they cannot be experts on every piece of information they find. Nor do they assume any responsibility for whatever underlying need or problem that has caused the patron to request information. The idea that reference librarians could be reasonably relied upon such they could be liable does not appear reasonable at all.

That hasn't stopped many writing in the library literature from assuming that such liability is possible. Angoff, and many subsequent writers on the topic, fail to comprehend the necessity of reasonable reliance. In Angoff's example of a book with improper information for building a deck,[3] the implication inherent in the claim is that the librarian either should have known that the book provided faulty information, or somehow assumed responsibility for the outcome of any project that used the book. Neither claim is in any way reasonable. Librarians cannot reasonably verify every piece of information in every source in their collection, nor can they assume responsibility for how the information they provide is used. Reliance on the librarian such that liability would result is just not reasonable.

The question of reasonable reliance as it relates to specific professional roles will be addressed in more detail in the specific chapters on branches of the information professions.

1.1.2 Proximate Cause

If a situation arose in which reliance was found to be reasonable, the next question that must be answered is that of proximate cause. The actions of the professional must have a direct causal connection to the plaintiff's harm in order for liability to result. This is often clear in situations where a professional assumes full responsibility for a client's problem, but is less so with information professionals. A doctor who fails to use reasonable care to diagnose and treat a patient's medical problem can be seen as the proximate cause of any further harm that occurs as a result of the failure to use reasonable care.

The question is, at what point do the actions of an information professional become so connected to what the client is doing that the information professional's actions would be the proximate cause of the client's harm? Information professionals tend to engage in activities that supplement the activities of their clients, rather than assuming full responsibility for solving a problem. To look at the Angoff example cited in previous chapters,[4] where someone built a deck using a book with faulty information and then tried to blame the library when the deck fell down, it is very hard to see how the librarian is the proximate cause of the harm. On the one hand, the library patron who built the deck made all of the decisions that went into its construction, and would have the responsibility of bringing sufficient skill and judgment to the task to do the job properly. If he lacked the skills to do the job, it is his own fault if the job was done poorly.

On the other hand, if the book he relied on provided faulty information, then his potential claim would be against the publisher of the book.[5] Librarians cannot guarantee the accuracy of every piece of information in every resource in their collection. It is simply not possible. Nor can a librarian assure that the information provided is truly applicable to the client's task, or that the information will be used properly. It is very hard to see how the actions of an information professional can be the proximate cause of the harm suffered by another.

Meeting a Standard of Care

1. A patient goes to a doctor for treatment of a chest cold. The doctor treats the patient, but the cold continues to get worse, eventually becoming tuberculosis, causing the patient to lose wages and pay medical and hospitalization expenses.

   Q: Is the doctor liable for malpractice?

   A: No. Although the patient did not improve, the doctor did nothing wrong. According to the court, the law "does not require that the instructions and advice given by a physician to a patient should be at all events and beyond question 'proper,' or that his treatment should be certainly such as to obtain an approximately perfect result. It requires only, first, that he shall have the degree of learning and skill ordinarily possessed by physicians of good standing practicing in that locality; and, second, that he shall exercise reasonable and ordinary care and diligence in treating the patient and in applying such learning and skill to the case."[6]

2. A patient goes to a dentist to have a molar removed. In removing the tooth the dentist breaks it, leaving fragments of the tooth in the patient's jaw. The dentist tells the patient that all of the tooth has been removed. The patient suffers ongoing pain and later must have surgery to remove the tooth fragments.

   Q: Is the dentist liable for malpractice?

   A: Yes. In this case the court said "The law exacts of physicians and dentists the degree of care usually exercised by practitioners in good standing in their calling or profession. A dentist. . . who, in attempting to extract a tooth, breaks it and fails to remove the fragments either because he is unaware that any remain, or otherwise, telling his patient that all parts of the broken tooth have been removed, is guilty of negligence. . . ."[7]

1.2 Is There a Duty of Care for the Information Professions?

The presence of a duty of care can arise out of two basic sources. The first is general standards for society as a whole. Thus, the duty of care that requires the library janitor to quickly mop up spilled water to prevent someone from slipping is not something that arises out of professional standards for janitors, or standards relating to libraries, but out of common law standards that apply to society as a whole. The second source of a duty of care arises out of professional standards, the violation of which leads to harm. If the information professions are to have a duty of care, the question then arises as to what professional standards will give rise to that duty. Professional standards are more easily discernible when a profession is licensed, or when lawsuits have provided a body of case law that defines professional duty of care. Because librarianship is not licensed and has no case law, there are no formal standards of this type.[8]

There is probably no one global answer to the question of whether a duty of care can exist in the information professions. As will be explained in the chapters on each branch of the information professions, some areas of the information professions, such as reference and technical services librarianship, do not appear to provide much of an opportunity for a duty of care to arise. Other areas, such as information brokering, provide more of a rationale for such a duty, although the issue is still not clear.

The idea of professional liability hinges on two important questions, each of which must be answered separately. The first question is whether the nature of the relationship between information professionals and their clients creates any kind of a duty of care, the violation of which could be proximate cause of the client's harm. The second question is whether the information professions have formalized standards that can be used to define a duty of care.

In the case of the first question, if a duty of care can be found between information professionals and their clients, then violation of that duty will lead to liability, providing the violation of the duty is reasonably the proximate cause of the client's harm. The second question speaks to whether standards of the profession will contribute to defining the duty of care.

Thus if the answer to the first question is no, and no duty of care exists, then information professionals do not face the threat of liability, and the answer to the second question is irrelevant. If the answer to the first question is yes, and a duty of care can exist, then information professionals are potentially liable for their actions regardless of the answer to the second question. If the answer to both questions is yes, then information professionals could be subject to liability in the form of malpractice.

While not a definitive and absolute answer, the information professions in general do not appear to meet the standards necessary to be considered a profession for purposes of liability. The lack of entrance requirements to the profession, the aspirational nature of the ethical codes within the information professions, and the lack of professional recourse for inappropriate actions makes it almost impossible to determine a professional duty of care that could form the basis of a malpractice action.

More important, the relationship of information professionals to their clientele is more like that of a nonprofessional to a customer than a professional to a client. Information professionals do not dictate solutions nor impose their authority on their clients. Instead, they provide information as a commodity to be used as the customer sees fit. In order to answer this question more fully, we need to take a close look at what constitutes a profession for legal purposes. We will do that in later sections of this chapter. Before we do, however, we should take a look at a particular court case that some have argued does create a duty of care for information professionals.

1.3 The *Sain* Case

In the context of duty of care and reasonable reliance, it is worth our while to examine the implications of a 2001 case from Iowa, *Sain v. Cedar Rapids Community School District.*[9] The *Sain* case is interesting because, while it takes place in an educational context, the harm complained of involves the provision of faulty information, and the court held that this act was a potential source of liability. Because of this, at least one writer has raised the possibility that *Sain* could apply to librarians.[10]

In this case, Sain, a high school student, who was by all accounts an excellent basketball player, aspired to earn a basketball scholarship to a major university. In order to qualify for such a scholarship, his high school coursework had to conform to requirements for student-athletes set by the National Collegiate Athletic Association (NCAA). Sain relied on the advice of his guidance counselor at the school in selecting appropriate courses. During his senior year, Sain was offered, and accepted, a full basketball scholarship to an NCAA Division I school. Unfortunately, after he graduated, Sain was informed that one of the courses he took in his senior year, as advised by his guidance counselor, did not meet NCAA academic requirements. The NCAA refused to allow an exemption, and declared Sain ineligible to play. Because of this he lost his scholarship and was unable to attend college.

Sain sued the school district for negligence and negligent misrepresentation. The trial court dismissed the suit, based largely on the fact that Iowa, like all other states, did not recognize the tort of educational malpractice. On appeal, the Iowa Supreme Court reversed the trial court's action, holding that a guidance counselor was a "person in the profession of supplying information to others,"[11] and that the relationship between a guidance counselor and a student gives rise to a duty of care.[12] In doing so, the Iowa court expanded the legal definition of negligent misrepresentation to include guidance counselors, saying that they have a duty of care, the failure of which could conceivably lead to liability.

A few points of explanation are in order here. The first is that the Iowa Supreme Court did not find Sain's guidance counselor liable for his actions. Rather, the court said that the decision of the trial court to dismiss the case before trial was improper because a guidance counselor could, in fact, potentially be held liable for negligent misrepresentation. The Iowa Supreme Court then sent the case back to the trial court for further action. There is no further published record, which in most cases means that the case was settled by the parties. This leaves us in the situation that, while the court has created the possibility for liability under these circumstances, we have no known cases where liability has actually occurred.

Another important point is that, to the extent the *Sain* case is good law, it only applies in Iowa. In order for the *Sain* decision to affect professionals in other states, it would have to be adopted as the relevant standard by courts in those states. Indeed, other states have not looked favorably on the *Sain* decision. For example, Arkansas specifically declined to follow it.[13]

What has raised the concern of those looking at liability issues for information professionals is the *Sain* court's statement that under Iowa law, the "duty" necessary to sustain a negligent misrepresentation claim "rises only when the information [upon which the claim is based] is provided by persons in the business or profession of supplying information to others."[14] This seemingly broad language would appear to create potential liability for information professionals, who must surely be seen as "persons in the business or profession of supplying information to others."

The problem with this discussion of *Sain* is that it leaves out the second, and more important, part of the analysis: that the duty of care imposed arises because the parties are in a "special relationship."[15] The operative question, then, is not simply whether information professionals are "persons in the business or profession of supplying information to others," but also whether their relationship with the persons they supply information to rises to the level of a "special relationship" such that a duty of care arises.

In the *Sain* case, the court said that a person in the business of supplying information to others "acts in an advisory capacity and is manifestly aware of the use that the information will be put, and intends to supply it for that purpose. Such a person is also in a position to weigh the use for the information against the magnitude and probability of the loss that might attend the use of the information if it is incorrect. Under these circumstances, the foreseeability of harm helps support the imposition of a duty of care."[16]

This definition implies a much closer relationship than that experienced by most librarians with their users, and indeed by most information professionals. It would be highly unusual for a reference librarian at a public or academic library reference desk to reasonably be seen as "act[ing] in an advisory capacity," of being "manifestly aware of the use that the information will be put," or "in a position to weigh the use for the information against the magnitude and probability of . . . loss." The bottom line is that, were the *Sain* standards to be applied to an information professional, it is not at all clear that a duty of care would be found.

In order for a librarian to find herself in a situation like that in the *Sain* case, she would have to essentially enter into a close, advisory relationship with a user, under circumstances that made it clear to both parties that the user would be relying on the librarian's advice, potentially to his detriment. For example, if a user approached a librarian looking for information on how to incorporate a business, and the librarian agreed to help the user, not just by finding information, but by guiding him through the incorporation process, she could be seen as acting in an advisory capacity, aware of the use to which the information will be put, in a position to weigh the use of the information against the possibility of harm. In such a situation the *Sain* standard could apply, and the librarian could be liable if the incorporation is defective and harm results. However, such actions would clearly be beyond the scope of the normal activities of a reference librarian.

It is interesting to speculate why the court used the language it did to open the door to potential liability in this case. A practical, if perhaps a bit cynical, possibility is that the court was looking for a way to provide relief for the harm Sain suffered without endorsing the tort of educational malpractice—a tort that has been held to be without merit in all other situations. Just as in the clergy malpractice case mentioned below, where the court avoided endorsing clergy malpractice by instead holding the minister to the standards of a counselor, in *Sain* the court used the concept of "persons in the business or profession of supplying information to others" as a way to describe a particular relationship with a duty of care without placing that relationship within the aegis of educational malpractice.

The key point to take from the *Sain* case is not that the court is endorsing the possibility of liability for all "persons in the business or profession of supplying information to others" when harm occurs, but that such harm must occur in a situation where the professional activity in question involved a "special relationship." This relationship requires "act[ing] in an advisory capacity," being "manifestly aware of the use that the information will be put, . . . intend[ing] to supply it for that purpose," and being "in a position to weigh the use for the information against the magnitude and probability of the loss that might attend the use of the information if it is incorrect." This definition is of a special relationship indeed, and it is hard to imagine a situation in which a librarian or other information professional would really qualify for such a definition.

2. THE IMPORTANCE OF "PROFESSION" IN LIABILITY ISSUES

Professionals whose profession makes them subject to the possibility of a malpractice claim face that possibility regardless of their employment status. While traditionally many professionals were not employees, having established an independent practice—for example, as a doctor, or lawyer, or psychologist—their personal liability for their professional actions arose not from their independent status, but from their actions as a professional. It is more common now for such professionals to be actual employees of institutions, but this does not change the fact that such professionals can be individually liable for their professional actions. Thus a lawyer who is an employee of a law firm will still be held personally liable for malpractice, as will a doctor who is employed by a hospital or group practice.

This distinction places the question of professional status at the heart of the analysis of personal liability for information professionals. If information professionals such as librarians are simply employees, and not professionals in the way that a doctor or a lawyer is considered a professional, then they would not be personally liable for harm they cause as long as what they did was within the scope of their employment. This is true even if there is a duty of care that was violated by the librarian and was the proximate cause of the claimant's harm. Liability for the harm would rest with their employer under the doctrine of respondeat superior.

While what might be called, for lack of a better word, "true" professional status is a highly desirable concept, it carries with it the undesirable side effect of making the professional potentially personally liable for harm that occurs during the course of his work. If information professionals are, in fact, simply employees, and not professionals in this legal sense, they would be protected from personal liability by their employment status. On the other hand, if information professionals are truly professionals in the formal and legal sense, then they could be personally liable for harm that results from their work, regardless of whether their employer was liable as well.

As was explained earlier, malpractice is a form of negligence in which the duty of care owed is determined by the standards of the profession involved. Thus the concept of malpractice is inextricably linked with the concept of a profession in the formal, legal sense, and depends on the presence of readily identifiable professional standards from which a duty of care can be derived. The essential question is whether information professionals, either as a whole or in particular roles within the information professions, qualify as professionals for the purposes of malpractice liability and thus are part of a profession that provides such standards. To answer this question we need to look at both sociology and law.

2.1 What Is a Profession?

There is a large body of research in sociology and other disciplines that attempts to define exactly what a profession is. Agreement on the topic is scarce,[17] and indeed, definitions of the term itself are confusing. In one sense, the term profession is used to indicate any specific line of work—for example, the lawn care profession or the computer programming profession. On the other hand, the term profession is used to delineate a group of occupations that are considered to have a special status in society, such as medicine and law. Which professions fall into which category can be very difficult to discern, and is the subject of much debate.

The term "professional" is a similarly slippery concept. The word is used in at least three ways: to do something for money, such as a professional dog walker or a professional musician; to do one's job in a conscientious and responsible manner, as in a receptionist who is very professional when receiving visitors to the firm; and to be a member of a formal profession. For example, doctors and lawyers are considered professionals by virtue of their membership in their profession, regardless of whether they are being paid or how they act while performing their duties.

We are concerned here with the concept of a profession as it affects the issue of malpractice. This is because it is professional standards that determine the duty of care in a malpractice action. It is important that we restrict our discussion of professions and professionals to this limited scope in this book. Because of the exalted status of formal professions in our society, it is only natural that information professionals would want to be considered part of such a group. Being so can lead to higher prestige, more credibility, and higher pay. There is nothing wrong with trying to enhance the position of one's occupation, and nothing in this discussion is intended to denigrate those efforts. Analysis of the concept of profession for malpractice purposes, however, may indicate that the information professions are not professions in that limited legal sense. If this is true it could have obvious benefits for information professionals from the standpoint of avoiding personal liability in most cases for professional activities.

Thus, in many ways asking what is a profession is to pose a big question with no certain answer.[18] One classic definition of a profession is "an occupation based on specialized intellectual study and training, the purpose of which is to supply skilled service or advice to others for a definite fee or salary."[19] Unfortunately, this is vague enough to leave us with more questions than answers. In fact, it has been said that current definitions of a profession could fit any occupation,[20] and that there is no one definite definition of what constitutes a true profession.[21] Any traits used in the definition of the term "profession" must be conceived as variables, forming a continuum along which a given occupation can move.[22] Occupations in a society distribute themselves along this continuum from unskilled jobs to well-recognized and undisputed true professions.[23]

The concept of a profession arose in Western civilization in the Middle Ages. The word profession has its roots in the Latin term for professing a belief, and was first attached to those professions that required public vows of faith or purpose.[24] Disagreement abounds as to what professions constituted this first exalted group. Some authors say they were just medicine and law,[25] while others say medicine, law, and theology,[26] and still others say law, medicine, theology, and university teaching.[27]

With such confusion about what the first professions were, it should be no surprise that there are many current definitions of a profession. Indeed, there are far too many to explore here. We will need to explore this further, but before we do, let's look at the legal approach to defining a profession.

2.2 The Legal View of Professions

Clearly the question of what qualifies as a profession is an open one from a sociological viewpoint. However, you may be wondering why all this debate is necessary, when all we are trying to do is determine whether the information professions are among those professions subject to personal liability for professional actions. The simple reason for all this is that the law doesn't really seem to know what a profession is either. The legal literature, and the body of law on the topic, is just as vague, confusing, and confused as the sociological literature.

In some cases, legislatures have tried to define a profession, but those definitions have been restricted to very specific groups. As such, they don't provide much guidance for other professions that are not directly part of the defined group. Absent a statute, the definition of a profession is a matter of common law. Unfortunately the common law approach has not resulted in any clear answers or even common approaches to the question. In fact, the courts have generally taken three approaches to defining a profession, all three of which have been criticized.[28]

The first approach to a legal definition of a professional has been to confine the definition to those professions recognized at common law. This approach would limit the definition of profession for legal purposes to medicine, law, teaching, and the clergy.[29] Most jurisdictions have rejected this approach as too restrictive.[30] The second approach has been to include as a profession every occupation licensed by the government.[31] This would leave the legal definition of profession in the hands of the legislature, as it determines what occupations should be licensed. The third approach has been to take some middle course, accepting that there are more professions than the original common law view, but that there is some other way to determine which professions qualify. Courts taking this approach have looked to such things as dictionary definitions and education requirements to determine if a particular occupation is a profession.[32]

In short, the courts have done no better job determining what a profession is than have sociologists and others who have studied the problem. We are left with a patchwork of case law and legal doctrine that has some professions subject to malpractice standards and others that are not, without any real guidance on how to judge a particular group. This, in turn fails to guide us as we try to assess whether it is possible for the information professions to be seen as professions subject to liability. Without a legal answer, we need to return to the sociological and library literature to further explore the topic.

2.3 Examining the Characteristics of a Profession

Can the sociological literature further guide us in identifying factors that might make the information professions subject to liability? Most current definitions of profession cluster around certain basic characteristics. Those include:

▶ A body of specialized knowledge[33]
▶ A formal educational process[34]
▶ Standards of admission[35]
▶ Licensure or special designation[36]
▶ Codes of conduct and a code of ethics[37]
▶ A public interest in the work performed[38]
▶ Recognition by the group of a social obligation[39]

Even in agreeing on these factors, a definition is elusive. These qualities can be examined in two ways: first, to see if they point toward those factors that would lead to professional liability by establishing professional standards on which a duty of care could be based; and second, to see how well they fit the information professions.

The characteristics that define a profession are important for malpractice because they point toward, or away from, the existence of a standard of care for a profession. For many professions these characteristics point to a clear set of standards that form the basis for malpractice liability for the profession. For others, including the information professions, the issue is not so clear.

2.3.1 Specialized Knowledge and Formal Education

A standard characteristic of most definitions of profession is that of requiring specialized knowledge and formal education. For example, only those who have successfully completed medical school and attained specialized knowledge of the human body and its diseases (as verified by an entrance exam for the profession) can be legitimately called a physician. The same is true for other true professions, such as law, dentistry, or even the ministry.

Most would agree that the information professions involve specialized knowledge, specifically knowledge of finding information and of using information sources. The question of whether being an information professional requires formal education is less clear. While a master's degree in library science is considered the professional degree for librarians, there is no actual requirement that those who call themselves librarians have such a degree. Because the information professions do not have a licensing system (see below), they do not have a mechanism to enforce formal educational requirements in the profession. In addition, there is no formal or enforceable standard that clearly delineates who can call themselves an information professional and who cannot. This is important from a legal standpoint because in the presence of formal educational requirements it is easier to determine enforceable standards for the profession that can lead to a duty of care. Without such standards, finding a duty of care for the information professions is much more difficult.

2.3.2 Standards of Admission and Licensure

Standards of admission for a profession allow it to uphold requirements of education, competence, and behavior by restricting membership to those who meet the requirements. Licensure, a related but separate topic, allows a regulating body to control who may or may not practice a particular profession. Licensing standards can demand that licensees have certain education or training, that they pass some sort of exam, and that they engage in continuing education. A licensing system also allows the regulating body to control professional behavior and punish misbehavior by being able to revoke the license.

Librarianship has long wrestled with the idea of certification or licensure.[40] There has been no comprehensive or widespread answer to the issue, although efforts on various fronts continue.[41] As a general rule, there are no standards of admission or licensing bodies for librarians and other information professionals, other than those imposed by employers as conditions for employment.

Without standards of admission or licensing, it becomes very hard to establish standards of performance, or to enforce those standards through any mechanism other than workplace discipline. As Leigh points out, the American Library Association has accreditation standards for library schools, but has not been able to establish minimum standards of performance for librarians.[42] Without such standards it becomes much more difficult to discern standards that would support a professional duty of care.

2.3.3 Ethics, Public Interest, and Social Obligation

One of the reasons for allowing "true" professions to take a prestigious place in society is that such professionals are generally required to place the interests of society and of their clients above their own. This can involve providing their services for free in some circumstances, and placing the interests of their clients above their own personal interests and wishes. For instance, many bar associations require lawyers to donate some of their time to representing clients who are unable to pay them. Doctors also routinely provide free care.

True professions also place a paramount emphasis on ethical behavior. This arises because of the serious matters that the professions deal with, and the responsibility they take for dealing with their clients' problems or interests. As a result these professions have clearly laid out ethical standards and rigorous enforcement mechanisms to deal with ethical violations.

Most branches of the information professions seek to serve the public interest, and see a strong social obligation in their work. This characteristic of a true profession is one of the strongest that the information professions put forth. The information professions generally have been concerned with the ethics of their work and have strived to codify those ethics in ethical codes. All of the major information profession national organizations have a code of ethics.[43] While a code of ethics is a key characteristic of a true profession, the codes of ethics of the national bodies of the information professions don't actually meet the criteria of a code of ethics for a true profession. This is because they are all aspirational in nature rather than proscriptive. This difference is crucial. For example, lawyers must abide by a code of ethics, called the Code of Professional Responsibility, that governs what they can and cannot do as they practice law. This code has aspirational elements, but also lays out strict behavioral requirements that must be met. Failure to meet those requirements can result in disciplinary action or even the loss of the lawyer's license to practice law.

By comparison, the ethical codes of the information professions do not proscribe any particular behaviors. More importantly, they do not provide any avenue for enforcement when an ethical standard is violated. This is inevitably the case because the information professions have no standards for admission or licensing authority, and therefore have no ability to level sanctions for inappropriate behavior.

2.4 Do the Information Professions Fit the Definition of "Profession"?

So what would be the distinction between a profession and a nonprofession for purposes of liability? According to Greenwood, a nonprofession has customers, while professionals have clients.[44] This distinction is important, because customers determine what services or commodities they want and shop around for them, while professionals dictate to the client who then accedes to the professional's judgment. Client subordination to professional authority gives the professional monopoly of judgment.[45] This distinction, between assisting someone as they continue to be responsible for their problem or activity (as in the case of a customer), and taking full responsibility for handling the matter (as with a client) appears to be a crucial matter for legal purposes.

2.4.1 Opinions on Librarianship as a Profession

With no clear answers on what constitutes an actual profession, or whether the information professions would qualify as such, we are left to sift through opinions of experts for some ideas. What literature there is by sociologists on this issue addresses only librarianship, although the other branches of the information professions are closely enough related to be guided by the same thoughts.

Robert Leigh, writing in 1950, said that librarianship "may best be characterized as a skilled occupation on its way to becoming a professional organization."[46] He does not specify what must happen on that progression for librarianship to finally become a profession. Harold Wilensky is similarly noncommittal, admitting only that librarianship is a "borderline case as to whether it is a profession."[47]

William Goode wrote about the topic several times. He is of the opinion that librarianship does not qualify as a true profession.[48] Among other things, he points out that there are no clear standards for what a librarian should know,[49] that the knowledge of librarians is not scientific enough to qualify as a profession,[50] that an experienced nonprofessional can do the same job that trained professionals can,[51] that librarians do not control their clients and cannot impose their authority on them,[52] and that librarians seek to implement standards imposed by others, such as faculty or the general public.[53] As a result, he says that society is not convinced that there is a real science to librarianship, as the skills involved are thought to be clerical and administrative.[54]

2.4.2 The "Semi-professions"

Sociologists studying the concept of professions have coined the term "semi-professions" to refer to professional groups that do not quite meet the standard criteria of being a true profession. Librarianship has been specifically mentioned in this context.[55] Semi-professions are seen as lacking autonomy, and lacking exclusive knowledge that gives them a public mandate to operate independently.[56] As a result, semi-professional organizations are more bureaucratic, place greater emphasis on hierarchical rank, and provide greater rewards for administrative and supervisory work than for professional work.[57]

Being a member of a semi-profession would serve to minimize the chance of professional liability for individual information professionals. The lack of autonomy of a semi-professional, combined with working in a hierarchical organization, would indicate that the status of the information worker is that of an employee rather than an independent professional. As we have seen, this would place any tort liability in the hands of the employer and would make the worker involved immune from personal liability, so long as the actions complained of occurred within the scope of their normal duties. This outcome is desirable, at least in the limited sense that it shields information professionals from personal liability for actions within the scope of their employment.

2.4.3 Comparisons with Teachers and Clergy

In the library literature, those who are anticipating liability for information professionals have used such professions as teaching and ministry as comparisons to support their point. The comparison between teachers or clergy and librarians is instructive and worth examining briefly. Of the two, claims against teachers have gotten the most attention.

2.4.3.1 Teachers

It would appear that malpractice claims against teachers would be more likely to be successful than those against librarians. This is true for a number of reasons. The teaching profession provides two important elements of a profession that are lacking in the information professions. First, teachers are licensed, which presumably allows for fairly concrete standards against which negligent activity can be measured. Second, there have been actual attempts to sue teachers for malpractice, and case law has been published.

Other less formal factors would also point to a greater likelihood for a successful malpractice claim against a teacher. One can assume that a teacher-student relationship is closer than that of an information professional with a user, and that it comes with more expectations of a measurable and identifiable outcome. In addition, a failure to perform the duties of an educator can be assumed to inflict a concrete type of harm on a student. Thus, in light of our examination of tort theory, it would appear logical that teachers might have a verifiable duty of care, the violation of which could be found to be the proximate cause of harm to a student. All of this would indicate that teachers are more vulnerable than librarians to a negligence or malpractice claim.

Just as in librarianship, the late 1970s saw predictions in the literature of a flood of law suits against teachers.[58] Although some suits were filed, the flood never materialized, and as of this writing, no successful educational malpractice case has been published.[59] This is in spite of the fact that some of the literature was not only predicting malpractice claims against teachers, but clamoring for it.[60]

The idea of educational malpractice has had absolutely no success in the courts, in spite of the close relationship between teachers and students, and the potential for identifiable harm.[61] Several courts have concluded that a duty of care for educators does not exist,[62] while others have refused to allow the tort as a matter of public policy.[63] Interestingly, at least one court notes that, while education is a collaborative effort, the ultimate responsibility for success remains with the student.[64] This collaborative effort is similar to the type of interaction that takes place in most of the information professions, with the qualification that such interactions are usually both brief and informal. To the extent that the comparison is accurate, the uniform refusal of courts across America to refuse to recognize a tort of educational malpractice makes the idea of information professional malpractice as a viable tort claim that much more unlikely.

2.4.3.2 Clergy

Another interesting example is that of clergy malpractice. As with teachers, the idea of holding clergy responsible for malpractice has found almost no favor in any court in America.[65] The single exception to this to date is a case involving a minister who became sexually involved with a person for whom he was also providing marital counseling.[66] In that case, the Federal 5th Circuit Court of Appeals found that the defendant was acting not as a minister, but as a counselor, and that the standards of the counseling professions should be applied to the case.[67] Other research on clergy malpractice has confirmed this view.[68]

3. A POSSIBLE SOLUTION: THE CONCEPTS OF FIDUCIARY AND CONSULTANT

As you can see, there has been quite a struggle to discern where the information professions fit in the grand scheme of society's professions, and how that placement might affect potential liability for professional actions. All of the writers, both in the library literature and in the general literature on professions, have struggled to define what a profession is and how this relates to professional liability. The basic assumption seems to be that those occupations which can be called professions will face professional liability, and those which cannot, will not. Clearly, such a bright line does not exist, and concepts like "semi-professions" have been put forward in order to fill the gap.

Perhaps another approach would be more fruitful, and provide more guidance on liability issues, not just for the information professions, but for all professions. This approach would look at the roles that professionals fill, and discern between those that assume a fiduciary role and those that assume a consulting role.

3.1 What Is a Fiduciary?

Put in simple terms, a fiduciary is someone who acts primarily for another.[69] The Restatement, (Second) of the Law of Agency defines a fiduciary as "a person having a duty, created by his undertaking, to act primarily for the benefit of another in matters connected with his undertaking."[70] The person for whom the fiduciary will act is referred to as the principal.[71] Fiduciaries have certain obligations to their principal. These include a duty of loyalty to the principal, and a duty to act only in the principal's interest, foregoing any personal advantage, aside from being compensated for their work.[72]

The term "fiduciary" is used most commonly to describe certain financial and business relationships, but the term can have a broader meaning. One case defined a fiduciary as "any person who occupies a position of peculiar confidence towards another."[73] Thus, almost anyone who agrees to undertake a responsibility to act for the benefit of another can be a fiduciary. However, one of the key aspects of a fiduciary relationship is that it must be undertaken by both parties.[74] This means that having someone assume that they have a fiduciary relationship, or a relationship of trust, with another is not enough.[75] As a result, even if information professionals acted as fiduciaries in certain circumstances, they would have to enter into that relationship knowingly and voluntarily in each case. It would not be enough for a user to simply assume that a fiduciary relationship existed.[76]

Those professions that take responsibility for a client's problem or situation can be seen as having a fiduciary role in the relationship. This is explicitly true in the case of some professions, such as law and accounting, but is implicitly true in other situations. Thus a doctor assumes a fiduciary duty to attempt to diagnose and treat a medical problem, as does an architect for the proper design of a building, or even a barber for providing an appropriate haircut. In each case the client presents a problem or need to the professional, and the professional assumes a fiduciary duty to render the service required, while upholding the duty of care of their profession.

3.2 What Is a Consultant?

While fiduciary is a common legal term, and thus has the benefit of being well defined as a result of much legal study and many court decisions, the term "consultant" has not been prominent in legal matters. A general definition of a consultant is one who offers professional advice or services regarding matters in his field of special knowledge or training.[77] One legal opinion defined the word "consulting" as "designating one called in conference regarding some case or project; as, a consulting engineer."[78] This describes a relationship in which a professional provides something of value, particularly information, but does not assume responsibility for the problem or outcome as a fiduciary does. As an example, it has been held that when a physician consults another physician concerning a patient's diagnosis, the consulting physician does not enter into a physician-patient relationship and cannot be sued for malpractice by the patient.[79]

3.3 Are Information Professionals Fiduciaries or Consultants?

If we accept the idea that a professional can fill either fiduciary or consulting roles and still be a professional, we can then ask which of these roles are assumed by information professionals. The crucial question is the extent to which information professionals assume responsibility for their client's need and assume responsibility for the outcome.

As a general rule, it seems clear that most information professionals are consulting, rather than fiduciary professionals. A possible exception to this would be information brokers. For librarians, archivists, and curators, it seems clear that the role they play is one of a consultant. Users come to them with an information need, and they provide possible sources to satisfy that need. Librarians do not dictate what sources the user can avail themselves of, nor do they follow through to assess how the information is used. This conclusion is bolstered by the gratuitous nature of reference interactions. There is no contract in place, and the user is not directly buying a service or compensating the librarians for the information.

Information brokers could be seen as assuming a fiduciary role under certain circumstances. By paying a direct fee for the information broker's service, and depending on the nature of the information request and the terms of the agreement between the information broker and the customer, the relationship between the two could rise to the level of a fiduciary.

The distinction between a fiduciary and a consultant can help us bring some order to the concept of profession for legal purposes. The fiduciary nature of the professional relationship is what gives rise to a duty of care, and makes the professional potentially liable for harm. It can also be true that consulting professions, such as the information professions, are true profession in every sense, but ones whose role does not require a fiduciary relationship. Without such a role liability would not be possible, except in very specific and unusual circumstances.

4. EMPLOYMENT STATUS AND PERSONAL LIABILITY

Whether or not our discussion of professional status solves the issues of potential liability, the issues of employment status also has a role. For most people in most careers in our society, employment status has a direct and important effect on the issue of personal liability for actions at work. Certain professionals, members of professions that assume a fiduciary responsibility for their client's problems or needs, are personally liable for harm that results from their professional activities regardless of their employment status. For just about everyone else, personal liability is not possible when they are an employee of some kind of organization or business, although the organization can be fully liable for their actions.

4.1 Employee Liability

As a general rule, employees are not subject to personal liability for harm that occurs in the normal course of their duties.[80] This concept, known in law by the Latin term "respondeat superior," simply means that an employer will be held responsible for the harmful acts of an employee, so long as those acts are within the scope of the employee's employment. For example, when a library janitor leaves a puddle of water in a library hallway, causing a user to slip and fall, it is the library that will be sued for the resulting damages. Although the janitor caused the harm, his employer is the one who will answer for it. This is true even if a law was violated. A library that employs a bookmobile driver who causes an accident while speeding in the bookmobile will still be liable for the employee's actions, even though the driver broke the law.[81]

The concept of being within the scope of employment is very important. If an employee's activities are found to be outside the scope of employment, not only would the employee not be protected by the respondeat superior doctrine, but it could serve to shift the entire liability to the employee, leaving the employer out of the claim. For this reason, all information professionals should be sure they understand the activities that are within the scope of their employment, and that their understanding matches that of the management of their employer.

There are a number of ways that a librarian or information professional could conceivably engage in activities outside the scope of their jobs. One possibility is an overly helpful reference librarian who involves herself personally in a user's information needs and problems. If harm were to result from activities she had been involved in, the library could argue that her overinvolvement was beyond the scope of her duties. It is also possible that excessively poor service could meet this argument, as would intentional torts conducted while working.

Scope of Employment

1. A user asks a reference librarian to help him find a particular section of the state code that he needs in order to pursue a legal matter. The librarian does so, but fails to notice that the code is out of date. It turns out that the code section the user wanted has been changed since the publication of the code the librarian consulted, and as a result the user's legal matter turned out badly.

   Q: Were the librarian's actions within the scope of her employment?

   A: Yes. Although she may have committed an error, finding information for library users is fully within the scope of her duties as a reference librarian. As an employee she would not be personally liable for any harm.

2. After finding the requested code section, the reference librarian offers the user her opinion about the legal matter, tells him how he should proceed, and even offers to help him write a document for use in the case. The user takes her advice, which turns out to be wrong, and as a result he is harmed.

   Q: Were the librarian's actions within the scope of her employment?

   A: No. Offering opinions and advice was not within the scope of the reference librarian's employment. As a result, she could be personally liable for the user's harm.

Members of professions that are subject to malpractice claims can be personally liable even if they are employees. If information professionals such as librarians are not members of a profession that assumes a fiduciary responsibility, then their employee status would protect them from any personal liability that might arise out of activities that were within the scope of their employment. This protection does not extend to independent contractors and those who are considered self-employed.

4.2 Self-employment and Liability

Someone who is self-employed loses the shield of vicarious liability that an employee has for actions that are within the scope of employment. This means that, were there a valid tort claim of some kind, a self-employed person would be fully liable for that claim. This exposure does not overcome the requirements for a valid claim, including an established duty of care, violation of the duty, probable cause, and harm.

Self-employment is, at present, relatively rare in the information professions. Indeed, apart from information brokers, the vast majority of information professionals are employed, usually by institutions such as public or academic libraries, school systems, or private industry. For such persons the self-employment issue is irrelevant. While self-employment can be an issue for information brokers, there are many other factors that are different for that branch of the information professions, as the chapter on information brokers will explain.

5. USER STATUS AND LIABILITY

The status of the user involved can have an effect on the potential for liability. We can look at users in terms of their relationship with the library or institution, and also in terms of their expertise. These factors can determine whether the user can bring any kind of action at all, and if so, to what extent their reliance on the actions of the information professional can be seen as reasonable.

In terms of their relationship to the institution, users can be classed as employees of the parent institution of which the library is part, students enrolled at the institution, members of the public, or customers. These categories of users will be discussed separately, but it is important to emphasize that the identity of a user is dependent on their actual activity at the time they use the library. For example, a janitor at a public library is an employee, but if he consults a reference librarian on a personal project, he would probably be considered a member of the public for our analysis, because his use of the library is not in the course of his employment. Similarly, a student who asks a reference question related to her schoolwork is in a different role than if she is asking for information related to a non-academic information need.

5.1 Employees

Employees are generally precluded from suing each other for harms that occur in the course of their employment. Originally, this doctrine arose under what was called the "fellow servant rule", in which an employee was held to have assumed the risk of the negligence of fellow employees.[82] By the 1940s this doctrine had been entirely supplanted by the workers' compensation system, which guarantees employees compensation for harm suffered on the job, in return for a complete bar against suing an employer or fellow employee for harms suffered during the course of employment.[83] The result would be that, should a fellow employee of a librarian suffer harm during the course of their employment due to the actions of the librarian, the recourse for that harm would be exclusively through the workers' compensation system. The librarian would not be personally liable.

5.2 Students

Students fall into two different groups. First there are students using academic libraries, which would include college, graduate, or professional students. This group needs to be considered separately from elementary, middle or high school students using a school library.

5.2.1 Students in Academic Libraries

When dealing with students, the crucial question would be the nature of the harm complained of. For students pursuing school-related tasks when seeking information, claims of harm related to the quality or nature of their education are clearly precluded under current law. Thus a student who wants to sue because she received a poor grade in a course that she blames on erroneous information supplied by an academic librarian would not be able to sue. The issue of liability would appear to be fully and firmly answered by the uniform refusal of American courts to endorse the concept of educational malpractice.

Other potential scenarios when dealing with students are less clear, but still highly unlikely, and would depend greatly on the facts of the particular claim. As an example, educational institutions, and sometimes educators, can be held liable for physical harm that occurs during educational activities. A specific example of this would be a class-related chemistry experiment in which an explosion occurs, injuring the student. Liability for the academic institution and educator involved would hinge on such issues as adequate instruction, proper supervision of the student's work, proper safety precautions, and so forth.

If we imagine that in this case the student caused the explosion when using erroneous information supplied by a reference librarian in the college library, it is possible to see how the librarian could be included in the claim. However, this simply raises the issue of reasonable reliance. Once again, it becomes a question of whether it was reasonable for the student to rely solely on the reference librarian, without otherwise verifying the information or taking other steps to assure that the information she was supplied was appropriate for her needs. In order to succeed with the claim against the librarian it would be necessary to show that the harm resulted directly from the work of the librarian, and that the student's reliance on the librarian was reasonable.

5.2.2 School Library Users

School librarians face three separate areas of analysis when considering liability issues. The first involves the constellation of risks associated with working in a school setting and dealing with K–12 students. The second are those issues that arise when students use the school library for their personal, non-school-related needs. The third is the liability issues that could arise when pursuing educational activities with students.

Although no court in America has adopted the tort of educational malpractice, there are a number of sources of potential liability for educators and professionals who work with K–12 students. Unless protected by governmental immunity, teachers and schools are subject to a reasonable duty of care when supervising and instructing students, and sometimes have an affirmative duty to protect students from harm.[84] Thus educators can be liable for such things as dangerous playground equipment, failing to supervise students, or failing to report suspected abuse. Because these liability risks adhere to everyone who works in a K–12 school, they necessarily also apply to school librarians. That said, most of these sources of liability are beyond our scope, as they do not arise out of a librarian's professional activities as a librarian.

A second area of concern for school librarians arises when students use the school library for their own personal information needs, as opposed to using it as part of some sort of class or other formal educational activity. At first glance, it would appear that such usage raises the same, admittedly limited, possibility of liability as a public or academic librarian might face when dealing with members of the public. However, with K–12 students there is the added factor that students, as minors, should be supervised in most or all of their activities. We can only speculate as to how such a case might transpire, but it would seem logical that, were a student to get information from their school library and then incur harm, the question of who should have been supervising and guiding the child at the time of the harm would be a far more important question than where the student got the information that was connected to the harm.

The third area of concern would be for liability that could arise during the school librarian's educational activities with students. In this case, unless the librarian was supervising students during activities that were somehow risky or dangerous, there appears to be little or no risk of liability. As with teachers, complaints about a school librarian's educational activities would have to come under a claim of educational malpractice, a liability claim that has had no success in American courts.

5.3 Members of the Public

Members of the public are those who have the right to use the library, but have no other formal affiliation with the library or its parent institution. Thus, the users of a public library would be members of the public, as would users of an academic library that is open to the public, unless the user in question is also a student, staff, or faculty member of the academic institution. For purposes of our analysis, employees pursuing information for non-work-related purposes, or students who similarly are looking for information for reasons other than pursuing their education, would be considered members of the public because their information seeking is not related to their status as an employee or a student. Thus, for example, a library employee who approaches the reference desk while not at work in order to find information about a personal matter or interest might be considered a member of the public when doing so.

Members of the public have the clearest theoretical chance of successfully bringing a claim against a librarian. This is primarily because, unlike employees and students, their status as a user does not have existing law that bars bringing a claim. This is not, however, the same as saying that such a claim would ever be valid. The analysis of the possibility of liability when dealing with members of the public is the same as that presented in other parts of this book. In order to succeed, the claimant would have to show not only that there was a problem with the supplied information, but that it was reasonable to rely on the work of the librarian to the extent that the librarian's efforts were the proximate cause of the harm. The purely consultative role of librarians when assisting users would make this a very difficult hurdle to get over.

5.4 Customers

Customers are those who are paying a direct fee for information services. The most common situation involving customers in the information professions is in the work of information brokers. This relationship is very different from the other user types described above. The exchange of value for information, and the probable presence of a contractual agreement, makes the possibility of liability very real. The ins and outs of dealing with paying customers will be discussed at length in Chapter Eight.

6. QUESTIONS AND ANSWERS

1. Why is the concept of "profession" important in liability issues?
The concept of profession is important in two ways. First, the existence of an established profession, especially if its members are specially trained, licensed, certified, or otherwise held accountable for a specialized body of knowledge, can provide standards that can delineate a duty of care in their professional activities. The second reason is that, for many professions, members can be personally liable for their professional activities regardless of employment status.

2. How does employment status affect liability?
Unless one's profession allows for personal liability regardless of employment status, being an employee will shield a worker from personal liability for harm caused on the job, provided the harm arose while the worker was acting within the scope of her employment. This is because liability for employee acts falls on the employer under the doctrine of respondeat superior.

3. What is the difference between a fiduciary and a consultant?
As they are used in this chapter, the term fiduciary describes someone who takes control of a client's problem in order to solve it or provide a needed service. A consultant is one who provides information or advice, but leaves clients to solve the problem on their own. The distinction is important in analyzing if there is a potential for liability because a fiduciary relationship creates a duty of care, where a consultant relationship does not.

4. Is there a standard of care for the information professions?
This question is unresolved, but there are important factors that militate against it for most activities of information professionals. Apart from information brokers, the generally arms-length relationship that information professionals have with their users, combined with the relatively limited role that they play in the user's information need makes a duty of care an unlikely possibility.

5. What effect does user status have on liability?
The relationship of the user to the institution is a key matter in determining the possibility of liability. Certain classes of users, such as employees or students, may be precluded from filing suit because of their status. On the other hand, customers who pay a direct fee for an information service might have both a stronger claim for relying on an information service, as well as a contractual claim if harm results.

7. IMPORTANT POINTS TO REMEMBER

▶ Whether or not an occupation is a profession can have a large effect on the possibility of liability, because a profession would have a duty of care toward its clients. This could lead to liability.

▶ Defining a profession is almost impossible to do. However, the lack of standards for admission, licensing, codes of ethics that punish violations, and other factors indicate that the information professions are not a profession in this sense.

▶ One helpful approach is to look at professions as either fiduciary, in which case they take control of their client's problem or need, or consulting, in which case they provide assistance and information but do not take control. While a fiduciary relationship would point the way to a duty of care, and liability, a consulting relationship most likely would not.

▶ Information professionals who are employees are most likely protected from personal liability under the doctrine of respondeat superior, in which the employer is liable for the misdeeds of employees, provided that the harm complained of occurred within the scope of the employee's duties.

ENDNOTES

[1] An excellent source of information about institutional liability for libraries is *The Library's Legal Answer Book* by Mary Minow and Tomas A. Lipinski (American Library Association, 2003).

[2] David F. Partlett, *Professional Negligence*, 26 (1985).

[3] Allan Angoff, *Library Malpractice Suit: Could It Happen to You?* 7 American Libraries 489 (1976).

[4] *Id.*

[5] While such a claim is possible, a number of cases take the stance that publications are not subject to product liability claims. See, *e.g., Cardozo v. True*, 342 So. 2d 1053, (Fla. Dist. Ct. App. 1977) (refusing to impose liability on a retail book dealer for illness suffered by a cookbook purchaser who ate certain ingredients called for by one of the book's recipes, where the cookbook failed to warn that such ingredients, if uncooked, were poisonous; decided under an implied warranty theory); *Jones v. J.B. Lippincott Co.*, 694 F. Supp. 1216, (D. Md. 1988) (products liability law does not apply to the dissemination of an idea or knowledge in books or other published material; to do so could chill expression and publication, which is inconsistent with fundamental free speech principles); *Way v. Boy Scouts of America*, 856 S.W.2d 230 (Tex. App. 1993) (ideas, thoughts, words, and information contained in a magazine are not products subject to strict liability).

[6] *Hesler v. California Hospital Co.*, 174 P. 654 Cal. 1918

[7] *Comeaux v. Miles*, 118 So. 786 (La. App. 1928).

[8] Blodwen Tarter, *Information Liability: New Interpretations for the Electronic Age*, 11 Computer L. Rev. & Tech. L.J. 490 (1992), at 491. Anne Mintz has argued that this lack of standards puts librarians at a greater risk for litigation, but it is hard to see how this could be so. In fact, it can be argued that a lack of identifiable standards lowers the risk of litigation because standards raise the expectations of patrons. See Anne P. Mintz, *Information Practice and Malpractice: Do We Need Malpractice Insurance?* 9 ONLINE 20 (1984), at 20.

[9] *Sain v. Cedar Rapids Community School District*, 626 N.W.2d 115 (Iowa 2001).

[10] John Cannan, *Are Public Librarians Immune from Suit? Muddying the Already Murky Waters of Law Librarian Liability*, 91 Law Lib. J. 7 (2007).

[11] *Sain, supra* note 9, at 126.

[12] *Id.*, at 129.

[13] *Key v. Coryell*, 185 S.W.3d 98 (Ark. App., 2004).

[14] *Sain, supra* note 9, at 124.

[15] *Id.*

[16] *Id.*, at 125.

[17] See, *e.g.*, William J. Goode, *The Profession: Reports and Opinions*, 25 Am. Sociological Rev., 902 (1960) (hereinafter Goode, *Profession*).

[18] Robert D. Leigh, *The Public Library in the U.S.* 187 (1950).

[19] A.M. Carr-Saunders, *Professions: Their Organization and Place in Society*, 5 (1928) (hereinafter Carr-Saunders, *Professions*).

[20] Partlett, *supra* note 2, at 2.

[21] E. W. Roddenberry, *Achieving Professionalism*, 44 J. Crim. L. Criminology & Police Sci. 109, 110 (1953).

[22] William J. Goode, *The Librarian: From Occupation to Profession?* 31 Lib. Q. 306, 307 (1961) (hereinafter Goode, *Librarian*).

[23] Ernest Greenwood, *Attributes of a Profession*, 2 Social Work 45 (1957), at 46.

[24] *Id.*, at 109.

[25] A.M. Carr-Saunders & P.A. Wilson, *The Professions*, 1933, at 3 (hereinafter Carr-Saunders & Wilson).

[26] Roddenberry, *supra* note 21, at 109; Carr-Saunders, *Professions*, *supra* note 25, at 4.

[27] William J. Goode, *The Theoretical Limits of Professionalization in the Semi-Professions and Their Organization: Teachers, Nurses, Social Workers* 266 (Amitai Etzioni, ed. 1969), at 267 (hereinafter Goode, *Theoretical*).

[28] Michael J. Polelle, *Who's On First, and What's a Professional?* 33 U.S.F. L. Rev. 205 (1998–1999).

[29] *Id.*, at 219.

[30] *Id.*

[31] *Id.*

[32] *Id.*

[33] Goode, *Theoretical, supra* note 27, at 276; Goode, *Librarian, supra* note 22, at 308; John A. Gray, *Personal Malpractice Liability of Reference Librarians and Information Brokers* 9 J. Lib. Admin. 71, 80 n. 1. (1988); Roddenberry, *supra* note 21, at 110.

[34] Good, *Theoretical, supra* note 27, at 276; Gray, *supra* note 33, at 80 n. 1; Leigh, *supra* note 18, at 188.

[35] Gray, *supra* note 33, at 71 n.1; Leigh, *supra* note 18, at 188

[36] Good, *Theoretical, supra* note 27, at 276; Gray, *supra* note 33, at 80 n.1

[37] Good, *Theoretical, supra* note 27, at 276; Gray, *supra* note 33, at 80 n.1; Greenwood, *supra* note 23, at 45; Leigh, *supra* note 18, at 188; Roddenberry, *supra* note 21, at 110.

[38] Gray, *supra* note 33, at 80 n.1.

[39] Goode, *Librarian, supra* note 22, at 308; Gray, *supra* note 33, at 80 n.1.

[40] John N. Berry, *Is Certification the Answer?* 128 Lib. J. 8 (1976).

[41] See Michael Gorman, *Strengthening Our Affiliated Body*, American Libraries, February 2003, at 3.

[42] Leigh, *supra* note 18, at 191.

[43] *E.g.*, American Library Association Code of Ethics, *available at* http://www.ala.org/ Content/NavigationMenu/Our_Association/Offices/Intellectual_Freedom3/Statements_ and_Policies/Code_of_Ethics/Code_of_Ethics.htm; American Association of Law Libraries (AALL) Ethical Principles, *available at* http://www.aallnet.org/about/policy_ethics.asp; American Society for Information Science and Technology (ASIST) Professional Guidelines, *available at* http://www.asis.org/AboutASIS/professional-guidelines.html; Association for Computing Machinery (ACM) Code of Ethics and Professional Conduct, *available at* http://www.acm.org/constitution/code.html; Association of Independent Information Professionals (AIIP) Code of Ethical Business Practice, *available at* http://www.aiip.org/ AboutAIIP/aiipethics.html; Association of Information Technology Professionals (AITP) Code of Ethics, *available at* http://www.aitp.org/organization/about/ethics/ethics.jsp; Institute of Electrical and Electronics Engineers (IEEE) Code of Ethics, *available at* http://www.ieee.org/portal/site/mainsite/menuitem.818c0c39e85ef176fb2275875bac26c8/ index.jsp?&pName=corp_level1&path=about/whatis&file=code.xml&xsl=generic.xsl; Society of American Archivists Code of Ethics, *available at* http://www.archivists.org/governance/ handbook/app_ethics.asp.

[44] Greenwood, *supra* note 23, at 48.

[45] *Id.*

[46] Leigh, *supra* note 18, at 192.

[47] Harold L. Wilensky, *The Professionalization of Everyone?* 70 Am. J. Sociology 137, 142 (1964).

[48] Goode, *Librarian, supra* note 22.

[49] *Id.*, at 311.

[50] *Id.*, at 312.

[51] Goode, *Librarian, supra* note 22, at 313.

[52] *Id.*, at 316.

[53] *Id.*, at 318.

[54] Goode, *Theoretical, supra* note 27, at 286.

[55] Richard L. Simpson & Ida Harper Simpson, *Women and Bureaucracy in the Semi-Professions and Their Organization: Teachers, Nurses, Social Workers* 196 (Amitai Etzioni, ed. 1969).

[56] *Id.*

[57] *Id.*

[58] See Julie O'Hara, *The Fate of Educational Malpractice*, 14 Educ.. L. Rep. 887 (1986).

[59] A search of LexisNexis and Westlaw in July 2008 found a total of 264 cases based on a claim of educational malpractice. In none of those cases was such a claim allowed. See also Laurie S. Jamison, *Educational Malpractice: A Lesson in Professional Accountability*, 32 B.C. L. Rev. 899 (1991); John G. Culhane, *Reinvigorating Educational Malpractice Claims: A Representational Focus*, 67 Wash. L. Rev. 349; Ryland F. Mahathey, Note, *Tort Law: Can an Educator be Liable for a Student's Failure? The Tort of Educational Malpractice* 34 Washburn L.J. 147 (1994).

[60] *E.g.*, Culhane, *supra* note 59.

[61] Dan B. Dobbs, *The Law of Torts*, 690 (2001); Stuart M. Speiser, et al., *The American Law of Torts*, 916 (1997, Supp. 2006); Joel E. Smith, Annotation, *Tort Liability of Public Schools and Institutions of Higher Learning for Educational Malpractice*, 1 Am. L. Rep. 4th 1139 (1980, Supp. 2006).

[62] Jamison, *supra* note 39, at 901; Irving J. Sloan, *Professional Malpractice* (1992), at 81.

[63] *E.g.*, *Brantley v. District of Columbia*, 640 A.2d 181, 183 (1994); *Nalepa v. Plymouth-Canton Community School Dist.*, 525 N.W.2d 897, 904 (1994).

[64] *Ross v. Creighton University*, 740 F. Supp. 1319, 1327-28 (N.D. Ill. 1990).

[65] John F. Wagner, Annotation, *Cause of Action for Clergy Malpractice*, 75 Am. L. Rep. 5th 750 (1990, Supp. 2006).

[66] *Sanders v. Casa View Baptist Church*, 134 f.3d 331 (5th Cir. 1998).

[67] *Id.*

[68] Maury M. Breecher, *Ministerial Malpractice: Is It a Reasonable Fear?* Trial, July 1980, at 11. In the face of marketed liability insurance for clergy, based on reported claims of ministers being sued for malpractice in their counseling activities, the author investigated a number of claimed instances of such suits. None of the claimed actions could be verified.

[69] William A. Gregory, *The Law of Agency and Partnership*, 13 (2001).

[70] Restatement, (Second) of the Law of Agency, § 13, comment a (1958).

[71] *Id.*, at § 1.

[72] Gregory, *supra* note 69, at 13.

[73] *Kinzbach Tool Co. v. Corbett-Wallace Corp.*, 1160 S.W.2d 509 (Tex. 1942).

[74] Gregory B. Westfall, comment, *But I Know It When I See It: A Practical Framework for Analysis and Argument of Informal Fiduciary Relationships*, 23 Tex. Tech. L. Rev. 835 (1992).

[75] *Id.*, at 847.

[76] *Id.*

[77] *Webster's Third New International Dictionary of the English Language*, unabridged, 490 (1993).

[78] *Goldenberg v. Village of Capitan*, 203 P.2d 370, 372 (N.M. 1949).

[79] *Oliver v. Brock*, 342 So.2d 1 (Ala. 1976).

[80] *Fowler V. Harper, et al., The Law of Torts*, §26.6 (2nd ed. 1986).

[81] Note, however, that this only applies to tort liability. Criminal liability is always personal. While the driver will not be sued personally for his actions, he may be prosecuted for his violation of the law and can suffer the full penalties.

[82] Dobbs, *supra* note 61, at 538.

[83] Edward J. Kionka, *Tort Law in a Nutshell*, § 8-13 (2005).

[84] Dobbs, *supra* note 61, at § 259.

▶Five

POTENTIAL SOURCES OF LIABILITY CLAIMS FOR INFORMATION PROFESSIONALS

IN THIS CHAPTER

Based on our understanding of the legal issues involved, any liability claim against an information professional would have to be based on some sort of harm perpetrated in the course of work activities. It will be useful to explore exactly where such harm could arise in the course of an information professional's work, and this chapter strives to do that by examining the following topics:

▶ When information is wrong

▶ When errors occur

▶ Types of errors

▶ Guarantees, authority, and expertise

Several things should be kept in mind. First, although we will withhold judgment at this point as to whether a claim arising from any of the activities listed below could actually result in liability, remember that the possibility of liability is dependent on harm that results from the violation of a duty of care. Any discussion of harm in information work must be framed within the context of violation of a duty. Thus, as with doctors or other professionals, the mere existence of harm resulting from a professional action is not enough to trigger liability. Rather, the act that caused the harm must fall below the standards of care of the profession and thus violate a duty of care.

Second, when harm does occur, it must have been reasonable for the claimant to have relied on the information professional in the way that resulted in the harm. For example, someone who is harmed after relying on information supplied by a reference librarian must show that it was reasonable to rely solely on the information supplied without further investigation or judgment on their part.

Third, any possibility of professional liability must, by definition, require some sort of deviation from standard or competent practices on the part of the information professional. This is because, without such a deviation, there is no possibility that the harm complained of resulted from a violation of duty of care. Because of this, our discussion of library activities in this chapter will focus not so much on the activities themselves as on possible errors, and the potential of those errors to cause harm.

1. HARM IN THE INFORMATION PROFESSIONS

Because no information professional has ever been found liable for professional activities, we can only speculate about what forms harm would take in such a situation. It is clear that both personal harm and economic loss could potentially be involved. In other words, someone would bring a claim because their reliance on the work of the information professional led to either a physical or emotional injury, or to some sort of economic loss.

The question then becomes what kind of activities could conceivably lead to harm. Most of the literature that envisions liability for an information professional does so by posing a situation where inaccurate, incomplete, or wrong information is the cause of the harm. Because the concepts of wrong information and professional error loom so large in the literature,[1] it would be useful to explore them in some detail before we look at other specific sources of potential harm in the information professions.

1.1 When Is Information "Wrong"?

Clearly there is a risk that a user might end up with the wrong information after dealing with an information professional. That said, what constitutes "wrong" can be very difficult to deduce, as can where an error actually occurs.

Without entering into a philosophical debate, it must first be pointed out that the idea of right and wrong information, or accurate and inaccurate information, can be very hard to pin down. There are many factors at play, including the extent to which a particular piece of information is subject to any kind of objective verification; how suitable a piece of information is for the purpose for which it is requested; issues of completeness, relevancy, currency, and appropriate relation to other information and the information need; and finally how the supplied information is interpreted due to experience, beliefs, and opinions. These and many other factors determine whether a particular piece of information is "right" or "wrong" in a given situation.

In the hypothetical scenarios proposed in the literature, this sort of conundrum is elided. Instead, a world of absolute certainty is proposed in which the erroneous information supplied by the information professional is clearly wrong, and it was somehow reasonable for the user to rely on it to their detriment. Unfortunately, in the real world such an easy determination of correctness is often elusive.

1.2 When Is There "Error"?

Apart from the issue of right or wrong, is the question of error. Even if we assume for purposes of discussion that a piece of information is "wrong" in a given situation, at what point is it an error for an information professional to have provided that information? Given the factors listed above, it can be very difficult to discern exactly what is appropriate in response to an information request. One approach to this has been the development of the reference interview, which attempts to understand more fully what the user is requesting. Even with that, though, a full understanding of exactly what is being requested, combined with a full understanding of what is available, is almost impossible to obtain. With such amorphous realities at work, the question of where an action can be said to be in error becomes very hard to identify.

Seemingly, the easiest situation in which to try to identify error concerning information is in those cases where the user is requesting some sort of certain and readily verifiable fact. In many cases simple facts are beyond argument, and cases of error are easily determined, should they occur. For example, the official capital of the Republic of Burundi is Bujumbura, and to provide a different answer, such as Gitega or Muyinga, would be an obvious error, even though these are also cities in Burundi.

Even with such simple fact requests, though, a question can arise as to the veracity of the answer. For instance, imagine that in June 2008 a librarian is asked for the population of the city of Dubuque, Iowa. The librarian responds that the population of Dubuque is 57,696, which is the figure listed as the 2006 estimate on the U.S. Census Bureau Web site.[2] Is the answer "right"? Given that the number was two years old at the time it was provided, there is an excellent chance that the actual population figure for Dubuque had changed, and that the number given was wrong. Further, since the number is an estimate, and indeed since all city population figures are actually estimates, it could very well have been wrong at the time it was generated. In fact, the figure 57,696 is almost certainly wrong, at least by a small amount.

But did the librarian commit an error? More to the point, did she violate a standard of care or competence for her profession? The standard answer would probably be no. After all, she consulted a reputable source, the U.S. Census Bureau, and got the most recent figures available. Even if the answer is verifiably wrong, there is no other or better source with the right answer. The librarian did her job correctly. This means that it is possible for an information professional to provide information that is objectively wrong, and yet not commit an error in doing so.

With a more complex or less certain information request, such complications multiply exponentially. This is why users must retain responsibility for determining whether or not they have satisfied their information need. Under such circumstances, for any error on the part of an information professional to be seen as the cause of any harm, it would have to be of such magnitude that it prevented the user from meeting all or a significant part of their information need; that it did so in a way that the user was powerless to prevent or change; and that it happened under circumstances that the user's reliance on the information professional was reasonable.

1.3 The Anatomy of "Error" in Practice

The idea that an information professional committed an error by providing the wrong information, such that a user's harm was reasonably caused by that error, is conceptually very easy to understand, and even to believe. But a careful analysis of the chain of assumptions in such a claim reveals a much more complicated environment in which it is very difficult to place the information professional in a position directly and reasonably related to the harm.

For purposes of discussion, let's go back to Allan Angoff's hypothetical claim in his 1976 *American Libraries* article.[3] The legal viability of Angoff's scenario already has been debunked several times,[4] but let us put that aside for now and consider the basic claim of the story: That the librarian committed an error in providing information that led to the user's harm.

In Angoff's hypothetical, a user came to the reference desk at his public library and requested information on building a deck. The librarian provided the user with a book from the library's collection that contained directions for building a deck. The book subsequently turned out to have faulty information. The user built the deck, and the deck subsequently fell down, so the user now feels the librarian should be liable for the harm of his deck falling down.

Again, for purposes of discussion, let's take as given a whole series of facts that the plaintiff would otherwise need to prove to make his claim (e.g., that he actually followed the directions in the book when building the deck, that he used appropriate skill in assembling the deck, that the materials he used were adequate and proper, that he didn't do anything to the deck that otherwise caused it to collapse, etc.), and let's ignore the obvious fact that any claim he has is actually with the publisher of the book, not its disseminator. After eliminating all of those complicating issues, we are left with a simple question: What was the error committed by the librarian in this situation?

The librarian responded to a request for information with a book from the collection that appeared to satisfy the user's information need. The implication of the claim, a claim also made in various forms in some of the library literature on liability,[5] is that the librarian should have known that the book had faulty directions. This is where the legal requirement of reasonableness comes in to play. To say that this is reasonable would require that every librarian know fully everything there is to know about every topic on which they assist users, and indeed on every topic to which every piece of information available in the library could apply.

Under such a standard, librarians would need to evaluate every piece of information in their collection, both for its own veracity, and also for its validity for every purpose for which a user would seek to use that information. This is simply impossible, and is certainly not reasonable. As an indication of how unreasonable this idea is, keep in mind the simple fact that it implies that, in the Angoff situation, the librarian should have understood that the directions for building the deck were faulty when no one else involved in producing, disseminating, or using the book was able to figure that out, including the person who used it to build the deck.

Indeed, as we look at all of the possible sources of error that led to the collapse of the deck, we see that the possible errors of the librarian are the least likely to have caused the claimant's harm. Starting with the author of the book on deck-building, it is entirely possible that the book was written with faulty information. This might be actionable if harm results, but as we saw in Chapter Three, publishers have generally not been held liable for faulty information, even when harm does occur. The Angoff scenario would seem most comparable to an example from that chapter, where a publisher was held not responsible for serious physical harm that occurred when a dictionary of mushrooms contained inaccurate information.[6]

Moving to the library, the purchaser and subsequent disseminator of the book, the two possible errors made were: (1) acquiring a book with faulty information and (2) recommending that book to a user. Once again, the question is how the librarians would have known that the book contained faulty information. Unless they were experts on building decks, and also read the book thoroughly to verify all of the information it contained, this is not reasonable. Alternatively, unless the library had been previously notified of a problem with the book, it is not reasonable that they should have any such knowledge.

If the publisher had notified the library of a problem with the book, it becomes more reasonable to find violation of a duty when harm results. If presented with such a notification, the library would most likely have an obligation to remove the book from the collection, or to provide clear notification, in the form of labels or other markings, that the book contained faulty information. If the book remains in the collection, it would also be advisable to include a clear notice that the user uses the book at his own risk. However, in Angoff's scenario, no such notice had been provided to the library.

Moving on to the user, we find many possible sources of error. There are the possible errors of not verifying the information in the book, of not bringing requisite building skill to the project to properly build a deck, of not following the directions properly, of doing a poor or incompetent job in building, of using inappropriate materials for the project, of not checking the final project properly, and so forth.

In the situation Angoff presents, the simple fact is that not only is the librarian not the reasonable source of the error that led to the claimant's harm, the librarian is also the only one who has not committed an error at all. In the end, Angoff's scenario shows not the possibility of a claim against a library, but how unlikely such a claim would be.

Although it may make us uncomfortable to do so, we can assume that for most information professionals errors of some kind are a regular occurrence. But as we look at possible sources of error in information work, it would be useful to keep in mind the larger point, that liability would only result when such errors are reasonably the cause of the claimant's harm.

2. FORMS OF ERROR

Our discussion of forms of error will be, by necessity, speculative. The purpose of this discussion is to highlight those activities that might conceivably be connected with a liability claim. To begin, we can divide errors into three categories: resource errors, service errors, and user errors.

2.1 Resource Errors

Resource errors involve problems that arise from the resources used themselves, rather than from the actions of the information professional involved. Resource errors are those that involve faulty, inappropriate, out-of-date, or incomplete information. In a claim based on this type of error, the information professional has consulted, used, or provided an inappropriate resource, with the result that harm has occurred. Providing a resource that is incomplete or does not supply all of the information required for the task would be a resource error. A resource error would be analogous to a doctor using an inappropriate instrument during surgery, or an architect relying on a faulty computer program to calculate some aspect of a building project. The result is that, while the professional made every effort to perform the job properly, the resource that was relied on resulted in an error.

The open question for information professionals is to what extent the problem with the resource is reasonably knowable, and therefore the responsibility of the information professional. The accuracy of some information is easily discernible. Older books on topics that have changed in recent times are one example. Therefore, a book on Russia published in 1985, or a book on sexually transmitted infections published in 1980, can both be assumed to have out-of-date and, by current standards, inaccurate information. With more technical information, or with topics that have not changed much, such an assessment is much more difficult. In many cases evaluating the quality of the information in a source is beyond the expertise of the average librarian.

It can be assumed that responsibility for resource errors would vary, depending on the exact nature of the job being performed and the relationship between the information professional and the client. An information broker who is being paid to find information on a particular company could probably be at fault if she uses inappropriate or out-of-date sources that miss important information. On the other hand, it does not appear reasonable to assume that a generalist reference librarian in an academic library can judge the adequacy of a chemistry reference book that appears to contain information requested by a library user.

Resource errors occur in various forms. The most prominent are situations in which the resource provides either inaccurate information, out-of-date information, or incomplete information.

2.1.1 Inaccurate Information

The most prominent form of resource error is that of inaccurate information. This error comes into play when the information provided by a resource turns out to be wrong in some definite sense. It is important not to confuse supplying inaccurate information as a resource error with supplying the wrong information as a service error. As a resource error, the inaccurate information is wrong in the resource itself, the result of mistake or some other error on the part of the producer of the information.

The Angoff example contemplates a resource error involving inaccurate information. The complaint was that the book supplied by the librarian contained faulty information about building a deck. It is important to keep in mind two things about resource errors involving inaccurate information. The first is that if the information is truly wrong in an objective sense, and the use of the information leads to harm, it is possible that the producer of the information—for example, the author or publisher—could be held liable for the harm. The second is that an information professional would not be liable for the harm unless she knew or reasonably should have known that information in the resource was wrong.[7] Even then, the fact that the user relied on the information professional without further action on the user's part must be reasonable under the circumstances before liability could ensue.

2.1.2 Out-of-date Information

Information that is accurate when produced or published can become inaccurate with the passage of time. The example of population figures was cited previously.

Other common types of information that can become out of date include scientific and medical information, legal information, and directories of all kinds. Once the information reflected in a resource has changed, the resource is in error as to that information.

2.1.3 Incomplete Information

Another form of resource error would be where the resource in question fails to provide all of the information required for an information need. An example would be a cookbook in which a recipe leaves out a key ingredient. In order for this error to occur, the missing information must be such that it normally would be included in the type of resource in question, although incomplete information errors will necessarily vary with the actual information need of the user.

Even then, the issue of liability is not clear. In *Cardozo v. True,* a Florida book seller was sued because a recipe book sold by the store neglected to inform readers that dasheen root, an ingredient in one of the recipes, was poisonous if uncooked.[8] Once again, the court found that it was not reasonable to hold a disseminator of information responsible for the accuracy of content. According to the court, "[i]t is unthinkable that standards imposed on the quality of goods sold

Resource Errors

1. A user approaches a public library reference desk looking for a recipe for whole wheat bread. The librarian finds a recipe in a cookbook in the library's collection and gives it to the user. By mistake, the recipe as printed omits yeast as an ingredient, which is essential to the recipe. The information is incomplete.

2. A library user asks for information about the penalties for being convicted of driving while intoxicated. The information is located in the state code. The copy of the state code in the library's collection is four years old, and within the last year the state legislature changed the code to significantly enhance the penalties for driving while intoxicated. As a result, the information in the copy of the state code that the user consulted was seriously out of date. Note that one could say that the librarian committed a service error by not checking for a newer version of the code. That said, the point of this example is that the resource itself contains an error by being out of date.

3. A book on snakes labels two highly poisonous snakes as nonpoisonous. The information is inaccurate.

In each of the situations above the error arose because of a problem with the resource itself, rather than because of the actions of the information professional.

by a merchant would require that merchant, who is a book seller, to evaluate the thought processes of the many authors and publishers of the hundreds and often thousands of books which the merchant offers for sale."[9] If the court is willing to hold the seller of a book to such a low standard, it would seem logical that a library would be in a similar situation.

2.1.4 When Is Liability Possible for Resource Errors?

While it can be assumed that there are pretty broad protections against liability for resource errors, there are some situations where a library or librarian might be held responsible for harm. The most prominent of these would be when the library, or the librarian, knew or should have known that information in a source is inaccurate, out of date, or incomplete.

The clearest case in which responsibility could redound to the library would be when an authoritative source, particularly the publisher, has informed the library of a problem with an item. Having such information, the library would be bound to take appropriate action, and could potentially be found liable if action is not taken and harm results.

Another situation is one in which it is reasonable for a librarian to know that information is out of date. A librarian may not be a lawyer or a pharmacist, but it is reasonable to assume that she would know when new versions of the state code or the *Physician's Desk Reference* are published, and that there could be problems with an out-of-date version of such an item.

Liability for Resource Errors

1. A publisher informs the library that a book on mushrooms has inaccurate information. The publisher supplies an errata sheet to be placed in the book, plus warning labels for the spine and title page. The library does not place the labels or errata sheet in the book, and subsequently a user is harmed because of the uncorrected information. The library is potentially liable in this situation because it knew the information was inaccurate and failed to take reasonable steps to correct the situation.

2. A user is looking for information in the state code. The librarian supplying the code to the user notices that it is four years old. She knows that the code is republished every two years. The librarians points out to the user that the print version is out of date, and offers to help him find the current version online. The user declines her help and uses the out-of-date print version. The information he consults has been changed, and he is later harmed because of this. In this case the librarian would not be liable because she took steps to inform the user of a problem with the material, which the user chose to ignore.

It is always advisable to inform users of any known issues or problems with information being supplied, including that it might be out of date. Doing so places responsibility back on users to satisfy themselves that the information is what they need.

2.2 Service Errors

Service errors occur when the activities of an information professional are themselves the cause of the harm. Put simply, service errors are errors made by information professionals as they go about their jobs. In such cases the appropriate resources were available, but the information professional failed to act in an appropriate manner. One example of this is a reference librarian who fails to do a complete or competent reference interview, and thus provides inadequate results. Another example is an information broker who fails to search all of the appropriate databases required to find the information that their client needs.

There is a crucial distinction between a resource error and a service error. In the case of a resource error, the information available is wrong in some way, but the information professional is either reasonably unaware of the problem, or has no better resource to turn to. With a service error, the proper information could be found, but the information professional does not act properly in order to find it. That said, service errors and resource errors are not mutually exclusive, and can blend together. For instance, if a librarian knows that an item, such as a state code, is out of date but neglects to inform the user of this, it would constitute both a resource error (an out-of-date source) and a service error (failure to inform the user).

All professionals make mistakes, both large and small. No one is contemplating the possibility that all mistakes can be eliminated from anyone's performance. The fact that a service error occurs doesn't necessarily imply anything about liability. The operative question from a liability standpoint is at what point an error committed by an information professional can reasonably be the cause of a user's harm.

It would be impossible to identify all possible service errors that could be committed by every branch of the profession. Rather than attempt that, the sections below will identify broader types of errors that can be extrapolated by the reader into particular work environments. We will look at the concept of service errors in the contexts of unsuitable information, guarantees, misplaced information, privacy, and misuse of donated items.

2.2.1 Unsuitable Information

The concept of unsuitable information threatens to become so broad as to be meaningless. What is meant here by unsuitable information is that the information supplied in response to a user's request is not the appropriate information for the request. Again, we are looking at this from the point of view of a service error, and not as a resource error. In other words, the information supplied is somehow wrong in the particular context of the request, even though the information itself is not wrong in the proper context.

As an example, if a user requested the population of the Dubuque, Iowa, meaning the population of the city itself, it would be a service error to respond with the population figure for the Dubuque metropolitan statistical area, which includes nearby communities in addition to the city of Dubuque. Note that the information itself is not wrong, it is simply unsuited to the specific information request of the user.

The concept of unsuitable information can take many forms, far too many to be listed here, but all are grounded in a fundamental mismatch between the information need and the information provided. It is possible to divide errors based on unsuitable information into two broad types: (1) information unsuited to the question and (2) information unsuited to the user. In both cases the error occurs because the information professional supplying the information provides resources that do not properly fit the information need.

2.2.1.1 Unsuited to the Question

When information is unsuited to the question, the information supplied does not meet the information need. Thus information that is wrong, incomplete, or otherwise lacking is unsuited to the question. Note that this type of error is always contextual. The information provided is not necessarily inherently wrong, nor unsuited to all questions. Rather, in this context the information does not meet the information need.

When information is unsuited to the question as a result of a service error, the problem is that the information professional did not act properly in finding the information requested. In other words, the correct information was reasonably available, but the information professional failed to act in a way that would have found it for the user.

2.2.1.2 Unsuited to the User

Information that is unsuited to the user may be correct and capable of meeting the information need, but is of such a type or quality that the user cannot access or understand it properly. This type of error, again, can take many forms. For example, a chemistry reference work may contain the answer sought by a high school student, but be written in such a way that the student cannot understand it.

In addition to problems of comprehension or understanding, information formats can make information unsuited to the user. For example, a Web site with good information is only useful if the user has access to the Internet. Similarly, users with special needs, such as vision impairments or low reading ability, may not be able to use information in the form that it normally exists in the library.

Unsuitable Information Service Errors

1. A library user would like to know the closing price of a certain stock on a specific date two years ago. The librarian provides a resource that indicates average stock prices for each month over the last ten years, but does not include information on closing prices on particular dates during that period. The information supplied is unsuited to the question.
2. An eighth-grade student goes to a law library to request information on freedom of speech for a school assignment. The librarian provides a professional legal text on constitutional law. The reading level of the work and the technical language it contains makes it incomprehensible to the student. The material supplied was unsuited to the user.

2.2.2 Miscataloged, Misorganized, or Misplaced Information

Another category of service error is that of making information inaccessible in some way. In most cases the effects of such errors on users would be minor, although understandably frustrating. It is very hard to see how such errors could conceivably lead to liability.

This category of errors takes a number of forms. Miscataloging would be the error of improperly placing the item within the library's cataloging scheme. Cataloging is both art and science, and differences of opinion will exist on proper placement regardless of the cataloging system in use. In order to truly defeat the user, the cataloging error would have to be of a scale and type that no search of relevant terms would retrieve the item or, in the case of a physical item, its placement on the shelf was too far from other similar items to be located by shelf browsing.

Thus, cataloging a book on landscape photography as one on portrait photography would clearly be an error, but still might be found with an appropriate search, and, depending on the size of the collection, might be spotted by browsing the shelf. On the other hand, cataloging a book on landscape photography as being about cloisonné would likely make it almost impossible to find by any rational method, even though it is still classified in the arts section.

Misorganizing information would involve placing it somewhere that makes it difficult or impossible to find, regardless of how it is cataloged or described. Improper organization can impede access to information both in the physical world and online. Poorly arranged stacks and a badly organized Web site can be equally frustrating for users. Similarly, poorly organized information that is presented to a user, such as a report delivered to a customer by an information broker, can suffer from this problem, and can be an error.

Misplacing information is the simple error of putting it somewhere other than where it belongs. Shelving mistakes are the most common form of misplacement errors in libraries.[10] Shelf reading can help find misplaced books, but in some formats, such as microfiche, misplacement can result in an almost permanent loss of the item. Similarly, misplacing a file online or creating broken links to a Web page can result in loss of information.

One area where misplacing information could be an important issue, with some potential for liability, is when controversial information is made available in inappropriate situations, particularly to children. For example, two famous children's books on gay parenting, *Heather Has Two Mommies*, by Leslea Newman, and *Daddy's Roommate*, by Michael Willhoite, have been subject to challenges when placed in the children's areas of the library. In most cases, such challenges were traditional book challenges, seeking to remove the book from the collection, and did not involve claims of professional liability.

In the only published case involving *Heather Has Two Mommies* and *Daddy's Roommate*, an attempt to force a public library to move them from the children's area to the adult section of the library was unsuccessful, and was found to violate the First and Fourteenth Amendments of the U.S. Constitution.[11] However, in deciding the case, the court placed considerable importance on the testimony of expert witnesses, who testified that there were important reasons for placing such books in the children's section. In essence, the court found that the placement of the books was proper.

2.2.3 Violations of Privacy

As we saw in Chapter Three,[12] people have a right to privacy in certain situations. Violations of the right to privacy can include intrusion into seclusion, public disclosure of private facts, false light, and appropriation. In addition, information professionals have a strong tradition of protecting the privacy of their users, and a violation of privacy would generally be considered a professional error, even if the violation is one of ethics rather than law.

Privacy concerns in information work focus primarily on the specific issue of confidentiality, or the obligation to maintain the secrets and confidences of our users. The concept of confidentiality is an important part of the ethics of librarianship.[13] Confidentiality can be protected by law; it encompasses the concepts of confidentiality, or preserving the secrets of another, and privilege, or the right not to be compelled to disclose those secrets while under oath.[14] The extent of a privilege is determined by state law, and generally (but not always), those professionals who are required to maintain confidentiality are also granted some sort of legal privilege concerning the confidential information.[15]

A legal privilege grants someone the legal freedom to do or not to do a given act. It immunizes conduct that, under ordinary circumstances, would subject the actor to liability. In relation to confidentiality, legal privilege would allow someone to refrain from disclosing information that he could otherwise be compelled to disclose, particularly when testifying in court. For example lawyers cannot be compelled to reveal their communication with their clients,[16] and priests can protect secrets told to them in confession.[17]

Confidentiality requirements and legal privilege can arise from statutory or common law, and are common for such professions as medicine, law and psychology. In the case of libraries, apart from circulation records, there are very few laws protecting confidentiality.[18] Confidentiality issues can arise at the reference desk, in relation to circulation records, as part of information brokering, and with museum and archive items.

2.2.3.1 Reference Services

While most librarians would agree that reference interactions should remain confidential, there is no actual requirement to do so. Any obligation to protect exchanges at the reference desk derives from ethics, not law. There is also no legal privilege to communications between librarian and patron, and no legal sanction for violation of confidentiality.[19]

This situation creates a clear conflict between law and librarian ethics, in two ways. First, and most obviously, this means that the ethics of librarianship require something that the law does not. This means not just that librarians are not required to maintain the confidences of those they serve at the reference desk, but also that those confidences are not legally privileged. In other words, librarians can be required by law to reveal what they know or have heard in an investigation, or testify about it in court. The second conflict is more subtle but still important. Implying or guaranteeing confidentiality at the reference desk could make it reasonable for a user to rely on that guarantee, such that liability could result.

This does not mean that librarians cannot or should not maintain the confidentiality of reference interactions. Rather, librarians should continue to respect confidentiality to the extent possible, without explicitly promising to do so. If asked by a user if the reference interaction will be confidential, the best answer would be for the librarian to say that she will do everything possible to respect the user's privacy but can make no guarantees.

As a practical matter, most library reference desks are in public spaces where confidentiality would be impossible to guarantee even if one wanted to. This can also be pointed out to the user. Once again, although it seems paradoxical given our professional ethics, this is probably for the best, as it both lowers the expectations of users and prompts users to maintain their own confidences as much as possible.

In spite of the fact that the reference desk is a public space, it is conceivably possible that a librarian could violate a user's right to privacy. If a user disclosed an embarrassing private fact to the reference librarian, and the librarian told others about the fact (in effect publicizing it), this act would meet the definition of public disclosure of private facts, and could be actionable. Alternatively, if a reference librarian discussed a user's information request in a manner that implied something damaging or salacious about the person, such an act could constitute placing the person in a false light.

There are three basic approaches that can help avoid such claims. The first, as mentioned above, is to remind users that confidentiality cannot be guaranteed at the reference desk. This, one hopes, would motivate users to keep potentially embarrassing information to themselves, and in any event would make unreasonable any claim that they had an expectation of confidentiality. The second approach is to actively avoid disclosure of private information by requesting that users not do so. Usually the information need can be identified without resorting to highly private information. Finally, reference librarians should honor the ethics of librarianship and maintain the confidentiality of their users. In addition to being ethical behavior, this would protect against a claim of violation of privacy rights by simply not revealing the private information.

2.2.3.2 Circulation Records

Circulation records are generally made confidential by state statute. Because of the variety of state laws involved, and the increasingly complex nature of this issue because of the USA PATRIOT Act and other legal developments, the confidentiality of circulation records is beyond our scope. Indeed, because of the variability of the laws in this area, it is not even possible to say whether personal liability is possible for violations of circulation records confidentiality laws. This will vary by jurisdiction. Legal repercussions for violating the confidentiality of circulation records are dictated by the terms of the statute in question.

2.2.3.3 Information Brokering

With information brokering, confidentiality enters an entirely different sphere. As with reference interactions, there are no laws protecting the confidentiality of information broker interactions. However, one assumes most information brokers would feel bound by the ethical requirements of confidentiality that other information professionals follow.

Another issue of concern for information brokers is that of trade secrets. If information obtained by an information broker—either from their own client or based on research on another company—constitutes a trade secret, that information could be protected, and revealing it could lead to liability.

What makes information brokering different is the paid nature of the service. As explored at length in Chapter Eight, charging a fee for a service occurs under circumstances that are ruled by the terms of a contract or other agreement. This agreement could have confidentiality terms, the violation of which would be actionable at law.

2.2.3.4 Museum and Archive Items

It is not uncommon for sensitive or confidential items to end up in museum collections or archives. How these items are treated will depend on a number of factors. Often, certain items will be required to remain confidential under the terms of the donation. These terms are generally legally enforceable.

2.2.4 Misuse of Gifts and Donated Items

Gifts and donated items, particularly items donated to archives and museums, can come with conditions. Generally speaking these conditions must be respected if the institution is to retain the items. The conditions of a donation may include a variety of terms that could limit how the item is treated and used. Two of the most common problems that can occur under this scenario are inappropriate display and wrongful deaccession.

2.2.4.1 Inappropriate Display

Inappropriate display involves displaying a donated item to the public in a way that violates the terms of the donation. The exact nature of the problem would depend on the terms of the donation, but could include displaying an item that was to be kept from public view, displaying an item without appropriate context or explanation, or displaying an item in a manner that the donor proscribed.

2.2.4.2 Wrongful Deaccession

Wrongful deaccession would be the act of removing from the collection an item that a donor demanded that the institution retain. Archivists like to point out that only about ten percent of records donated to archives are usually worth keeping. It is therefore not uncommon for much of what is donated to be disposed of. Institutions may accept donations of items that they do not wish to retain for any number of reasons. These could include to get another item that was part of the donation that the institution wanted, to remain in the good graces of an important donor, or to gain publicity of the donation process.

When the institution ends up with items it does not need or want, it must be careful about disposing of them in light of donor requirements.

Misuse of Donated Items

A museum has received a donation of the personal effects of a prominent local judge. Included in the effects is a letter to the judge's mistress. The terms of the donation included a restriction that correspondence between the judge and this person were not to be displayed to the public. The letter ends up being included in a display on the judge's personal life. This is an example of inappropriate display.

An archive is donated the papers of a famous author. The donation agreement specifically requires that all of the correspondence in the donation be retained, regardless of quality. An assistant, unaware of this requirement, goes through the correspondence and culls items of little or no significance. This is an example of wrongful deaccession.

2.2.5 When Is Liability Possible for Service Errors?

Service errors are the most commonly envisioned form of error that could lead to liability. Liability for service errors depends on the presence of a duty of care. This duty depends, at least in part, on how reasonable it was for the person claiming harm to rely on the service to the extent that harm resulted.

2.2.6 Guarantees and Real or Apparent Authority

One possible way that an information professional could make a user's reliance reasonable, and thus incur liability, would be by offering guarantees, or assuming, or appearing to assume, authority about the information supplied. Providing guarantees or claiming special authority about the information being provided would make it reasonable for recipients of the information to assume that they could rely on that information as being accurate or complete without further investigation on their part. Guarantees are slightly different from claims of authority, but in practice they present the same dangers.

2.2.6.1 Guarantees

Guarantees are assurances that the information provided is complete, accurate, or entirely suited to the intended use. Although we have no cases involving information professionals, other professions providing information have been successfully sued when they provide guarantees about the information they give their clients. For example, surveyors have been held liable when they certified the result of a survey, but the survey turned out to contain errors. In one such case, the court stated that when a surveyor undertakes to certify that something has been done or not done, or done in a certain way, the client has a right to rely on the professional knowledge and skill of the surveyor in making that certification, and that a surveyor's duty of reasonable care to the client is breached when such a certification is negligently made. If such breach results in injury to the client, she may recover damages.[20]

Although as an information professional it is always unwise to offer a guarantee or imply authority about a topic, there is a subtle distinction between types of guarantees that is worth exploring. This distinction is between offering guarantees about the information itself and offering guarantees about the nature or quality of the information service being provided. Both types of guarantees are ill advised, but they function differently and have different implications. Along the same lines, there is a difference between claiming to be an authority on the topic of the information request and claiming authority on the process of finding that information.

It is always inadvisable to offer any kind of a guarantee on the actual information provided in response to an information request. This is not just a cautionary statement. In fact, most such guarantees would, in fact, be in error. As we have seen, there are a huge number of variables at play in the process of providing information. Most of those variables are outside of the knowledge and influence of the information professional. The professional did not produce the information, and is generally not able to verify or certify it, beyond having consulted a credible source. The information professional also usually does not know how the information will be used, under what conditions, and for what purposes. Under such conditions a guarantee about the information supplied would have little actual validity. At the same time, however, a guarantee would serve to create a reasonable expectation that the information can be relied on by the user. It is this reasonable expectation that can lead to liability.

2.2.6.2 Authority or Expertise

This same basic concept applies to holding forth as an expert on the topic being researched. Claims of authority occur when an information professional holds forth as an expert on the subject of the information need. Doing so also serves to create a situation in which it would be seen as reasonable for the user to rely on the information professional to their detriment. In some limited situations, an information professional might actually be a subject expert—for example, an art librarian with a PhD in art history, or a law librarian with a JD—but in most cases, information professionals are not experts on the specific topics about which they find information. Even if they are, the inherent risks of allowing reasonable reliance to take place make implying or stating subject expertise inadvisable.

Again, we have no cases against information professionals involving authority or expertise, but other professions have been successfully sued on that basis. As an example, a real estate broker was successfully sued for claiming that the well on a property was good even though she had not investigated it. The court held that it was reasonable for the buyer to rely on her statement because of her expertise as a real estate broker.[21]

Advertising or implying authority on finding information, as opposed to authority on the information itself, is less risky, but still problematic. While it may be reasonable in most cases to make such statements as "I can find that for you" or "this is a good source," one should be careful to do so in a way that makes clear the limitations of such a statement. The trick is to express your confidence in the service you provide without doing so in a way that would reasonably shift the responsibility for resolving the information need from the user to the professional. Once again, the problem arises because the process of claiming authority or providing a guarantee makes more reasonable the idea that the user should rely on the information professional. Such reasonable reliance can potentially lead to liability.

This discussion has the understandable ability to rankle information professionals who take pride in their work, feeling that they should be able to guarantee their work and provide reasonable claims of expertise in finding information. The problems with this are twofold. First, while most information professionals can and do provide excellent, expert service, the kind of results implied by such guarantees or claims of expertise are beyond the abilities of even the most competent and diligent information professionals. This is not intended to denigrate the efforts of information professionals, but simply points to the reality that the work is generally dependent on the nature and clarity of the information request, the quality and nature of the information they have access to, and the use to which that information is put. Important aspects of all of these are outside of their control, and thus any guarantees they provide make promises that they cannot be sure will be fulfilled in any given situation.

The second problem with offering a guarantee or claiming expertise in finding information is that it unnecessarily, and dangerously, raises the expectations of users and creates the possibility of reasonable reliance. This in turn could lead to liability.

The simple fact is that, in spite of obtaining assistance from an information professional, users must remain responsible for their information needs. Information professionals are not in a position to assume such responsibility for a user's situation

---

Guarantees and Authority

1. Guarantees imply that the information provided is complete, accurate, or otherwise entirely suited for the user's purpose without further review or judgment on their part:

   "This is all the information that you require."

   "This information is absolutely correct."

   A better approach is to avoid judgments about quality or completeness, and to explain the limitations of the sources.

   "This is the information I found using [source]. There may be other information related to your topic that you might want to consult as well."

   "I used [source] to find this information. It was published two years ago, so newer information might be available."

2. Authority implies that you have knowledge about the subject itself, and that the user should rely on you or your opinion, rather than referring to sources:

   "I have a bachelor's degree in engineering, and I can tell you that this information on replacing a load-bearing wall is correct."

   "I have been divorced several times, and I know that this is the law on custody."

   Even if you are an expert on a given topic, it is best to avoid expressing your opinion or knowledge. Your role as an information professional is to find information, not interpret or apply it.

   "This is the information that I can find. You should evaluate it to see if it fits your needs. If you need help finding further information I'd be glad to assist you."

   "I can't tell you what the law is or how it applies in your situation. I can, however, help you locate the laws that you are interested in."

that they can control the outcome. In such a situation, making reliance on the information professional seem reasonable does a disservice to the user, and exposes the information professional to the potential for otherwise avoidable liability.

2.3 User Errors

User error is mentioned here because it must be included to give a complete picture of the possible sources of error in information work. While it might be natural for a user or customer to blame an information professional when harm occurs, the relatively large role that users play in information transactions means that user error would most likely be a major question in any claim.

Drawing on the Angoff example, the possibility that user error contributed to or caused the collapse of the deck is almost impossible to avoid. This would be true with many, if not most, interactions between users and information professionals.

3. IMPORTANT POINTS TO REMEMBER

▶ Only errors that violate a professional duty of care and cause harm can result in liability for an information professional.

▶ Resource errors are errors that result because of a problem with the information resource itself, and not because of actions by the information professional.

▶ Service errors are errors committed by an information professional in the process of providing information services.

▶ Guarantees about information should always be avoided, as should claims of authority or expertise on a given topic.

ENDNOTES

[1] *E.g.*, Nasri sees one who supplies inaccurate information as liable for the harm caused by it (William Z. Nasri, *Malpractice Liability: Myth or Reality?* 1 J. Lib. Admin. 4, at 5 (1980)), while Dunn says, "by inference 'says' that the information is accurate."(Susan Dunn, *Society, Information Needs, Library Services and Liability*, 26 Iowa Lib. Q. 18 (1989)). Similarly, Ebbinghouse envisions a librarian who did not search for patents properly. See Carol Ebbinghouse, *Disclaiming Liability*, 8 Searcher 3 66–71 (March 2000).

[2] Available at http://factfinder.census.gov (last visited July 2, 2008).

[3] Allan Angoff, *Library Malpractice Suit: Could It Happen To You?* 7 American Libraries 489 (1976).

[4] See, e.g., Martha J. Dragich, *Information Malpractice: Some Thoughts on the Potential Liability of Information Professionals* 8 Info. Technology & Libr. 265 (1989). John A. Gray, *Personal Malpractice Liability of Reference Librarians and Information Brokers* 9 J. Lib. Admin. 74 (1988); Paul D. Healey, *Chicken Little at the Reference Desk*, 89 Law Lib. J. 515 (1996).

[5] *E.g.*, Dunn, *supra* note 1; Nasri, *supra* note 1.

[6] *Winter v. G.P. Putnam Sons*, 938 F.2d 1033 (10th Cir. 1991). For further discussion see Chapter Three, section 4.

[7] Gray, *supra* note 4.

[8] *Cardozo v. True*, 342 So.2d 1053 (Fla.App. 1977).

[9] *Id.*, at 1056.

[10] In libraries open to the public, users can be one of the largest sources of misplacement errors, a problem that is frustrating for users and librarians alike.

[11] See *Sund v. City of Wichita Falls, Texas*, 121 F.Supp.2d 530 (N.D. Tex., 2000).

[12] Chapter Three, section 6.

[13] RASD, *Guidelines for Medical, Legal, and Business Responses at General Reference Desks*, 2.3.

[14] See, *e.g.*, Robert I. Karon, *Privilege and Confidentiality: Confusing Principles*, 23 Tax Advisor 406 (1992); Fred C. Zacharias, *Privilege and Confidentiality in California*, 28 U.C. Davis L. Rev. 367 (1995); Gary W. Paquin, *Confidentiality and Privilege: the Status of Social Workers in Ohio*, 19 Ohio N.U. L. Rev. 199 (1994).

[15] Robert I. Karon, *Privilege and Confidentiality: Confusing Principles*, 23 The Tax Advisor 406 (1992).

[16] Brian Sheppard, J.D., *Views Of United States Supreme Court As To Attorney-Client Privilege*, 159 A.L.R. Fed. 243 (2000).

[17] Claudia G. Catalano, J.D., *Subject Matter and Waiver of Privilege Covering Communications to Clergy Member or Spiritual Adviser*, 93 A.L.R.5th 327 (2001).

[18] Rosemary Del Vecchio, *Privacy and Accountability at the Reference Desk*, 38 Reference Lib. 137 (1988). In some states things like registration records and other library records are protected by statute.

[19] Mark Stover, *Confidentiality and Privacy in Reference Service*, 27 RQ 242 (1987).

[20] *Bell v. Jones*, 523 A.2d 982 (D.C. 1986).

[21] *Bevins v. Ballard*, 655 P2d 757 (AK 1982).

►Part II

LIABILITY ISSUES FOR SPECIFIC SEGMENTS OF THE LIS PROFESSIONS

►Six

SPECIFIC PROFESSIONAL LIABILITY ISSUES FOR LIBRARIANS

IN THIS CHAPTER

Librarians have been the focus of much of the literature that discusses professional liability for information professionals. In most cases, it appears that the chances for liability are small during the course of normal library work. This chapter discusses the legal issues at play for librarians, examining the particular legal situations for public, academic, school, and special librarians.

In order to make the issues presented understandable in the library context, this chapter presents four case studies that illuminate the types of situations in which liability could arise. While the case studies are specific to a particular type of library, each raises issues that can apply to all libraries. As such, all four case studies should be worthy of your attention.

Issues examined in the case studies include:

► Governmental and statutory immunity
► Employment and user status
► Malpractice and duty of care
► Defenses
► Failure to act
► Expertise and guarantee
► Due diligence

1. CASE STUDY: THE BUILDING PROJECT

Harry Stern came to the reference desk of the West Mournwood Public Library looking for information on home construction. He told reference librarian Shirley Stanis that he planned to take out a wall between his kitchen and the adjoining family room, so as to make it into one big room. He said that he had never done this kind of project before, and wanted materials that would show him how to go about it. Shirley found materials on construction in the library catalog and took Harry to the relevant part of the stacks. He selected several books and took them to the reading room to peruse.

A while later, Harry came back to the desk and said that the materials he had found were too technical and complicated. He wondered if the library might have something more basic. Shirley couldn't find anything more basic in the collection, and so she suggested that they look on the Internet. She went with Harry to one of the library's public computers and helped him construct a Google search. They found several sites on home construction and remodeling. Having found this, Shirley then left Harry to explore the results. Harry read for a while, printed out some materials, and then left the library.

Six months later the library was served with a lawsuit filed by Harry Stern. The suit was against the library, claiming negligence, and also personally against Shirley Stanis, claiming she had engaged in professional malpractice. The suit said that the materials that Harry had obtained from the Internet were faulty, and among other things, failed to warn Harry that some walls in a house may be load bearing, and cannot be removed without damaging the structure of the house. The wall between the kitchen and family room that Harry had removed turned out to be a load bearing wall, and its removal resulted in the partial collapse of the kitchen ceiling. Harry's wife was slightly injured when the ceiling collapsed. The suit alleged that Shirley was negligent in finding a site on the Internet with faulty information, that she "knew or should have known" that the information on the Web site was faulty, and that further she should have pointed out to the user that the library materials she had first offered him contained verified, correct information.

This suit raises a number of issues, including potential immunity, employment status as a shield to liability, and malpractice and duty of care. Each will be discussed in turn.

1.1 Issue: Governmental Immunity

Are the library and Shirley immune from being sued under the doctrine of governmental immunity?

A preliminary issue for any publicly owned institution when faced with the type of legal action mentioned here would be potential governmental immunity from being sued. As explained in Chapter Two section 6, there is a distinct and plausible possibility that a governmental employee is immune from suit for discretionary actions that took place in the course of employment. Whether the librarian's actions are discretionary, as opposed to ministerial, is open to debate, but the fact that the librarian exercised professional judgment in finding the materials would strengthen the argument that they were. The argument would be that the librarian was asked to assist with finding information, and that this activity is both discretionary in nature, because it requires professional judgment, and fully within the scope of her employment as a government employee.

Whether a librarian is covered by governmental immunity as a matter of common law will vary from state to state, as will any grants of or exceptions to immunity that may appear in each state's governmental immunity statute. In some cases, though, immunity appears to be specifically in place by statute. For instance, the Illinois Local Government Tort Immunity statute[1] provides tort immunity for "local public entities,"[2] and specifically includes libraries in the definition of a local public entity.[3] Further, the tort of misrepresentation is specifically included as one of the acts for which immunity is granted.[4] Finally, and most definitively, the code grants specific immunity for injuries that arise from the provision of information and includes libraries as protected entities as follows: "A local public entity is not liable for injury caused by any action of its employees that is libelous or slanderous or for the provision of information either orally, in writing, by computer or any other electronic transmission, or in a book or other form of library material."[5]

Thus, if the West Mournwood Public Library were in Illinois, there appears to be no question that it would be immune from suit under the facts in the case study. Other states may not be as explicit in including libraries in their state immunity statutes, but often the basic immunities reserved by the state will often create the same effect. Once again, the effect of immunity is to prevent the suit from being brought, regardless of the fault of the government or its employees. Even if the reference librarian in this case had done something for which she could be found liable if employed by a private entity, she cannot be sued at all as a public employee. In such a case, the library's attorneys would ask the court to dismiss the suit because of the immunity statute, and that would be the end of the matter.

1.2 Issue: Statutory Immunity

Do the library and Shirley have statutory immunity for materials downloaded from the Internet?

Even if governmental immunity did not apply in this case, there is the issue of statutory immunity. Recall that the faulty materials Mr. Stern used were obtained from the Internet. As discussed in Chapter Two section 6.2, the legislature can extend immunity to anyone if it chooses to do so. In this case, immunity under the Communications Decency Act (CDA)[6] would probably come into play. Although the CDA was primarily intended to govern obscene materials accessed over the Internet, it contains a fairly broad grant of immunity for information found on the Internet. The CDA says, in part, that "[n]o provider or user of an interactive computer service shall be treated as the publisher or speaker of any information provided by another information content provider."[7] This would appear to preclude Mr. Stern from treating the librarian as responsible for the quality of the information he found using the Internet while in the library. Keep in mind that this is true because Stern did his own evaluation of the information he found. If librarian Stanis had searched for him and evaluated the information before recommending it to him, then CDA immunity might not apply.

1.3 Issue: Employment Status

Does the status of Shirley as an employee preclude personal liability?

As far as Shirley's personal liability for the claimed damages is concerned, a major factor would be whether she is considered an employee or an independent professional for purposes of liability. Section 5.2 of Chapter Two and section 4 of Chapter Four lay the groundwork for this discussion. In sum, if she is a fiduciary professional she is potentially liable for harm that occurs as a result of her actions, regardless of her employment status with the library. If she is not a fiduciary professional, and is considered an employee, then she is immune from personal liability, even if she caused the harm, so long as her actions were within the scope of her employment. Thus, even if it were possible for Harry Stern to sue the library for damages, he cannot successfully sue Shirley personally as long as she is considered an employee.

But can she be sued personally as a professional? This is the great unanswered question that was the focus of sections 1 and 2 of Chapter Four. Without any law to guide us, it is hard to answer this question definitively. However, the point was made in section 2 of Chapter Four, that most librarians, as professionals, appear to take a consulting role, as opposed to a fiduciary role, in assisting users. Consulting activities leave responsibility for the user's information need with the user. Under such circumstances, it is hard to see how a duty of care can arise, such that the librarian's actions can be seen as the proximate cause of the user's harm. As a result, even if the librarian can be seen as a professional who is potentially subject to being sued, the real question becomes one of whether a duty of care exists, and if so, if it was violated.

1.4 Issue: User Status

The status of the user complaining of harm is always a factor in a liability claim. User status can determine if liability is possible at all, or, if it is, what form it can take. Put simply, for liability to result for Shirley as the librarian, her actions would have to be the reasonable cause of the harm, and the claim of liability must not be otherwise barred by law. Thus, a fellow employee who seeks information for employment-related purposes could not sue the librarian if harm results because such suits are barred by law. Similarly, a student who seeks redress against an academic librarian would not be able to sue because the courts have not allowed such claims.

As will be discussed in more detail in Chapter Seven, professionals seeking information for their professional work, particularly doctors and lawyers, would retain responsibility for the adequacy of the information they received, and could not seek to make a librarian liable if there were problems. Similarly, a person seeking information for a third party would not be able to make a claim if the harm happened to that other party. Whether or not the third party involved could sue the librarian would be subject to the same analysis of reasonable reliance as any other claim, but with the additional complicating factor of needing to show that the person who requested the information and passed it to the third party was not the actual source of the harm because of how they made the request or handled or interpreted the information they received.

For public and academic librarians, the possibility of liability would seem to exist solely when dealing with users who are members of the public, and who are seeking information that affects their own personal interests. This could be information on how to get a divorce, or how to build a deck, but in all cases would need to involve an activity from which identifiable harm could arise. Even in that situation, it would be necessary that the harm complained of arose under circumstances in which it was reasonable for the user to rely solely on the actions of the librarian without applying further analysis, investigation, or corroboration of the information supplied. In this case, Harry is a member of the public, and so his claim would not be barred outright based on his status as a library user.

1.5 Issue: Malpractice and Duty of Care

The claim against Shirley is that she committed malpractice. As we saw in Chapter Three section 2.5, malpractice is a form of negligence that uses the standards of a profession in order to determine the duty of care. In order for Shirley to have committed malpractice, there must be an established duty of care based on professional standards, she must have performed her job in a way that failed to meet that duty of care, and her failure of the duty must have been the proximate cause of Mr. Stern's harm. In order to analyze this situation, we need to look at each of these in turn.

The issue of whether a duty of care can ever exist between a librarian and a user cannot be definitively decided here. For librarians, true professional standards have been elusive, although much sought after. Much like U.S. Supreme Court Justice Potter Stewart's famous test for obscenity—"I know it when I see it"[8]—many reference librarians feel they can recognize good reference service when it occurs, but they cannot articulate specific standards for it. The issue of evaluating the work of librarians, particularly in reference work, has been the subject of much study, but few standards have been developed that could conceivably lead to a standard of care.[9]

In the current case, the allegation is that Shirley "knew or should have known" that the information retrieved in the Google search was somehow faulty. It is highly unlikely that such a standard would be upheld. Rather, any duty of care would relate to Shirley's skill in finding information, not her expertise about the information itself. It would be very unreasonable to claim that the average professional librarian would be able to act as an expert on specific topics, such as home construction, or that such expertise is part of the normal professional knowledge of a librarian.

On the other hand, it might be possible to look into Shirley's actions in finding information. Here again we have two separate questions to be answered. The first is what standards can be applied to finding information, and the second is what actions, or lack of action, would constitute violation of those standards. Given the elusive nature of professional standards for librarians, in this case it might actually be easier to work backwards. In other words, is there anything that Shirley did when helping Harry that seems somehow wrong? The answer to that is most likely no. She took the information request as presented by Harry and found information in the collection that appeared to relate to his information need. When Harry decided that the materials she'd found were not what he wanted, Shirley had helped him search the Internet for other information. These are all appropriate and adequate steps for a reference librarian to take in providing information.

The distinction between a consulting and a fiduciary professional can also shed some light here. A fiduciary professional, the type of professional who would clearly be subject to malpractice standards, would have taken over responsibility for the user's information need, and would have delivered a final product that had been carefully designed to meet that need. The user would have minimal input, and would be relying on the professional to deliver a total solution, without further input or review. This would not be possible on this scenario without extensive subject expertise as well as searching expertise. A consulting professional, on the other hand, would only attempt to find information that might satisfy the information need. Evaluating the information would remain the responsibility of the person requesting it, as would responsibility for the need itself. This latter description more correctly fits the role of a librarian.

The question really is whether the reference librarian had a duty not just to find information on request, but to find information that is guaranteed to be correct and appropriate for the use intended. The short answer is that such a standard would be impossible to meet, and does not exist. This is not to say that librarians do not try to provide fully accurate information. They do, and should be justly proud of those efforts. However, there is a big difference between aspiring to do something and implying that succeeding in doing so is a professional standard, the failure of which can lead to liability.

The other interrelated issue is reasonable reliance. Put simply, was it reasonable for Harry to rely on the information Shirley helped him find on the Internet without further verification? Once again, such reliance would only be reasonable if Shirley had assumed a fiduciary role in the transaction, and in the process provided some sort of guarantee that no further assessment or review was necessary on Harry's part. If Shirley's role was as a consultant, as it almost certainly was, then Harry remained responsible to verify the information he received, and reliance on Shirley's actions would not be reasonable.

1.6 Issue: Defenses

A final factor to consider in the face of Harry's claim is one of legal defenses. Assuming, for the sake of argument, that Harry's claim is not barred because of governmental or statutory immunity, and that Harry is able to show a breach of professional standards in some way, it does not automatically follow that Harry will win the suit. Even if all this is true, Shirley will have a number of defenses she can raise that could defeat Harry's claim.

For instance, Shirley could raise the defense of contributory negligence. This would claim that regardless of Shirley's actions, Harry caused the harm himself by the way he went about the work. Because he is responsible for his own harm, Shirley cannot be held liable. Another defense would be to claim that Harry, by undertaking the construction project himself, had assumed the risk of harm resulting. These defenses could be raised in addition to claiming that there is no duty of care for Shirley to violate, and that nothing about Shirley's activities were the proximate cause of Harry's harm. All of these defenses are explained in detail in section 5 of Chapter Three.

2. CASE STUDY: THE PERILS OF POISONOUS MUSHROOMS

In February 2005, the Yorken College Library purchased a book titled *The Complete Illustrated Encyclopedia of North American Mushrooms* and added it to its reference collection. The book contained descriptions and photographs of mushrooms, along with prominent notices as to whether a particular mushroom was edible or poisonous. In March 2005, Plottswarth Publishing, publisher of the book, issued an errata notice to all known purchasers of the work, including Yorken. The notice explained that four photographs in the book had been misprinted, with the result that in two cases, entries for edible mushrooms contained pictures of what were actually poisonous mushrooms. The errata notice contained labels for the spine, the cover page, and the affected pages of the encyclopedia that notified readers of the error. It also contained an offer for a corrected copy of the book at a reduced price.

When the errata notice arrived, it was routed to the head of public services, who was in charge of the reference collection. She immediately removed the book from the shelf and met with the library director to discuss what to do. The outcome of the meeting was a decision to put the book back on the shelf with the errata labels attached, rather than buy a new copy. The book and the errata notice was given to the head of technical services, who gave it to the library aide who labels books. Unfortunately, the aide misunderstood the directions and put the book back on the shelf without the errata labels.

In May 2005, Jennie Carpenter, a sophomore at Yorken, came to the reference desk along with two friends, both nonstudents. The girls wanted to go mushroom hunting in the woods near campus, and were looking for pictures of edible mushrooms that grow in the Yorken area and might be in season. Betty Lange, the reference librarian, found *The Complete Illustrated Encyclopedia of North American Mushrooms* in the reference collection, and gave the book to the girls. In the process, Betty suggested that the girls might want to look for Chanterelle mushrooms. She flipped the book open to the entry on Chanterelles, then went on to explain that she and her husband hunted for them often, describing their favorite hunting sites and how she liked to cook the mushrooms. The girls asked several questions, which Betty answered off the top of her head, giving them the impression that she knew quite a bit about mushrooms. During the interaction they all, including Betty, looked at the picture of the Chanterelles in the encyclopedia, but did not comment on it. Eventually the girls made a photocopy of the entry and left the library.

Unfortunately, the picture of Chanterelles they photocopied from the encyclopedia was one of those in error, and was in fact a picture of *Amanita brunnescens,* a highly toxic mushroom. The girls went on their outing, found and subsequently ate *Amanita brunnescens,* and became severely ill. They later filed suit against Betty and the Yorken library, claiming that the library was responsible for their harm by having in its collection a book that contained factually wrong information, and that Betty was also responsible for their harm because she held herself out as an expert on mushrooms, but did not notice or point out that the picture they copied was in error. The girls claimed that it was reasonable for them to rely on the accuracy of a book in the library's collection, and on Betty's professed subject expertise, such that a duty was created, and the failure of the duty was the proximate cause of their harm.

Issues raised in this scenario include the effect of user status on liability, the issue of failing to act on a publisher's errata notice, and the issue of expertise.

2.1 Issue: User Status

As we saw with the first case study, the status of the user can be an important issue in whether a claim can be brought. Because this case study deals specifically with an academic library, as opposed to a school library in an elementary, middle or high school, when we speak of students we are talking about college, graduate, or professional students. When dealing with students, the crucial question would be the nature of the harm complained of. For students pursuing school-related tasks when seeking information, claims of harm related to the quality or nature of their education are clearly precluded under current law. Thus a student who wants to sue because she received a poor grade in a course that she blames on erroneous information supplied by an academic librarian would not be able to sue. The issue of liability would appear to be fully and firmly answered by the uniform refusal of American courts to endorse the concept of educational malpractice.

Other potential scenarios when dealing with students are less clear, but still highly unlikely, and would depend greatly on the facts of the particular claim. It is true that educational institutions, and sometimes educators, can be held liable for physical harm that occurs during educational activities. As a specific example of this, a school district was liable for an injury to the hand of a high school student incurred by using a bench saw without a guard, due to lack of proper instruction and supervision by his teacher.[10] If we imagine that in this case the student harmed himself when using erroneous information supplied by a reference librarian in the college library, it is possible to see how the librarian could be included in the claim. However, this simply raises the issue of reasonable reliance. Once again, it becomes a question of whether it was reasonable for the student to rely solely on the reference librarian, without otherwise verifying the information or taking other steps to assure that the information she was supplied was appropriate for her needs. In order to succeed with the claim against the librarian, it would be necessary to show that the harm resulted directly from the work of the librarian, and that the student's reliance on the librarian was reasonable.

In the present scenario, the three girls were seeking information for their own non-school-related recreational activities. In this case, they would most likely be considered casual users who are not precluded from pursing a claim. This would be true even though one of them was a student at Yorken. If, however, Jenny had been seeking the information for a class project or activity, this analysis might not apply.

2.2 Issue: Failure to Act on Publisher's Warning

One issue of concern in this case is the library's failure to act on the errata notice sent by the publisher. While a library cannot be expected to verify every fact in its collection, when it is put on notice by the publisher of a flaw in a publication, it is safe to assume that the library has a duty to act. This is particularly true when, as in this case, the error is one that could potentially lead to harm. The fact that the failure to put the errata labels in the book was due to an inadvertent error, and not simple neglect, does not change this outcome. Although it is possible that the library would be liable in this situation, it is much less certain that any of the people involved in the process of putting the labels on the book could be held personally liable. The library aide who neglected to do the labeling is clearly not a professional, and would be protected from liability as an employee. The professionals involved in the process did not violate a duty of care in how they performed their jobs. In sum, the failure to label the book could have resulted in liability for the library, but most likely not in personal liability for professional actions on the part of anyone involved in that process.

2.3 Issue: Expertise and Guarantee

Personal liability does become an issue when we look at Betty's actions during the reference interview. By putting herself forward as an expert on mushrooms, rather than as an expert on finding information about mushrooms, Betty may have created a situation in which it was reasonable for the girls to rely on her knowledge and expertise about Chanterelle mushrooms. They might also have been justified in assuming that as an expert, Betty would have noticed if the picture was in error. Betty's liability here is not a certainty, but it appears very possible. By acting as an expert on mushrooms she, in essence, took responsibility for the girls' information need, and implied that they could rely on the information she gave them without further review.

3. CASE STUDY: EVADING EVOLUTION

The sixth-grade class at Hearnwhistle Elementary School was doing a unit on biology, and was scheduled to spend a week studying evolution. The parents of Anne Watson, a sixth-grade student, objected to her participation in the unit because of their religious beliefs. After some negotiation, it was decided that Anne would go to the school library each day that week during the biology lesson, where school librarian Jane Treadway would supply Anne with material on a noncontroversial aspect of biology. During that hour, Anne was to read the material and write a two-paragraph report on what she had read. The report was to be handed in to her teacher each day when she returned to the classroom.

When the week of the evolution unit arrived, Anne went to the library, and for the first four days Jane supplied her with an entry from the *School Encyclopedia of Biology*. Anne was extremely well behaved during these sessions, and each day read the material quietly, wrote her reports, and handed them in to the teacher. On the last day of the week, Jane decided to let Anne pick whatever topic she wanted to read, and left her to her task. She did not check to see what Anne had chosen. In the Friday rush, when Anne returned to her classroom, her teacher forgot to collect her report. Later that weekend, Anne's mother discovered the report in Anne's book bag and found that the topic was evolution. The Watsons are now threatening to sue Jane Treadway for educational malpractice because she failed to supervise Anne's work, and that Anne was harmed by being exposed to the material on evolution.

3.1 Issues for School Librarians

School librarians face three separate areas of analysis when considering liability issues. The first involves the constellation of risks associated with working in a school setting and dealing with K–12 students. The second involves those issues that arise when students use the school library for their personal, non-school-related needs. The third involves liability issues that could arise when pursuing educational activities with students.

Although no court in America has adopted the tort of educational malpractice, there are a number of sources of potential liability for educators and professionals who work with K–12 students. Unless protected by governmental immunity, teachers and schools are subject to a reasonable duty of care when supervising and instructing students, and sometimes have an affirmative duty to protect students from harm.[11] Thus educators can be liable for such things as dangerous playground equipment, failing to supervise students, or failing to report suspected abuse. Because these liability risks adhere to everyone who works in a K–12 school, they necessarily also apply to school librarians. That said, most of these sources of liability are beyond our scope, as they do not arise out of a librarian's professional activities as a librarian.

A second area of concern for school librarians arises when students use the school library for their own personal information needs, as opposed to using it as part of some sort of class or other formal educational activity. At first glance, it would appear that such usage raises the same, admittedly limited, possibility of liability a public or academic librarian might face when dealing with members of the public. However, with K–12 students there is the added factor that students, as minors, should be supervised in most or all of their activities. We can only speculate as to how such a case might transpire, but it would seem logical that, were a student to get information from their school library and then incur harm, the question of who should have been supervising and guiding the child at the time of the harm would be a far more important question than where the student got the information that was connected to the harm.

The third area of concern would be for liability that could arise during the school librarian's educational activities with students. In this case, unless the librarian was supervising students during activities that were somehow risky or dangerous, there appears to be little or no risk of liability. As with teachers, complaints about a school librarian's educational activities would have to come under a claim of educational malpractice, a liability claim that has had no success in American courts.

In the scenario presented above, the risk of liability for Jane Treadway would depend on how the liability claim was framed, and on how it was perceived by a jury or judge. If presented as an educational malpractice claim, the chances that Jane would be found liable are very small. The tort of educational malpractice has simply not been accepted by American courts. On the other hand, if the Watsons claim that their daughter was harmed by her exposure to evolution materials, exposure that only took place because of Jane's failure to supervise her, then the claim becomes more like an injury in gym class where failure to supervise led to harm. The question would then be one of whether the "harm" of having Anne exposed to evolution is actually compensable. One suspects not.

A more reasonable form of harm in this situation would be the harm the Watsons suffered because of violation of their agreement with the school concerning Anne's activities during the week of the evolution unit. Such a claim is more one of contract than tort, but even so, personal liability for Jane is unlikely. This is because she was not personally involved in making the agreement. Even if she had been, she would have done so as a representative of the school, and would not have been entering into the agreement personally.

4. CASE STUDY: DUE DILIGENCE

The Kresge-Stacy Chemical Corporation is a major manufacturer of industrial lubricants and solvents. Kresge-Stacy had agreed to buy Overland Petroleum Distributors as a way of diversifying its business, because Overland would provide Kresge-Stacy with an entry into the lucrative oil distribution business. While negotiating the sale, Overland had provided figures that projected a substantial rise in its operating revenues and profits, as well as ample opportunities to increase market share, in the next three years. Kresge-Stacy was able to negotiate what seemed like a very good purchase price for Overland, especially given the projected growth of the company.

As part of the acquisition, the Kresge-Stacy legal department engaged in a due diligence exam of Overland. This involved searching for all available information about the company in order to verify its claims about its financial condition and assets. Kresge-Stacy librarian Bill Skegness was given the task of performing searches to obtain the information the company's lawyers needed to review. In doing so, he searched a number of online business and financial databases, as well as databases of federal securities and regulatory filings and proceedings. He also searched online news sites for information about the company.

Based on the results of Bill's searches, the Kresge-Stacy legal department approved the purchase of Overland, and the sale was completed. However, over the next year, sales and profits at Overland stagnated. Overland officials claimed this was due to an unexpected market downturn that would reverse itself soon. In fact, the next year was even worse. Finally, it came to light that the oil distribution industry was overbuilt, and that new methods of distribution, including more reliance on trucks and an increase in pipeline terminals in ports not serviced by Overland, had effectively shut Overland out of the market.

Stacy-Kresge sued the Overland board of directors for securities fraud, claiming that they had been fed false information about the company's potential. In their defense Overland pointed out that information about trends in the oil distribution market was readily available on the Internet, and that several industry bloggers were discussing Overland's perilous market situation at the time of the sale. Overland contended that Kresge-Stacy had essentially deceived itself, because Bill's search had not included this publicly available data. The court agreed, and dismissed Kresge-Stacy's suit.

4.1 Issues

As with school librarians, the user population of special libraries would appear to preclude the possibility of a claim that would result in personal professional liability for the librarian. To recap, the law has long made it difficult or impossible for employees to sue fellow employees for negligence that occurs in the course of employment. The development of workers' compensation in the first half of the twentieth century formally precluded employees from suing their employer or fellow employees for physical harm, in return for a guarantee of care and benefits for work injuries.

Liability to third parties, such as customers of the company that employs the librarian, would be precluded by principles of vicarious liability. This would potentially make the employer liable for harm, but shields any employees from personal liability. Once again, nothing about this would prevent an employer from disciplining or terminating a librarian employee whose work was judged to be substandard, or whose work resulted in harm to a fellow employee or a third party.

Bill Skegness could be in trouble with his employer, and indeed could be terminated as an employee, for missing the information on Overland's market outlook in his due diligence search, but there is really no scenario that allows him to be personally legally liable for the errors.

5. AVOIDING AND MINIMIZING LIABILITY

In spite of the lack of articulated standards and the resulting low risk of liability, all librarians would be well advised to take certain prudent steps to minimize the possibility of liability, and if possible, avoid it altogether.

5.1 Consulting vs. Fiduciary

At its heart, the most important step to take to avoid liability is very simple. Librarians should assume a consulting rather than a fiduciary role in their work, leaving responsibility for information needs with the user. Put another way, librarians can be experts on finding information for users, but should not present themselves as experts on the information they find. Avoiding the role of an expert on the topic of the information request encompasses not only the idea of being a subject expert, but also of avoiding claims that the information provided is necessarily complete or adequate for the user's needs.

There are several specific tactics that can help make this distinction when assisting a user. On the public services side, it is best to avoid making guarantees, avoid promoting subject expertise, and take steps to preclude reasonable reliance. For technical services librarians, it is useful to take reasonable steps to assure the accuracy and appropriateness of materials added to or in the collection.

5.2 Guarantees

While it may seem counter to some professional standards, librarians should always avoid making guarantees about their services. This includes not trying to guarantee having found the right information, or all the information, or guaranteeing that the information is necessarily correct, complete, or appropriate for the user's purpose. The purpose of this stance is to reinforce the simple fact that the librarian is acting in a consulting capacity, and that users remain responsible for their information needs.

In many ways, and in spite of how "wrong" it may feel from a professional standpoint, refusing to make guarantees is only logical. Precisely because a librarian fills a consulting role, most of the things she might have the urge to guarantee are outside of her control. Thus, while a librarian might have provided the best possible information from the collection in a manner that seems to fully address the expressed information need, there is no way to actually know whether the information is adequate or appropriate, if it actually meets the user's real need, or how it will be used. The only guarantee that a librarian should ever give is to exert her best effort to find information that will help meet the user's information need.

5.3 Promoting Expertise

Expertise takes many forms. We know that librarians can and should promote themselves as experts in the task of finding information for users. The problem, which in many ways is a compliment to the profession, is that librarians are often seen by users as highly educated and capable of being experts on the topics of user information needs, as well as experts on finding information. Some users see these two things as synonymous.

In some cases, a librarian may have actual expertise in the topic of the information request. A librarian might have an advanced degree in a particular subject, or substantial personal or work experience with this subject. Sometimes simpler personal experience can feel like expertise. For example, someone who has been through a divorce might feel that the experience left her with expertise about that process. Similar to providing guarantees, librarians should not promote their own expertise on the topic of an information request. Once again, this is in order to retain the consultant role, and further avoid reasonable reliance. Even if a librarian has expertise on a particular topic, to be present in the interaction as anything but an expert on finding information is to change roles in a substantial way.

There are two approaches that librarians should take in relation to their own expertise on a topic. The first is not to express their expertise in response to a user's request. This means that even if the librarian knows a direct answer to the user's request, she should still refer the user to a source that contains the information. She should also not hold herself out as an expert on the topic, regardless of whether or not she provides a direct answer. The idea is to let the user rely on the information, not the librarian, in satisfying their information need.

The second approach to take is to proactively assert to users the limitations of reference work and the necessity that they satisfy themselves about the adequacy and accuracy of the information they've been provided.

Language to Reduce Potential Liability

1. Setting the tone:
   "I am not an expert on this topic, but I can help you find information on it."
   "I can show you what we have in our collection so that you can decide what you'd like to use."
2. Presenting results:
   "Here is some information I was able to find. You should look it over to see if it is what you had in mind."
   "You should satisfy yourself that this is what you need."
   "This is what is in our collection, but I don't know if it will answer your question."
   "There may be other information or sources that you will want to consult."
3. Terminating the interview:
   "I have given you what information that I can find. Please let me know if this does not turn out to be what you need."
   "I can't guarantee that this is everything you need, but I would be happy to do further searching for you if you feel that you need more."

5.4 Reasonable Reliance

Most of the articles that envision liability for librarians either gloss over the issue of reasonable reliance or take the view that reliance could be found to be reasonable in normal reference interactions. As we have discussed elsewhere, legal theory really doesn't support this idea, and the fact that the issue has never been tried in court leaves it as only a theoretical possibility. For reference interactions, the suggestions in the previous section are intended to minimize the possibility that reliance on the actions of the librarian would ever be seen as reasonable for purposes of tort liability.

As an example, let's look once again at the scenario proposed by Allan Angoff in his 1976 *American Libraries* article.[12] In it, the user who got a book from the library about building decks, and then had the deck he built fall down, was claiming that the library was liable for this problem. We've already discussed several times how his claim was actually with the publisher, but let's leave that aside for this example. The simple fact is that for liability to ensue, for the library or the librarian, it would have been reasonable for the user to have relied on the actions of the librarian.

Whether reliance was reasonable in general is the open question that has not been answered. However, building on the previous section, we can see that certain actions by the librarian could serve to create reasonable reliance, or make reliance more reasonable, while certain other actions could serve to minimize the possibility of reasonable reliance.

For example, if the librarian, when presented with the user's request for information on building a deck, had held herself out as an expert on deck building, it would be far more reasonable for the user to rely solely on the information she gave him as expert advice on building a deck. Similarly, if the librarian were not to claim deck building expertise, but were instead to claim that all library materials are accurate and correct, or claim that she was guaranteeing that she was giving him the correct information, then once again the user's reliance on the information could be found to have been reasonable.

On the other hand, if the librarian in the Angoff situation had presented the information she found to the user with a disclaimer, then that would serve to minimize the possibility of reasonable reliance. For instance, if she had said to the user, "This is a book from our collection on deck building. You might find it useful, but you should satisfy yourself that it contains the information you need. There might also be other information available that you could check. I'd be happy to help you find such information, but only you can determine if it is what you need." Such a statement has two beneficial effects for the librarian. The first is that it makes reasonable reliance much less plausible. The second is that it reinforces the purely consultative role of the librarian in the user's information gathering process.

It is unlikely that a reference interaction would ever lead to a legal conclusion that the user's reliance was reasonable, such that liability could result. However, it is both prudent and professionally responsible for a librarian to avoid projecting subject expertise, avoid providing guarantees, and also to remind users that they remain responsible for their information needs.

5.5 Collections Decisions and Accuracy of Materials

For the most part, collections decisions do not pose issues that could lead to personal professional liability. That said, there is one theoretical, if improbable, exception to this. This exception would be in the situation in which a librarian knew or reasonably should have known that a book being collected or in the collection contained wrong or inaccurate information that, if disseminated, could lead to physical harm. Reasonable reliance is once again an issue in this case, but the key factor at play would be the fact that the librarian knew or should have known about the harmful information and disseminated it anyway.

Thus, in the example of the person building a deck, if the librarian had been informed that the information in the book she supplied was dangerously wrong, and she supplied it anyway, liability is a theoretical possibility. This standard does not require that librarians carefully investigate every fact in every book in the collection. It only holds that, should they become aware through reasonable channels that information in a book is wrong, they should either remove the book from the collection or make users aware of the problem.

The other very real issue is that of libel. It is clear that, should a library become aware that materials in the collection are libelous, they have an obligation to remove these from circulation. While this is certainly the case, there is no precedent for individual professional liability for such libel. Rather, the libel claim would almost certainly be against the library as an institution.

ENDNOTES

1. 745 ILCS 10/1 et seq.
2. 745 ILCS 10/1–101.1.
3. 745 ILCS 10/1–206.
4. 745 ILCS 10/2–106.
5. 745 ILCS 10/2–107.
6. 47 USC 230.
7. 47 USC 230(c)(1).
8. *Jacobellis v. Ohio*, 378 U.S. 184, 197, 84 S.Ct. 1676, 1683, 12 L.Ed.2d 793 (1964) (Stewart, J. concurring).

[9] See, *e.g., Professional Competencies for Reference and User Services Librarians: RUSA Task Force on Professional Competencies* 42 Ref. & User Services Q. 290 (2003); for a discussion of the challenges of evaluating reference work, see William A. Katz, *Introduction to Reference Work, Volume II: Reference Services and Reference Processes* (7th ed., 1997) 263–266.

[10] *Matteucci v High School Dist.*, 281 NE2d 383 (Ill. App. 1972).

[11] Dan B. Dobbs, *The Law of Torts,* at 259.

[12] Allan Angoff, *Library Malpractice Suit: Could It Happen to You?* 7 American Libraries 489 (1976).

▶Seven

LIABILITY ISSUES FOR LAW AND MEDICAL LIBRARIANS

IN THIS CHAPTER

This chapter covers the legal issues that arise for those who work in law and medical libraries. While most of the chapter is oriented toward such specialized libraries, the issues it addresses apply to any librarian who assists users with legal or medical questions. Most of the material in this chapter will use legal questions as the context, but most of the concepts covered can be applied to answering medical questions as well. Indeed, the concepts covered here extend to any topic of professional expertise, whether in a specialized or general library.

The topics covered include:

▶ Who is asking legal and medical questions and why
▶ Liability implications for different library user types
▶ The special challenges of pro se library users

1. CASE STUDY: LEGAL REFERENCE QUESTIONS IN THE LIBRARY

It is a Friday afternoon in the law library of the Yorken School of Law. At the reference desk, the head of public services, Gillian Knauss, is training April Warren, a new reference librarian. Like many academic law librarians, Gillian is also an attorney and is licensed to practice law. She has been a law librarian for ten years. April recently joined the law library staff after spending three years as a reference librarian at the Yorken City Public Library. She has an MLS, but no legal training.

As a training exercise, Gillian has April assist her in fulfilling a reference request from one of the law school faculty members. The professor is teaching a course on family law, and would like the library to assemble a complete set of materials and example forms that would be required in order to pursue a divorce action. The professor plans to have his students use the materials in a mock divorce exercise. Gillian spends some time showing April the specialized divorce form books that the library has, as well as practitioners' materials on divorce. They also look at annotated statutes and other divorce-related materials. When the materials are assembled, Gillian has April deliver them to the professor. Upon her return, April sees that Gillian is busy assisting two students. At this point, a middle-aged man approaches the reference desk, and April decides to try to assist him without Gillian.

The man tells April that he has been served with a divorce petition, and that he wants to represent himself in the matter. He asks her if she can show him the library's divorce materials—in particular the form for something called an "answer," which the petition he's been served with says he must file within ten days. Pleased to be asked about something she'd just learned about, April shows the man some of the divorce materials that she and Gillian had just been going over. The man asks several technical questions that April cannot answer. She suggests that he ask Gillian, because Gillian is a lawyer and could probably help him.

At this point Gillian joins them. When the man asks her his questions, Gillian's demeanor changes noticeably. She tells him that she cannot give legal advice, and that he will have to find the answers to his questions himself. He mentions that April said she is a lawyer, to which Gillian replies that her role here is that of librarian, and that all she can do for him is show him where information on divorce is located in the library. The man reluctantly takes the materials April found and goes to a table to read them. April is surprised by this seemingly unhelpful attitude on Gillian's part. After thinking about it, she decides that it must be because the man is not a member of the college community, but she is not sure that's it. April is about to ask Gillian about it, when a well-dressed woman approaches the desk.

The woman introduces herself as a local attorney. She explains that she is looking for discovery materials, particularly pattern deposition checklists, for a car accident case she has. Gillian responds to this request enthusiastically. With April accompanying them, Gillian takes the attorney to the materials she wants. In addition to showing her what she requested, Gillian makes several suggestions of other materials. She also tells the attorney about her credentials as a lawyer, and even makes some tactical suggestions for approaching the case. April is amazed at how forthcoming Gillian is, and feels completely confused about Gillian's different approaches to these two users.

When they get a free moment April decides to ask about the difference. Gillian explains that her treatment of each of those library users was based on the risk of liability they posed. She explained that answering questions for the professor and the attorney provided no risk of liability, but that assisting the man with the divorce, whom Gillian referred to as a "pro se," provided not only the risk of liability should he be harmed, but also the possibility of having April thrown in jail for unauthorized practice of law. April was stunned. Clearly she had a lot to learn.

2. LAW AND MEDICAL REFERENCE QUESTIONS: WHO IS ASKING, AND WHY?

The risk of liability when answering legal and medical reference questions revolves around two issues: the role, or status, of the person asking the question, and the purpose for which they want the information. The role of library users can be divided between laypeople and subject experts. The purpose of the use can be divided between simple curiosity or scholarship, professional purposes, or pursuing one's own interests.

Much of this chapter will be devoted to understanding the interactions of these roles and purposes. For purposes of introduction, we can summarize the topic in this way: Assisting subject experts (e.g., lawyers or medical professionals) poses no risk of liability, regardless of the purpose for which the professional is seeking the information. Similarly, laypeople who are asking legal or medical questions do not pose a liability risk if they are asking simply to learn more about the topic, as opposed to pursuing their own interests. On the other hand, laypeople who are asking for legal or medical information in order to pursue their own interests pose a very real threat of liability. In addition, if these laypeople legitimately see the reference librarian as a subject expert, and reasonably rely on them to provide information, which then results in harm, the librarian could be subject to charges of unauthorized practice of law or medicine, or a medical or legal malpractice claim. It is this reality that results in the very different treatment that certain library users receive when asking legal or medical reference questions.

To sort this out in detail, let's begin by looking at the users librarians don't have to worry about, users we can refer to as benign.

2.1 Benign Users and Uses of Legal and Medical Materials

The danger of liability when dealing with professional information only exists when the information is to be used in a way that could lead to harm. Essentially this means when the person seeking the information is pursuing his own interests. Put another way, liability would only be an issue when the person seeking information is a layperson (i.e., someone who is not a member of the profession about which they want information) and who is seeking information to pursue their own interests. Thus, someone who is looking for medical information poses a threat of liability only if they are not a doctor or other relevant health professional, and further, only if they are seeking information related to their own medical need or problem.

While laypeople seeking professional information are by definition those who raise the risk of liability, keep in mind that it is entirely possible for a layperson library user to be seeking professional information for entirely benign purposes.

For example, someone might want information on a medical procedure or a legal doctrine out of simple personal interest, in order to write a school report, or to settle a bet. In those cases, the user can be treated as any other library user. This is because, even though they are a layperson seeking professional information, their use of the information is not such that it could conceivably lead to harm. Because such people pose no particular threat of liability, they will not be discussed further in this chapter.

The second category of benign users is professionals, particularly licensed professionals. Although they do not raise concerns of liability, this is for different reasons than for lay users.

2.2 Services to Licensed Professionals

A professional, such as a doctor or lawyer, also poses no risk of liability when asking reference questions. This is because such professionals remain responsible for their professional activities, and cannot displace liability to those who work for or serve them, such as secretaries or librarians. This concept is very important, and although the details differ from profession to profession, the basic concept is that professionals remain responsible for their own work product. The legal rationale for this takes two forms. First is the obligation of professionals to be responsible for the professional activities they engage in or supervise. The second comes under the doctrine of vicarious liability. The following sections explain this concept separately for law and medicine.

2.2.1 Lawyers

With lawyers, personal responsibility for their work product is a settled fact both under the *Model Rules of Professional Conduct* and in attorney malpractice case law. The *Model Rules of Professional Conduct* are the ethical rules of the legal profession. The *Model Rules* are just that, a model, but all fifty states have adopted them in some form. Although there is some variability in lawyer practice rules from state to state, the basic concepts we are discussing are treated the same way in all states.

The *Model Rules* make lawyers responsible for their work product in two ways. First, it is the affirmative duty of a lawyer to conduct adequate research as stated in rule 1.3 of the *Model Rules of Professional Conduct*. This rule states that a lawyer is responsible for adequate investigation of the facts and law in a client matter, and that delegation of the work to another does not relieve the lawyer of this obligation.[1] This concept has been adopted in each of the states.[2]

The second is Model Rule 5.3, which states that lawyers remain responsible, and liable, for the actions of those who do work on their behalf.[3] This responsibility extends to both employees and non-employees who do work or perform tasks for an attorney.[4] As long as the tasks performed are within the scope of the person's employment and are done at the attorney's request, the attorney remains responsible. This means that a librarian who provides information to a lawyer will not face personal professional liability, because the information was supplied at the lawyer's request, and supplying information is within the scope of her employment. Of course, an employee of a lawyer, such as a firm librarian, while protected from personal liability to the person harmed, could still face discipline as an employee when her work is seen as inadequate or in error.

The idea that lawyers are personally responsible for the quality of their legal research is well settled in the law on legal malpractice,[5] as is the idea that lawyers remain responsible for their work product even if they have delegated it to a non-lawyer.[6] This is true in all states.[7] Once again, there are two broad rationales used to support this doctrine. The first is that improper or poorly done research is a violation of the state's equivalent of Model Rule 1.3, requiring diligence and competence on the part of the lawyer, and is thus malpractice regardless of who actually performed the research. The second is under the doctrine of vicarious liability. Vicarious liability is "Liability that a supervisory party (such as an employer) bears for the actionable conduct of a subordinate or associate (such as an employee) based on the relationship between the two parties."[8] This is basically the same concept as respondeat superior; it means that an employer is responsible for harm caused by employees who were acting within the scope of their employment. Under either rationale, the attorney remains legally responsible for any harm that results from inadequate legal research, and that responsibility cannot be diverted to a librarian.

2.2.2 Doctors

The twin rationales for leaving the responsibility for information with lawyers holds true for doctors as well. This means that doctors have an affirmative duty to assure themselves that they have adequate and current medical information, and are also responsible for the actions of employees in treating a patient.[9] Unlike with lawyers, the role of licensing, with its concomitant ability to pursue disciplinary actions based on ethical rules, has not played as large a role with doctors.[10] The result is that the standards for medical care have come from the large body of medical malpractice law.

Like lawyers, doctors also have a requirement for diligence in practice.[11] Doctors are responsible for meeting the standard of care for medicine in their locality, and assuring that they have current knowledge is both a legal requirement and an ethical one.[12] Doctors are fully subject to vicarious liability, and are responsible for harm that occurs to their patients as the result of the actions of their employees, so long as those employees are acting within the scope of their employment.[13] This responsibility exists not only under respondeat superior, for direct employees of the doctor, but also under the "borrowed servant" doctrine, which makes the doctor responsible for the actions of employees of other entities when those people are working under the doctor's direction.[14] Thus, a self-employed surgeon performing surgery at a hospital would be liable for the actions of a surgical nurse attending him who was employed by the hospital.

The result is that in a case in which a doctor was provided with inadequate or improper information, which led to harm, liability would lie with the doctor. This would be true either because of the requirement that the doctor apply appropriate knowledge to patient care as part of the general standard or care for medicine, or because liability for the actions of the librarian who provided the information inures to the doctor under vicarious liability. The doctor would be vicariously liable for the actions of his employees because of the doctrine of respondeat superior, or for employees of other entities under the borrowed servant doctrine.

2.3 Who Is Asking Legal Questions?

Having established the categories of users for questions on professional topics, and having looked at the concept of benign users, let us now look specifically at the users of a law library. Those who approach the law library reference desk with a law-related information need can be divided into three basic groups: legal experts, law students, and lay users. Experts include lawyers, law professors, and certain other legal professionals, such as paralegals. Law students are those pursuing a legal education. Lay users include everyone else asking a legal question. Once again, all of our concern about liability is with the lay user category. As discussed above, legal experts remain personally responsible for their information needs, and law students, in seeking legal information for their studies, are not pursuing their own legal interests. If a law student has a legal question that is about their own legal interests or situation, they would be considered a lay user, as discussed below.

2.4 Pro Se: A Special Category of Law Library Users

In the American legal system, those who are pursuing their own legal interests, including representing themselves in court, are referred to as "pro se". This Latin phrase means "for oneself," and is used as a specific designation for those who are pursuing a legal matter without being represented by an attorney.[15] Law librarians follow this usage, but broaden it to refer to any layperson doing legal research in the library. For purposes of liability, there are actually significant distinctions between types of lay law library users, and the term "pro se" tends to blur those differences in ways that create difficulties for analysis.

Laypersons doing legal research can be divided into three distinct categories, the characteristics of which are important to understanding how librarians deal with the pro se issue. The first group of lay law library users are those who are doing research on legal topics, but not pursuing their own legal interests. A student writing a paper on an important Supreme Court decision, or someone interested in the history of jurisprudence are examples of this group. For librarians, such library users are benign in the sense that they bring no real or perceived legal or ethical problems, and can generally be treated like any other library user.

A second group consists of those who are pursuing their own legal interests, but are not involved in a court action. Examples include those looking for information on writing their own will or on drafting a contract without the assistance of an attorney. The legal and ethical issues such library users raise are significant, but because they are not currently involved in an active legal dispute, they don't present with the urgency that self-represented litigants do. Librarians should treat such library users with the same caution that they would treat a self-represented litigant.

The third group of laypersons using the library are self-represented litigants. This group historically has been the focus of discussion on the topic. These are people who are involved in some sort of active legal action and are trying to pursue or protect their own legal interests without an attorney.

In the case study scenario above, the professor was asking for information for his class, and was not pursuing his own legal interests. As such his request poses no threat of liability. Similarly, as was explained above, the attorney remains responsible for her case, and could not sue the librarian. On the other hand, the man who had been served with divorce papers was a pro se library user, and presented a very real risk of liability.

Differentiating Lay Users, Pro Se Users, and Self-represented Litigants

▶ Lay users include any person without legal training who is using the library to research a legal topic.

▶ Pro se users are those lay users who are actively pursuing their own legal interests or problems, whether or not they are engaged in litigation.

▶ Self-represented litigants are those pro se users who are actively engaged in litigation.

2.4.1 The Special Problems of Being Pro Se

Self-representation, whether in litigation or not, is an extremely dangerous undertaking, for a number of reasons. The practice of law requires education and expertise that the self-represented litigant usually does not have, and most people cannot bring to their own problems the kind of dispassionate judgment required to effectively handle a serious legal situation. Litigation is adversarial in nature, and a self-represented litigant cannot be assisted by the judge or the other side. People who decide to proceed in a legal matter without an attorney are taking the very big gamble that they will be able to overcome these obstacles.

Most legal issues create significant risks for those involved, and can affect such fundamental interests as the right to liberty. In criminal matters, there is the threat of prison or jail, while in competency matters, the threat of forced hospitalization or treatment. In addition, other constitutional rights can be at stake. Those convicted of felonies can lose their right to vote or own guns. In a divorce, people can lose the ability to live in their home. Landlord-tenant conflicts can lead to eviction, while mortgage foreclosures or condemnation actions can result in the loss of one's home.

Interests in real and personal property can be at stake. Civil litigation can result in large damage awards, as well as fines, court costs, and the obligation to pay attorneys fees incurred by other litigants. Contract disputes can involve significant money or property, and zoning issues can affect how land can be used. Rights and duties relating to one's family and children can be affected. Divorce affects rights to property, where one lives, and the relationship with one's children, while custody proceedings can fundamentally affect both relationships and monetary interests. Paternity actions can lead to the creation, or loss, of rights related to children and also significant financial obligations. There are few legal actions so trivial in nature that they do not affect significant interests of those involved.

Pro Se Users

What are the legal activities that pro se library users might be pursuing?

Some of the nonlitigation activities that pro se users can be engaged in include:

- ▶ Drafting wills or trusts
- ▶ Negotiating leases
- ▶ Handling legal issues related to their business
- ▶ Negotiating contracts or agreements
- ▶ Pursuing change in government
- ▶ Pursuing other advocacy issues

Self-represented litigants are those who are representing themselves in litigation. This can include civil litigation or some sort or criminal defense. Common types of actions for self-represented litigants include:

- ▶ Divorce and custody
- ▶ Paternity
- ▶ Criminal matters
- ▶ Government benefits
- ▶ Disputes involving government actions (such as zoning or property issues)
- ▶ Driving and vehicle issues
- ▶ Tax problems
- ▶ Constitutional issues, including discrimination

Self-representation

Why do people represent themselves?

Given the dangers associated with self-representation, one might reasonably ask why someone would choose to proceed pro se. The reasons are varied, but some of the main reasons include:

▶ Money: Legal representation is very expensive, and is not guaranteed or provided by the court for anyone other than certain criminal defendants. Many people simply cannot afford an attorney, no matter how serious the situation is. They feel that they have no choice but to represent themselves. Some people have the resources to pay for representation, but perceive of lawyers as being unduly expensive. They refuse to spend money in this way, and prefer to represent themselves.

▶ Distrust of lawyers: Some people feel that lawyers are dishonest and untrustworthy. They feel that a lawyer will not protect them or their interests.

▶ Belief that the system will protect them: Some people feel the court is obligated to do justice, and will protect them no matter how bad a job they do representing themselves.

▶ Belief that law is simple: Much about the practice of law looks simple to the casual observer. Media portrayals have exacerbated this impression. Many self-represented litigants have a persistent belief that the answers to legal problems and instructions on how to proceed are written in a book somewhere, if they could just find it. This belief is a major source of pro se reference requests.

▶ Mental illness: It is an unfortunate fact that a certain percentage of pro se library users are mentally ill. Their desire to represent themselves arises from impaired judgment about their situation, their skills, the nature of the other parties, their interests, or the risks involved.

▶ Seeking a tactical advantage in litigation: Some self-represented litigants may believe that if they represent themselves they will be treated more favorably by the court, and given breaks and advantages because they are perceived as the weaker party.

▶ The actual benefit of previous experience: In some cases, laypersons who have extensive experience in court may actually know enough to represent themselves well. A person with an extensive criminal background may know more about criminal defense than an inexperienced lawyer. A landlord who has experience in landlord-tenant legal issues may be able to adequately handle such an issue.

▶ A blind belief in their own innocence and in the inherent ability of the legal system to see their innocence or the justice of their cause: Many people believe that the justice system is bound to do justice, no matter what. If they are innocent or otherwise in the right, they believe the court will see that and act accordingly. For this reason they feel that they do not need a lawyer.

Many of the problems experienced by pro se library users arise out of the unique nature of law practice and legal information. By definition, lawyers are highly trained professionals who are licensed to practice law in a given jurisdiction. The tools of the legal profession are legal information and the ability to analyze and use that information in a legal setting. Many people errantly suppose that law school is a process of mastering legal information, when in fact legal training is intended to develop and hone legal thinking and analytical skills. The heavy reliance on such thinking and analysis means that much of the practice of law is unseen by outsiders. This, in turn, can lead to the assumption that the only real tools for practicing law are the sources of legal information available in the library.

Pro se library users can thus approach legal research with a number of misapprehensions. In addition to being unfamiliar with legal materials, pro se users often appear to misunderstand essential aspects of law and the legal process. The fluid nature of the law often comes as a surprise, including the lack of clear answers to most legal questions. They often underestimate the skill required for effective representation in almost any legal matter, as well as the value of a dispassionate, but fully informed, point of view on a legal case. This often results in frustration for the pro se user, a condition which they hope the librarian will help alleviate.

2.4.2 Are Pro Se Users a Big Issue for Libraries?

Pro se users are considered a major presence in law libraries, and most law librarians in institutions open to the public feel that a significant portion of their users are members of the lay public.[16] One would assume that public and academic libraries see their share of pro se users as well. There do not appear to be any statistics available on pro se users in public, academic, and other non-law libraries open to the public. Statistics on pro se use of law libraries are also hard to come by, but at least one study from the 1970s confirmed that pro se law library users were a significant percentage of the users of university law libraries.[17] The study concentrated on law school libraries, but found that in tax-supported law school libraries in particular, an average of 20 percent of users were laypeople or pro se litigants, and that at some institutions this number was as high as 48 percent. More recent figures, admittedly based on a very informal survey, indicate that members of the public generate between 30 and 70 percent of reference questions at public law libraries in major metropolitan areas.[18]

There is no question that the high number of people proceeding pro se in legal actions is very real. Unfortunately, although pro se representation is a national issue, statistics on it are frustratingly hard to come by. The National Center for State Courts has produced a Web page that collects what statistical reports are available for state courts on pro se representation, but the offerings are far from complete (see following shaded box).[19] Authors writing in legal journals provide some figures for state court litigation. According to McEnroe,[20] 88 percent of litigants in Washington, D.C., family court are proceeding pro se, as are 60 percent in

Santa Monica, California (an increase from 30 percent five years earlier). In Hennepin County, Minnesota (the county containing Minneapolis), over 30,000 people a year represent themselves in Conciliation Court.[21]

The total volume of cases in the federal courts is less than those of the state courts, but at the federal level, the most recent available statistics indicate 69,919 pro se cases were filed during the 12-month period ending September 30, 2006, compared to 189,622 non-pro se cases.[22] This makes pro se filings 26 percent of all federal court filings. Of the pro se cases filed during that period, 50,451 were filed by prisoners, and 19,468 were filed by non-prisoners. Non-prisoner pro se litigants thus accounted for 28 percent of pro se filings, and 7.5 percent of all federal court filings. Note that these statistics only track the pro se status of the person filing the petition, and not that of other parties to the action. For this reason, the actual incidence of pro se representation in the federal courts may be higher than these statistics indicate. With such numbers, it is only logical to assume that pro se litigants are coming to libraries for information and assistance.

Pro Se Statistics

Some figures on pro se litigation supplied by the National Center for State Courts[23] from individual states include:

▶ California: In 2004 over 4.3 million court users are self represented in California. For family law cases, 67 percent of petitioners at filing (72 percent for largest counties) are self-represented and 80 percent of petitioners at disposition for dissolution cases are self-represented.

▶ Florida: In 2001, 73 percent of court hearings involved at least one pro se participant, up from 66 percent in 1999.

▶ Iowa: In 2005 a random survey of a week of district court schedules in one county showed that 58 percent of cases set for trial that week involved at least one pro se party.

▶ New Hampshire: In 2004 one party was pro se in 85 percent of all civil cases in the district court and 48 percent of all civil cases in the superior court.

▶ Utah: In divorce cases, 49 percent of petitioners and 81 percent of respondents are self-represented. For small-claims cases, 99 percent of petitioners and 99 percent of respondents are self-represented. Seven percent of pro se litigants reported using a law library for assistance.

▶ Wisconsin: In 2000, as many as 70 percent of family cases involved litigants who represented themselves in court. There was an increase in pro se litigants in family law cases from 1996 (43 percent) to 1999 (53 percent) in the Tenth Judicial Administrative District, and an increase in pro se litigants in family law cases from 1996 (69 percent) to 1999 (72 percent) in the First Judicial Administrative District.

2.4.3 Librarians' Perceptions of Pro Se Users

The general view of the pro se library user in the law library literature is neither complimentary nor welcoming. The pro se user has been referred to as ignorant of the law and in general, and proceeding pro se has been referred to as comparable to self-surgery.[24] Yvette Brown says that pro se users are "seeking legal advice" and are "unaware of the fundamental differences between the services of an attorney and the services of a librarian."[25]

Pro se users are seen as presenting a variety of problems for the law reference librarian. It has been pointed out that pro se users tend to dominate the reference librarian's time, requiring instruction in legal bibliography and needing direction concerning the collection, and then demanding interpretation of the materials they find.[26] As additional users of the library, they place demands on library resources, including books and library seating, as well as presenting a threat for the theft of materials.[27]

One of the feelings expressed in the literature is that the lay public will confuse a law librarian with a practicing lawyer.[28] Because of this, some law librarians have argued that legal information is more appropriately dispensed by public libraries, partly with the idea that pro se users in a public library will be less likely to regard the librarian as a subject expert in law.[29] By contrast, other authors question whether pro se users, even when they see law librarians as subject experts in law, actually confuse this with being a lawyer, and contend that pro se users in a law library are seeking reference help, not legal advice, and know the difference between the two.[30]

2.4.4 Perceptions of Reference Service vs. Legal Advice

One of the great problems with the issue of assisting pro se library users is that there are no clear standards with which to determine what constitutes legal advice. Librarians have thus been left to their own devices to determine which reference activities are allowable, and which are not.

Perceptions of where the line is between reference assistance and legal advice are not at all uniform. Indeed, the argument has been made that almost any reference interaction involving legal materials is, in some sense, practicing law.[31] Schanck says that suggesting a book, index terms, or a source might all be activities that constitute interpretation of the law.[32] Those who take this view worry that reference interviews can lead to unintentionally dispensing legal advice,[33] and that any difference between legal reference service and legal advice is a fallacy.[34] Mills raises the possibility that there might be an implied attorney-client relationship at the reference desk through the concept of agency, or that an attorney-librarian might be held to an attorney-client relationship with pro se users and liability could result.[35] This area of liability is completely undefined in law. In such a situation it is very important to understand what the unauthorized practice of law is, and how it affects law librarians.

3. FORMS OF LIABILITY ARISING FROM ASSISTING LAY USERS

With such confusion about how to deal with lay library users who are pursuing their own interests, we should concentrate on the two forms of liability they make possible. The first is that of unauthorized practice of a profession, in this case law or medicine. The second is the possibility of tort liability arising from the librarian being seen as a subject expert. These two forms of liability are not mutually exclusive, and can or would operate independently.

3.1 Unauthorized Practice of a Profession

When dealing with a licensed profession, such as law or medicine, there is a very real risk that the assistance provided by a librarian might go too far into the realm of the profession, by offering advice or diagnosis. In such a case, the librarian could be guilty of unauthorized practice of a profession. This is particularly true of law and law librarianship, because the practice of law includes giving legal advice, and legal advice is very hard to discern from standard reference services. Under the circumstances, a thorough discussion of unauthorized practice of law will be instructive.

3.1.1 Unauthorized Practice of Law

Librarians, including law librarians, have not traditionally been part of the discussion of unauthorized practice. Unauthorized practice of law by librarians is not discussed in standard works relating to unauthorized practice of law,[36] and there are no actual court cases concerning librarians and the unauthorized practice of law discussed in the law library literature.[37] A recent online search also failed to find any such cases.[38]

The confusion that librarians feel about what is permissible or not when answering legal reference questions has its basis in what is, at best, a fractious, confusing, and vague area of law. Unauthorized practice is covered in rule 5.5 of the *Model Rules of Professional Conduct*.[39] A majority of states have adopted the model rules, and those that haven't have largely borrowed its content,[40] but the definition of legal practice varies by jurisdiction.[41] The ability to practice law is regulated at the state level, and unauthorized practice issues are dealt with at that level as well. Depending on statutes and court rules, states can bring criminal actions against those accused of unauthorized practice, but more often use civil suits, injunctions and contempt actions.[42]

In most states the unauthorized practice of law is clearly proscribed, but what constitutes practice is not defined.[43] What is and is not the practice of law thus remains unsettled,[44] and any attempt to define the practice of law in order to determine rational limits to legal activity is doomed to failure.[45] As general concepts, the *Model Rules of Professional Conduct* state that a lawyer is a representative of clients, and serves as advisor, advocate, negotiator, and intermediary.[46]

The rationale for prohibiting the unauthorized practice of law varies, but usually includes protection of the public from practice by unqualified persons,[47] and meaningful regulation of the legal profession.[48] At its heart, the prohibition of unauthorized practice protects the ability of a layperson to get assistance with their legal interests by establishing a relationship with someone adequately schooled in law. The result should be that a licensed attorney is in the best position to protect a client's interests because the attorney has better access to the facts, and a more complete knowledge of the law.[49] An attorney can also research the law at leisure, and understands the practical functioning of the legal system.[50]

The basic statutory law provides very little guidance for librarians. A survey of cases from various jurisdictions reveals certain common tests for the unauthorized practice of law. A few of these are that more than lay knowledge is required for the task, that the services rendered concern the legal rights of others, that the activity is one customarily performed by a lawyer,[51] and that the activity involves a personal relationship of confidence and trust.[52]

In a similar way it might also be helpful to look at what activities have been prosecuted as unauthorized practice of law. In addition to taking action against obvious violations, such as the practice of law by disbarred or suspended attorneys, or by laypeople who hold themselves out to be lawyers, the organized bar has most often sought to limit the activities of title abstract and insurance companies, trust departments, accountants, collection agencies, insurance companies, and similar groups.[53] The presence or lack of material gain in such activities is clearly a factor.[54] Generally speaking, unauthorized practice prosecutions have focused on fraudulent activities, or those that actively seek to advise or represent others on legal matters, usually with some monetary gain. In spite of the vagueness of this area of law, none of the activities described above resemble the type of interaction that takes place at a library reference desk.

Exceptions have evolved from the prohibitions barring non-lawyers from performing services customarily performed by lawyers. These include parties acting for themselves, legal activities incidental to a regular business or profession, laymen of special expertise, incidental activities done without compensation, scrivener activities, and activities providing a public benefit.[55]

Pro se activity is a specific exception to unauthorized practice proscriptions.[56] The right to self-representation in federal court has been protected by statute since the creation of the American government,[57] and the right to proceed pro se in state court was granted by the U.S. Supreme Court in *Farretta v. California*[58] but is limited and conditional.[59] Lawyers are permitted to counsel those who wish to proceed pro se without violating the proscription against assisting the unauthorized practice of law.[60] Indeed, some writers see a requirement that the legal profession assist those who wish to proceed pro se.[61]

This leaves law librarians uncertain whether any reference activity can be interpreted as unauthorized practice of law. The only state authority that has addressed the issue is the Virginia State Bar Association, whose unauthorized practice of law opinion 161 addresses assistance provided by non-lawyer library staff to law library users.[62] Under that opinion, when assisting pro se users, "Library staff may only respond to specific questions or requests rather than attempt to interpret the user's need as to do more would constitute the unauthorized practice of law."[63] This explains why, in the case study above, Gillian refused to help the pro se library user, even though she had expertise in the topic.

Avoiding Legal Advice

Many, if not most law librarians take the view that they should be very careful about any activity that might constitute legal advice. In doing so many will avoid:

▶ Interpreting any term, statute or case
▶ Suggesting search terms or topics
▶ Advising users about what kind of law to look for
▶ Selecting, discussing, or assisting with any forms
▶ Agreeing or disagreeing with any legal opinion or argument made by a user

3.2 Subject Expertise and Liability for Librarians

The unauthorized practice of law is a different issue from the kind of tort liability that this book is concerned with. Unauthorized practice of law would involve the librarian being prosecuted by the state, rather than by the person harmed. The kind of tort liability that we have been discussing in the rest of this book would arise from the pro se library user reasonably seeing the librarian as a subject expert, and therefore as someone on whose expertise they can reasonably rely. When dealing with subjects like law or medicine, liability for the librarian is possible under a tort based on reasonable reliance, or on malpractice.

While one of the main messages of this book is that professional liability is unlikely for most information professionals, there are several specialized areas of librarianship for which the idea of liability is more reasonable. Such areas are those where the librarian might legitimately be seen as a subject expert, and therefore as someone who could reasonably be seen as giving professional advice on the topic at hand, in addition to, or instead of, simply providing information in response to a request.

The essential issue here is one of expertise. While being seen as an expert on finding information does not provide an opening for liability under normal circumstances, being seen as an expert on the information itself does provide such a possibility. Once the librarian puts herself forward as an expert on the topic being researched, as opposed to an expert on research, her involvement in the user's information need moves to a different level. In some cases this might be relatively benign—for instance, if the topic is a purely academic one, such as philosophy or history—but if the topic is a professional one or one that has an impact on important personal interests, then the involvement can have serious implications.

Once again, in the event that reliance on the librarian leads to harm, the essential question will be whether that reliance was justified. However, if a library user sought information from a librarian, and circumstances were such that he reasonably concluded that the librarian was an expert on the topic of his information need, liability for the librarian is a realistic possibility in the event the information or advice provided by the librarian somehow leads to harm.

This is especially true in two circumstances. The first is where a librarian is, in fact, an expert on the topic of the information need. The second is in a specialized library, where it might be seen as reasonable to assume that everyone who works there is a subject expert. Of the two issues, the idea of actually being a subject expert is worth some discussion.

Many librarians have advanced degrees in other fields, including professional fields. For example, about one third of the more than 5,000 members of the American Association of Law Libraries have law degrees.[64] Such librarians are legitimately experts in law, and many even have a license to practice law. If, while assisting a user, a lawyer-librarian were to offer advice on the user's legal issue, it would be entirely reasonable for the user to rely on that advice, and liability could result.

While this chapter concentrates on law and medicine, reasonable reliance is possible for other disciplines as well. An example of this would be a librarian who has an advanced degree in engineering and who makes this known to users seeking information on an engineering question. In such a situation, the user might decide that the librarian could be relied on as an expert and rely solely on the information she provided, resulting in harm. Under these circumstances a court might find that it was reasonable for the user to rely on the librarian for engineering advice, and hold the librarian liable for the harm.

Two important points flow from this possibility. The first is that, should someone bring a claim based on relying on a librarian as a subject expert, as opposed to an expert on finding information, the claim would be based on the idea that the librarian violated a duty of care related to the underlying subject or profession, rather than that the librarian violated any duty of care related to librarianship.[65]

The second point is that this reinforces a foundational idea: All librarians, regardless of training or background, should present themselves as experts in finding information, rather than being an expert on the information they find. This basic concept is the single most important step to take in order to avoid liability for providing information.

3.2.1 Malpractice and Tort Issues for Law Librarians

There actually are two separate issues here: malpractice as a lawyer and general liability for harm. Librarians who are lawyers, and who are found to have allowed a lawyer-client relationship to come into being with a pro se library user, could quite reasonably be held to lawyer malpractice standards. For lawyer-librarians this is a serious issue. It is clear that lawyer-client relationships can be found to exist unless the lawyer affirmatively acts to negate its existence and it is reasonable to do so.[66] This means that the issue of whether a lawyer-client relationship exists will revolve around whether it is reasonable for the putative client to believe that one does.[67] A librarian who presents herself as a lawyer and renders what can be seen as legal advice could very easily be held to lawyer malpractice standards.

There is no reason to believe that a lawyer-librarian who is not licensed to practice in the jurisdiction where she works will be held to any lesser standard, and the danger of tort liability to the putative client would be just as great. Lawyer-librarians licensed in the jurisdiction where they work would also face potential disciplinary action from the bar, but it can be assumed that lawyers licensed elsewhere could face similar discipline from the jurisdiction where they are licensed.

A librarian who is not a lawyer would presumably not be held to legal malpractice standards, providing that she did not hold herself out to the user as an expert on law. The key issue would be the extent to which the librarian implied that substantive legal help was being provided, as opposed to help with finding legal information. Librarians who take an advocacy approach to pro se problems could conceivably face liability if problems resulted from their activities.

There is a fairly simple form of guidance on this issue. Lawyers are required to hold non-clients at arm's length[68] in order to protect the interests of all parties. A librarian, whether a lawyer or not, serves library users best by assuming a similar stance.

4. LIABILITY ISSUES FOR MEDICAL AND HEALTH LIBRARIANSHIP

While there are some minor differences, most of the cautions that apply to legal information also apply to medical and health information. Once again, the crucial question is whether it would be reasonable for a user to rely on the information or advice received from a librarian in the event of harm. Also, as with law, potential liability exists in the twin forms of liability to the user under medical practice standards and liability to the state for the unauthorized practice of medicine.

There are some practical differences between law and medicine. On the one hand, most library users are less likely to confuse medical information with the practice of medicine itself, or assume that medical information is the only necessary element required to treat an illness or disease. This arguably makes reasonable reliance on a medical librarian less likely. On the other hand, while legal issues can be very serious, medical issues can involve serious physical harm or even death. At least one writer has made the point that physical harm that results from negligent provision of information could lead to liability.[69]

The literature of medical and health librarianship has registered liability concerns that are similar to those of law.[70] However, much of the literature has done a better job of emphasizing the relatively low risk of personal liability for medical and health librarians.[71] The basic advice given in the medical and health librarianship literature is also similar to that given for law librarians. In broad terms, the recommendations include to avoid giving advice, and to use acceptable sources for information.[72] A number of articles emphasize the need to be a conduit to the source of information, not the source itself.[73] This stance is also endorsed by a Medical Library Association policy statement.[74] Many articles also suggest posted disclaimers.[75]

5. PRACTICE SUGGESTIONS FOR LAW AND MEDICAL LIBRARIANSHIP

In spite of the ambiguity of the law and the lack of legal precedent, there are some basic steps that all librarians can take to minimize liability risks when dealing with requests for medical and legal information.

5.1 Basic Concepts to Guide Your Approach to Medical and Legal Questions

Librarians should understand and keep in mind the following basic concepts when preparing to assist users with medical and legal information requests. There is no precedent for legal liability for legitimate reference activities. This doesn't mean that such liability can never occur, but the chances are slim as long as librarians restrict themselves to legitimate reference activities.

There is no legal precedent for librarian malpractice liability per se. That said, it is conceivable that lawyer-librarians working in the jurisdiction where they are licensed could be considered to have formed an attorney-client relationship with a pro se user. If so, a malpractice claim could result. For medical librarians with advanced degrees or training in a health-related field the same risk could arise. The key point concerning librarian liability is that the librarian should restrict her activities to those of helping users find the information they seek.

There is a theoretical risk of engaging in the unauthorized practice of law or medicine while performing legal or medical reference services. As with other forms of liability, the risk is theoretical and has never actually happened. The law in this area is exceedingly unclear and subject to much legitimate disagreement and debate. Given the totality of the law and literature in this area it seems unlikely that a librarian could be successfully prosecuted for legitimate reference activities. That said, it is still imperative that librarians should be careful to avoid holding themselves out as experts on law or medicine, or trying to advise users with legal or medical problems.

In addition to any legal or liability issues presented by assisting users with legal or medical questions, there are also ethical and professional issues to consider. Librarians must balance the ethical need to assist all users fairly and professionally with the potential that the librarian's activities could lead to harm. As an example, the American Association of Law Libraries Ethical Principles contains the following text under the rubric of service:

1. We promote open and effective access to legal and related information.
2. We uphold a duty to our clientele to develop service policies that respect confidentiality and privacy.
3. We provide zealous service using the most appropriate resources and implementing programs consistent with our institution's mission and goals.
4. We acknowledge the limits on service imposed by our institutions and by the duty to avoid the unauthorized practice of law.[76]

Librarians have an ethical obligation to provide zealous service and open and effective access to legal information to pro se users, within the limits imposed by the missions and goals of their institution.

When asked a legal or medical reference question, librarians must be sensitive to issues of confidentiality, conflict of interest, and reliance or harm. There is no law that protects the confidentiality of reference interactions. However, the ethical imperative to protect confidentiality is clear. Users should be made aware that confidentiality of reference requests cannot be guaranteed. Librarians should never discuss reference requests with other users or persons not on the library staff. Confidentiality can be protected by urging a user to omit unnecessary details about their situation.

In providing reference services, librarians need to avoid any conflicts of interest. In the case of legal questions, this includes treating both sides of a legal dispute equally and fairly, should both sides seek reference help. Librarians should never become involved or take sides in a legal issue or between pro se users. Librarians dealing with any professional topic, including law and medicine, should treat all users consistently and in accord with policy.

Perhaps the most important issue that arises in medical or legal reference work is the potential for reliance and harm. Reliance occurs when a user assumes that the librarian has given accurate complete legal or medical advice, as opposed to simply providing information. Librarians must always make it clear that they are providing information and not advice. Proceeding pro se or self-diagnosis and treatment is inherently dangerous. It is highly likely that users who try to do so will be harmed by their attempts to represent themselves or treat their own illnesses. While we cannot prevent this, we can make sure that the library does not contribute to their harm.

Users must be made to understand that the help they receive at the reference desk is not legal or medical advice, and that the information they receive may not be adequate for their needs. In offering to help users in ways that are beyond the bounds of normal reference service, librarians run the risk of creating unrealistic expectations. Among other things, they may come to believe that they have received full and complete legal or medical advice, that the librarian has given them everything they need for their situation, or that they have received the advice of an expert and do not need to do further research or analysis, or consult an actual expert. The result of overinvolvement by the library can be that users are harmed by the librarian's activity more than they would have been otherwise. Sometimes allowing a user to encounter the complexity and difficulty of legal or medical materials can motivate them to seek legal advice. A librarian should never attempt to overstate the complexity or difficulty of materials. On the other hand, a librarian should not minimize this complexity or attempt to give advice.

Avoiding Liability

When one looks at the larger picture provided by the legal and ethical theory related to answering legal or medical reference questions, several themes appear:

▶ Liability for such activity is possible but unlikely, provided that librarians restrict themselves to legitimate reference activities.

▶ Ethical considerations indicate that doing anything other than providing regular reference service could inadvertently lead to harm for the user.

▶ Taken together the ethical and legal considerations indicate that librarians should:

• give fair, balanced, and complete reference service to those with legal or medical questions;

• avoid becoming involved in a user's research or problem;

• avoid holding themselves out as an expert on law or medical matters; and

• avoid advising users on legal or medical topics.

5.2 Tips and Tools for Serving Library Users with Legal or Medical Information Needs

Good preparation is the best way to deal with the ethical and legal concerns about answering legal or medical reference questions. All libraries should consider a variety of measures including:

- Policies
- Staff training
- Pathfinders and handouts
- Public notices
- Referrals

Policies: The library should develop and consistently apply policies for dealing with medical and legal information requests. The policies should:

- State the activities that are allowed and not allowed in providing legal and medical reference service.
- Use both legal and ethical considerations to form policy.
  - Describe who does and does not provide legal or medical reference service.
  - Lay out a procedure for users to pursue complaints about reference services.
  - Provide for referrals for users who need or request them.

Training: Staff training is essential.

- Staff should be trained on the library's policies and procedures.
- Staff should be trained to refer user questions to the reference desk.
- All staff should understand the seriousness of attempting to provide legal or medical reference services.

Handouts, Pathfinders, and Publications: Many libraries find handouts and pathfinders to be highly useful in assisting pro se users. Handouts can describe:

- Legal or medical reference policies
- Library resources available

Pathfinders can describe:

- Resources available for legal research in various areas
- Resources available for medical research in various areas

Public Notices:

- Posting notices of library policies can help users understand the parameters of reference service before they ask a librarian for help.
- Posted notices can also provide authority for a librarian in limiting service and setting boundaries.

▶ Notices can also point out the impossibility of guaranteeing confidentiality or privacy.

Referrals: A list of referrals can be very useful for pro se users. Referrals can be of the following types:

▶ To other libraries with better collections or services for the user's particular problem.

▶ For legal questions:
  • Legal services organizations.
  • Lawyer referral services.

▶ For medical questions:
  • Free or reduced cost medical clinics
  • Government or other health care resources.

ENDNOTES

[1] Center for Professional Responsibility, American Bar Association, *Annotated Model Rules of Professional Conduct*, 47 (5th ed. 2003) (hereinafter *Model Rules*).

[2] American Law Institute, *The Restatement of the Law: The Law Governing Lawyers*, § 16 (2000) (hereinafter *Restatement*).

[3] *Model Rules, supra* note 1, at 454.

[4] American Bar Association, *ABA/BNA Lawyer's Manual on Professional Conduct*, 301:1012.

[5] *E.g.,* "[A]n attorney may be liable for a failure to conduct adequate legal research." *Kempf v. Magida*, 832 N.Y.S.2d 47 (2007) (citing sources); "It is prima facie negligent conduct for an attorney to misadvise a client on such a settled point of law that can be looked up by the means of ordinary research techniques." *Lopez v. Clifford Law Offices, P.C.*, 841 N.E.2d 465 (Ill. App. 2005).

[6] In re Opinion No. 24 of Committee on Unauthorized Practice of Law, 607 A.2d 962 (N.J. 1992).

[7] *Restatement, supra* note 2, § 58.

[8] *Black's Law Dictionary* 934 (2004).

[9] Arthur W. Haffner, *Medical Information, Health Sciences Librarians, and Professional Liability*, 81 Special Libraries 305, 306 (1990).

[10] David W. Louisell, Harold Williams, *Medical Malpractice*, § 8.01 (2007).

[11] Norman S. Blackman, Charles P. Bailey, *Liability in Medical Practice: A Reference for Physicians*, 94 (1990).

[12] *Id.;* American Medical Association Council on Ethical and Judicial Affairs, Code of Medical Ethics, § 9.011 (2002-2003 ed.).

[13] C. Kerns, C.J. Gerner, C. Ryan, *Health Care Liability Deskbook*, § 1.3(c) (2007).

[14] Scott Becker, *Health Care Law: A Practical Guide*, § 13.01(2) (2007).

[15] Some parts of the country use the term "pro per" for the same purpose. "Pro per" is a contraction of the Latin phrase "In propria persona" meaning "in one's own person."

[16] Robert T. Begg, *The Reference Librarian and the* Pro Se *Patron*, 69 Law Lib J. 26, 28 (1976).

[17] Cameron Allen, *Whom We Shall Serve: Secondary Patrons of the University Law School Library*, 66 Law Lib. J. 160 (1973).

[18] K. L. Fitz-Gerald, *Serving Pro Se Patrons: An Obligation and an Opportunity*, 22 L. Ref. Serv. Q. 41, at 55 (2003).

[19] Madelynn Herman, Memorandum, *Pro Se: Self-Represented Litigants: Pro Se Statistics* (September 26, 2006). *Available at* http://www.ncsconline.org/WC/Publications/Memos/ProSeStatsMemo.htm#statecourt (last visited July 2, 2008).

[20] Paul McEnroe, *Going It Alone: Pro Se Litigation*, Bench & Bar, Feb. 1996, at 18.

[21] *Id.* Conciliation court is the Minnesota equivalent to what most jurisdictions refer to as small claims court. See Minn. Stat. 487.30 (1996).

[22] Administrative office of the U.S. Courts, *2006 Annual Report of the Director: Judicial Business of the United States Courts, Table S-24 Civil Pro Se And Non-Pro Se Filings, by District, During the 12-Month Period Ending September 30, 2006. Available at* http://www.uscourts.gov/judbus2006/tables/s24.pdf (last visited July 3, 2008).

[23] Herman, *supra* note 19.

[24] Begg, *supra* note 16.

[25] Yvette Brown, *From the Reference Desk to the Jail House: Unauthorized Practice of Law and Librarians*, 13 Legal Ref. Services Q. 31 (1994), at 32.

[26] Begg, *supra* note 16.

[27] *Id.*

[28] Brown, *supra* note 25.

[29] Robin K. Mills, *Reference Service vs. Legal Advice: Is It Possible to Draw the Line?* 72 Law Lib. J. 180 (1979).

[30] Madison Mosely Jr., Commentary, *The Authorized Practice of Legal Reference Service* 87 Law Lib. J. 203 (1995).

[31] Mills, *supra* note 29, at 187.

[32] Peter C. Schanck, *Unauthorized Practice of Law and the Legal Reference Librarian* 72 Law Lib. J. 57, at 60 (1979).

[33] Brown, *supra* note 25, at 37.

[34] Maria E. Protti, *Dispensing Law at the Front Lines: Ethical Dilemmas in Law Librarianship*, 40 Lib. Trends 234, 238 (1991).

[35] Mills, *supra* note 29, at 191.

[36] *E.g.,* American Bar Foundation, *Annotated Code of Professional Responsibility* (1979); H. Glenn Boggs, *What Is the Practice of Law? Really?* 57 Fla. B. J. 369 (1983); Center for Professional Responsibility, *American Bar Association, Model Rules, supra* note 1; Geoffrey C. Hazard, Jr & W. Willam Hodes, *The Law of Lawyering: A Handbook On the Model Rules of Professional Conduct,* 814 (2nd ed. 1996).

[37] Schanck, *supra* note 32, at 57.

[38] A search was conducted of Westlaw and LexisNexis on July 5, 2008. The search utilized Boolean search terms and was conducted on the federal and state databases in each

service. None of the cases returned by the searches dealt with a librarian accused of engaging in the unauthorized practice of law.

[39] *Model Rules, supra* note 1, at 464.

[40] Hazard, *supra* note 36, at 1255.

[41] *Model Rules, supra* note 1, at 464.

[42] Mills, *supra* note 29, at 183.

[43] See *e.g.,* Boggs *supra* note 36.

[44] Defining the outer limits of the practice of law is practically impossible. Hazard, *supra* note 36, at 814; Mills, *supra* note 29, at 183.

[45] Moses Apsan, note: *Assisting the Pro Se Litigant: Unauthorized Practice of Law or the Fulfillment of a Public Need?* 28 N.Y.L. Sch. L. Rev. 691, 694 (1983).

[46] *Model Rules, supra* note 1, at 7.

[47] *Model Rules, supra* note 1; Hazard, *supra* note 36, at 813.

[48] *Model Rules, supra* note 1, at 465.

[49] Schanck, *supra* note 32, at 59.

[50] *Id.*

[51] *Model Rules, supra* note 1, at 466.

[52] *New York County Lawyers Association v. Dacey,* 21 N.Y.2d 694, 234 N.E.2d 459, 287 N.Y.S.2d 422 (1967) (reversing on the dissenting opinion in 28 A.D.2d 161, 283 N.Y.S.2d 984 (1967)). (Holding that a book on avoiding probate does not constitute practice of law because it provides no personal contact or relationship with a client.)

[53] Mills, *supra* note 29, at 182 (citing sources).

[54] Gerome Leone, *Malpractice Liability of a Law Librarian?* 73 Law Lib. J. 45 (1980), at 50–51.

[55] Apsan, *supra* note 45, at 704–05.

[56] Helen B. Kim, *Legal Education and the Pro Se Litigant: A Step Towards a Meaningful Right to Be Heard,* 96 Yale L.J. 1641 (1987).

[57] Apsan, *supra* note 45, at 692; Begg, *supra* note 16, at 28.

[58] 422 U.S. 806, 95 S.Ct. 2525, 45 L.Ed.2d 562 (1975).

[59] Begg, *supra* note 16, at 28.

[60] *Model Rules, supra* note 1, at 472. (Comment on Model Rule 5.5.)

[61] *E.g.,* Apsan, *supra* note 45.

[62] Virginia UPL Opinion 161: *Assistance Provided by Non-Lawyer Library Staff to Library Patrons.* Available at http://www.vsb.org/site/regulation/virginia-upl-opinion-161 (last visited July 2, 2008).

[63] *Id.*

[64] American Association of Law Libraries, *The AALL Biennial Salary Survey & Organizational Characteristics,* 2007.

[65] John A. Gray, *The Health Sciences Librarian's Exposure to Malpractice Liability Because of Negligent Provision of Information,* 77 Bull. Med. Lib. Assoc. 33, 34 (1989).

[66] Hazard, *supra* note 36, section 1.3:107.

[67] *Id.*

[68] Hazard, *supra* note 36, section 1.3:107.

[69] Gray, *supra* note 65.

[70] Nicholas G. Tomaiuolo, Barbara J. Frey, *Computer Database Searching and Professional Malpractice: Who Cares?*, 80 Bull. Med. Libr. Assoc. 367 (1992); M. Sandra Wood, *Public Service Ethics in Health Sciences Libraries*, 40 Library Trends 244, 255 (1991).

[71] Arthur W. Hafner, *Medical Information, Health Sciences Librarians, and Professional Liability*, 81 Special Libraries 305 (1990).

[72] Eva F. Eisenstein, Julia B. Faust, *The Consumer Health Information Library in the Hospital Setting*, 5 Medical Ref. Serv. Q. 63, 66 (1986).

[73] Jana C. Allcock, *Helping Public Library Patrons Find Medical Information: The Reference Interview*, 18 Public Library Q. 21, 22 (2000); Robert Berk, *Access to Consumer Health Information*, 12 Reference Librarian 195, 202 (1985); Eisenstein, *supra* note 72, at 66.

[74] *The Librarian's Role in the Provision of Consumer Health Information and Patient Education*, 84 Bull Med Libr Assoc 238 (1996), *available at* http://caphis.mlanet.org/resources/caphis_statement.html (visited July 2, 2008).

[75] Allcock, *supra* note 73 at 24.

[76] American Association of Law Libraries Ethical Principles, http://www.aallnet.org/about/policy_ethics.asp (visited July 2, 2008).

►Eight

SPECIFIC PROFESSIONAL LIABILITY ISSUES FOR INFORMATION BROKERS

IN THIS CHAPTER

This chapter covers the possible sources of liability for information brokers. In it we will look at the possibilities for liability on the part of information brokers, and also look at ways of controlling liability. Topics include:

► Tort issues, including reasonable reliance, duty of care, and negligent misrepresentation.

► Contract and self-employment issues.

► Minimizing liability, including the use of letters of agreement and disclaimers.

1. CASE STUDY: SETTING UP SHOP

Melinda Farken has been a reference librarian at the Yorken City Library for 12 years. During that time she has come to specialize in business information requests. Melinda has an entrepreneurial streak, and it seemed to her that the library could make money by providing a fee-based information retrieval service for local businesses. She drew up a formal proposal that the library do so. However, the director of the library didn't like the idea; she didn't think the library board would be interested in having the library entering into a for-profit scheme, so she turned down Melinda's proposal.

Melinda decided that the proposal would work just as well as a business plan, so she decided to go into business for herself as an information broker. Several months later, after marshaling her savings and, with the library's permission, doing some networking with business users of the library, Melinda set up her own shop in a bedroom of her home and hung out her shingle as a solo information broker.

Because of her networking, Melinda began to get requests right away. She wanted to seem accessible and cooperative, and so she took requests over the phone, emphasizing quick results. She didn't do an extensive interview unless the client seemed to want that. She learned early on to mention her fees, which she would itemize and present to the client with her final product.

For a while things went well, but then small problems began to crop up. Several clients were not paying their bills, although she billed them repeatedly. There were several instances when a client was unsatisfied with her work product, claiming that she had misunderstood their request. Since she had no record of the request, it was hard to fight the claim.

About six months into her new career, Melinda received a request from a major client for all publicly available information on fast food restaurants in the Yorken area, which Melinda took to mean the city. She also assumed that by "fast food" the client meant drive-in–type restaurants. Melinda supplied the information and billed the client for her work. After billing them twice, Melinda received a phone call from an attorney representing the client. The attorney told Melinda that the client was refusing to pay her fee because she hadn't done the work properly. He said that the client had requested information on fast food restaurants in Yorken County, not just the city, and that the definition of fast food included certain types of restaurants that Melinda hadn't included in her search.

Melinda disagreed with the client's version of the request. In response, the attorney offered to send her a copy of the client's internal memo that recorded the information request. The attorney went on to say that the client's business opportunities had been damaged by Melinda's poor search, and that they were considering suing her for the tort of negligent misrepresentation, based particularly on the idea that her work failed to meet the required duty of care. Alternatively, they would allege that Melinda's performance violated the unwritten contract that governed the transaction.

Melinda was both scared and angry by this point. She challenged the attorney about the idea that such a thing as an unwritten contract could exist. In response, he suggested she consult an attorney of her own.

2. LEGAL ISSUES OVERVIEW

Among information professionals, information brokers are in a unique position concerning liability. The fact that information brokers are essentially selling a product changes the reasonable reliance calculation significantly, and contributes to the existence of a duty of care. In addition, information brokers often have a contract or other agreement with their clients, the terms of which are legally enforceable. Finally, it is not uncommon for information brokers to be self-employed, and thus without any possibility of being protected by vicarious liability.

As an independent for-profit business, information brokers, whether sole proprietorships or corporations with employees, face all of the legal and other issues faced by any other business. Our concern here is with the issue of personal liability for professional activities, and so many of the other issues facing such a business are beyond our scope.[1]

2.1 Reasonable Reliance and Duty of Care

As with any information work, the main issue to be explored when considering professional liability is that of reasonable reliance. Reasonable reliance, and any consequent duty of care, rest on a number of factors. In the case of information services rendered gratuitously, such as in a public or academic library, there is clearly a lower standard at work.[2] This is reinforced by the idea that public policy promotes the availability and circulation of information in society.[3] However, when an information broker charges a fee for providing information, this all changes. According to the Restatement of Torts, someone who provides information in the course of their business, and who has a pecuniary interest in the transaction, is subject to liability for harms caused by justifiable reliance on the information, if the provider failed to exercise reasonable care or competence in obtaining or providing the information.[4]

The exact nature of this duty is not defined, and will depend on the circumstances. It is clear, though, that liability must be the result both of justifiable reliance by the customer, and a failure to exercise reasonable care or competence on the part of the information broker.

In this light, it is worth a reminder that a duty of care is not the same as an absolute guarantee. The fact that the customer has a poor outcome from using the information supplied by the information broker does not, in and of itself, indicate liability. The reasonableness of the customer's reliance on the information will be a factor, and will be judged based on the totality of the circumstances.[5]

Information brokers can assume that they have a duty of care that requires them to exercise reasonable care and competence in finding and providing information to paying customers. How exactly that duty would be defined, and what standards would be applied, is not clear. One would assume that the easiest cases would involve blatant errors that a reasonably competent information professional would avoid. In any event, a claimant would have the burden of showing that that information professional's actions were done incompetently or without reasonable care.

Thus, a liability claim against an information broker will not succeed if the customer's reliance on the information was not justifiable under the circumstances, or if, despite justifiable reliance, the actions of the information broker were not incompetent or lacking in reasonable care. Both justifiable reliance and a lack of reasonable care or competence must be present for a claim to have merit.

2.2 Contract Issues

For information brokers, almost every task performed for a customer will involve a contract. There is a common misunderstanding that in order to be valid and enforceable, a contract must be in writing and signed by both parties. While most people think of contracts as formal, signed documents, in fact any agreement to provide a service for a fee is most likely enforceable in the same way as a formal signed contract. This misconception is common. In *The Information Broker's Handbook*, Sue Rugge and Alfred Glossbrenner point out that the often rushed nature of information brokering doesn't allow for "drawing up and exchanging signed contracts."[6] This idea that a contract can only exist in the presence of a carefully drafted, written, and duly signed agreement is not only wrong, but can be dangerously misleading.

In fact, a contract is simply "a promise . . . for the breach of which the law gives a remedy."[7] In essence, a contract consists of an agreement between two or more parties in which there is an exchange of value. Contracts can be oral or written, and can be formal or informal. The essential elements are an agreement and a promised exchange of value. If the agreement meets these requirements, it is a contract and can be enforced in court. Whether or not it is reduced to a formal writing, any agreement to provide information for a fee is a form of a contract.

While written contracts are common, and generally a good idea, oral promises can also constitute a contract. The danger in unwritten agreements is in leaving the full terms of the agreement unspoken or undefined. In order to be enforceable, the agreement must be sufficiently defined for a court to be able to determine the relative obligations and rights of the parties.[8] Under the Uniform Commercial Code, a contract for a sale with terms left undefined will not fail for indefiniteness if the parties intended to make a contract and there is a reasonably certain basis for providing a remedy.[9]

Information brokers should conduct their affairs under the assumption that every transaction with a customer involves a contract. As we shall see below, this can be as much an opportunity as a burden. Knowing that agreeing to find and supply information for a fee involves a legally binding agreement simply means that the information broker has the ability, and opportunity, to define the terms of that agreement. Doing so will turn the contract into a prime tool for limiting professional liability.

2.3 Self-employment

One aspect of the work environment that often sets information brokers apart from other information professionals is self-employment. While it is rare for a librarian or archivist to be self-employed, it is fairly common for information brokers. This has a major effect on the possibility of personal liability for the information broker. As explained earlier in this book, the question of personal professional liability can be greatly affected by employment status. As a general rule, employees are not personally liable for their actions as an employee. Further, employees of governmental bodies may further be simply immune from suit.

The important dichotomy is that employment status can, and often does, protect an employee from personal liability for their professional actions. Should the employee's activities result in harm, the institution could be successfully sued, but the employee would not be personally liable. By contrast, a self-employed person is, in essence, their own employer. This means that there is no shield provided by employments status or governmental immunity. A self-employed information broker is fully liable for any activity that would allow for either institutional or personal professional liability in any other context.

2.4 Negligent Misrepresentation

The tort of negligent misrepresentation, as discussed in Chapter Three section 2.6, appears to be relevant to information brokers. That said, none of the major sources on tort law specifically discuss information brokers (or librarians or information professionals) in the context of this tort.[10] Negligent misrepresentation is related to other misrepresentation torts, but comes into play when the activity that led to harm arose out of negligence, rather than out of an intentional misrepresentation or deceit.[11] According to the Restatement, negligent misrepresentation occurs when:

> One who, in the course of his business, profession or employment, or in any other transaction in which he has a pecuniary interest, supplies false information for the guidance of others in their business transactions, is subject to liability for pecuniary loss caused to them by their justifiable reliance upon the information, if he fails to exercise reasonable care or competence in obtaining or communicating the information.[12]

The pecuniary interest that an information broker has in a transaction is clear, especially if the broker is self-employed. However, even with that in place, the standards of the Restatement for this tort raise a fairly high bar. For example, the comments state that holding the supplier of information to a duty of care would only be appropriate when the supplier was "manifestly aware of the use to which the information was to be put, and intended to supply it for that purpose."[13] Whether this is actually the case when an information broker assists a client would depend on the facts of the case. If the client laid out exactly what they were trying to achieve, and asked for the information broker's assistance, the requirements could be met. On the other hand, if a client simply requested a certain piece or type of information, without explaining why, or for what use, it is hard to see how an information broker would be "manifestly aware of the use to which the information was to be put."

The Restatement also makes it clear that that negligence can only occur if the person supplying the information fails to exercise the care or competence of a reasonable person in obtaining or supplying the information.[14] Establishing a duty of care is a difficult issue in the information professions, as we have seen, although it certainly would not be impossible. A final issue is that the Restatement requires that the person relying on the information be justified in doing so.[15] In the case of information brokers, especially given the fact that information is supplied for a fee, reliance is very likely to be seen as justified.

It is clear that negligent misrepresentation is a risk for information brokers. Whether or not it applies will depend on how much the information broker knew about the use to which the information would be put and, more problematically, whether the information broker failed to exercise due care and competence in supplying the information.

Although the tort of negligent misrepresentation is possible, and should not be ignored, for a variety of reasons liability is still more likely to arise out of a contract claim than a tort claim. In other words, it is more likely that a client will complain that that faulty information violated the terms of the agreement between the client and the information broker, than that it constituted a tort. This is both a problem and an opportunity for information brokers. As will be discussed below, the fact that a claim might arise under the contract between the parties provides an opportunity for information brokers to negotiate the terms of the contract, and thus minimize liability.

3. MINIMIZING LIABILITY

While the bad news may be that the threat of liability is very real for information brokers, because of the nature of their relationship with their customers, the good news is that this very factor also provides tools for minimizing liability that other information professionals don't have access to. Information brokers are in a position to shape and define their relationships with their customers in ways that many other information professionals cannot. By carefully using this factor to their advantage, information brokers can take some very effective steps to limit their liability.

3.1 Reasonable Reliance and Duty of Care

Although justifiability of reliance and the duty of care for an information broker would be defined by the court based on the circumstances of the claim, there is much an information broker can do to help avoid liability. As a basic step, information brokers should be cautious about taking work or assignments that are outside their areas of expertise. Many information brokers find a niche of the information world in which to operate, and this is probably advisable.

The purpose of concentrating on an area of expertise is to avoid the incompetence claim that could underlie a successful suit. An information broker should be knowledgeable enough about the information she is retrieving to know what appropriate sources are, how they are updated, and what the warning signs are that the information is out of date or inappropriate for the customer's purposes. This type of expertise can best be attained by concentrating on a particular area of information work.

Information brokers can also work to control the reasonableness of having their customers rely on the information provided such that they would be responsible for any harm. This is largely a matter of managing expectations. As will be discussed below, by avoiding unnecessary guarantees and making their customers aware of limitations to their services, information brokers can help keep customers from relying on the information provided such that harm results.

3.2 Contracts and Agreements

As discussed above, it is true that it would be unusual to sign a formal contract for every information transaction. But as we have also seen, almost any agreement to provide information for a fee is probably a contract in the eyes of the law. This raises the issue of what to do to adequately control the nature of the agreement. Rugge and Glossbrenner suggest the use of letters of agreement instead, an excellent suggestion and one that is discussed in detail below, but they apparently fail to understand that a letter of agreement can be, and often is, a contract.

With this in mind, information brokers should use this reality in their favor. By realizing that every job or task involves an agreement, the information broker can take the initiative to make sure that the terms of the agreement are in their favor. Just as an information broker would surely take the time and care to explain, and if necessary negotiate, the fee to be charged for the information service requested, so should she take the time to explain the limitations and parameters of the service. While this sounds cumbersome, with some advance planning and the development of routines, it will become easy to be sure that any customer knows exactly what service is being provided and what they remain responsible for.

3.2.1 Letters of Agreement

A letter of agreement is exactly what the name sounds like: It is a letter, sent to the customer, outlining the terms of the agreement to provide information services. While it is true that a letter of agreement is not a signed contract, it can be a legally binding agreement, enforceable as a contract. The key is that the letter lays out the terms of the agreement and provides notice of those terms to all the parties. Once the letter has been shared with everyone involved, it becomes incumbent upon all the parties involved to object if any of the terms are not what they wish to agree to. Absent such an objection, the letter will generally be taken as legally sufficient evidence of the terms of the agreement in the event of a dispute.

Because so many transactions that an information broker engages in are similar, it should be possible to draft a standard letter of agreement. This letter can be used, with suitable modifications, for each transaction. By spelling out the nature of the services to be performed, the standards to be applied, the product to be delivered, and the expectation of payment, an information broker can quickly and easily define the terms of each transaction, setting appropriate expectations for their customers.

> **Basic Elements to Include in a Letter of Agreement**
>
> ▶ Define the product, including when and how it will be delivered to the customer.
> ▶ Describe payment terms, including when payment is expected and in what form.
> ▶ Define the duty of care in providing the information.
> ▶ Define limitations of the services and the information.
> ▶ Address any warranties or guarantees.

3.2.2 Disclaimers and Limitations of Service

Disclaimers are commonly used by businesses to attempt to limit liability, but their actual efficacy in doing so can be doubtful. This is because the courts will often ignore a disclaimer if allowing it would be contrary to good public policy. As a result, it is generally not possible to simply disclaim away a duty of care or responsibility for harm.

Even though that is the case, it is possible, and advisable, to inform customers of the exact limitations of the services being provided. This should include a number of things:

▶ That the information is provided based on the description of the information need from the customer and is subject to the limitations of that description

▶ The limitations, if any, on your ability to find information in the area requested

▶ Potential limitations of the timeliness or completeness of the information provided

▶ The need for the customers to satisfy themselves as to the adequacy and usefulness of the information provided

3.2.3 Guarantees

Guarantees are best avoided. While it may be tempting to offer a guarantee for information work, the immense number of variables outside the control of the information broker makes guarantees a risky business indeed. Information brokers can promise to do the best job possible within the constraints of the project and the information request, but to claim anything beyond that is unwise. Indeed, one of the purposes of a letter of agreement would be to reduce customer expectations about any guarantees concerning the information broker's work.

4. OTHER APPROACHES TO LIMITING LIABILITY

In addition to the measures listed above, there are other avenues that can be used to limit or reduce potential liability for the information broker.

4.1 Expertise and Collaboration

As mentioned above, the more expertise an information broker has in the area of the information request, the less likely it would be that incompetence or lack of reasonable care would come into play in the event of a claim. Information brokers should build and hone expertise, and may want to restrict their work to those areas where they are knowledgeable.

Another approach that might be useful would be to form collaborative relationships with other information brokers. Issues of competition aside, such collaborations could provide a sounding board and access to further expertise in handling a request. Collaborating with other information professionals would serve to enlarge the resources available to an information broker and help avoid mistakes that could result in liability.

4.2 Communication

Many legal disputes, especially commercial disputes, arise not so much because of harm suffered, but because of miscommunication or lack of communication between the parties. The opposite of this is also true: Good and careful communication can go a long way toward preventing or avoiding problems that could otherwise blossom into a full lawsuit. The beauty of placing an emphasis on communication is that it allows for both a clearer understanding of what is being agreed to, but can also serve as an early warning system for problems, allowing them to be identified and dealt with earlier, and resolved more simply.

Careful communication means not only making sure that the customer knows exactly what the information broker will do, and for what fee, but also explains the information broker's responsibilities, and the limitations of the services and work product. In addition, good communication should be an ongoing process with the customer, carefully tracking and communicating progress, changes to the project, results, and levels of satisfaction.

An essential part of good communication is making sure that every aspect of the agreement and the product are, at some point, written down and shared. This is true regardless of how the information was initially communicated. As an example, if a customer requests information during a phone call, the information broker should write down the details of the request and send it to the customer in some form. If a customer later requests a change to the initial project, that change should be written and sent to the customer, or, if the change was requested in writing, a written response should be sent indicating agreement. Finally, results should be at least summarized in writing to the customer, even if they are first communicated orally.

A second essential step in good communication is to always document the agreement and process with every customer, no matter how regular they are or how routine their request is. When an information broker has an ongoing relationship with a customer, it might be tempting to operate on a more informal basis. However, familiarity does not reduce the risk of liability. Since good communication can only help, the same procedures of writing and sharing all important aspects of the project and its performance should be followed in every instance.

An information broker really cannot communicate too much with a customer, but the idea of reducing everything to writing may seem daunting. There are, however, a number of ways to make the process easy, and even automatic. As usual, it is the computer that makes this possible. As Rugge and Glossbrenner point out, "In these days of fax machines and e-mail, it is very easy to get a written agreement into someone's hands almost instantly."[16] A simple e-mail memo to the client summarizing every request, change, and result communicated could be your greatest weapon against the possibility of liability.

4.3 Records

An essential part of any information broker's work should be the careful creation and retention of records. There are many good reasons for this. Good records can help the information broker become more efficient by providing records of past searches. They can help track the development and growth of a relationship with a client. They can be used to replace information previously supplied to a client and subsequently lost.

In the case of a liability claim, good records can serve as evidence of the entire body of the transaction. The letter of agreement will state the terms of the agreement for the information service. Records of searches can show the adequacy and competence of the services performed, and a copy of the final product supplied to the customer can show that a product of sufficient quality was delivered.

Good records are an important part of any business, and once proper routines are established, keeping them can become a simple habit.

4.4 Ethical Behavior

One of the simplest and surest ways to face a liability claim would be to engage in objectionable behavior, even if that behavior itself doesn't rise to the level of being legally actionable. A customer who has been treated badly or unethically will be especially motivated to find fault with an information broker's work and, accordingly, bring a claim.

There are some basic aspects to ethical behavior that all information professionals should observe. Among these are confidentiality, fair dealing, and remaining neutral when dealing with customers who are competitors.

4.4.1 Confidentiality

Most information professionals have a strong sense that they should respect and maintain their customer's or user's confidences. This is especially important for an information broker. There are a number of instances where revealing information from a customer could, in and of itself, lead to liability. In the case of trade or business secrets shared with the information broker, revealing such information is actionable. Even relatively innocent-seeming information can be used by competitors to obtain an advantage in business. Information professionals should observe strict confidentiality about all dealings with their customers. Indeed, the very identity of customers shouldn't be revealed to others without the explicit permission of the customer. This practice will prevent inadvertent harm, reduce potential liability, and strengthen relations with the customer.

4.4.2 Fair Dealing

No one likes to feel cheated. When customers are charged different fees for what is essentially the same work, the customer charged more will have reason to feel slighted. Similarly, to treat one customer's request as a greater priority than another's, or to provide a better or more enhanced product to one client at the same price is to treat the other customer less than fairly. Treating customers differently is a recipe for trouble. At best, such behavior risks losing customers. At worse, such behavior could serve as the motivation, or even the basis, for a liability claim.

Information brokers should establish standards for their work methods, operational practices and timelines for completing work. They should establish prices in advance that they will charge all similarly situated customers. It is a good practice to be as transparent as possible about all the practices, so that a customer always knows what to expect. On the plus side, having a reputation for fair dealing is a great way to enhance an information broker's business reputation.

5. CONCLUSIONS

Information brokers do face an enhanced possibility of liability. This is primarily because the commercial nature of their information transactions creates a realistic duty of care. In addition, self-employed information brokers do not have the protection of being shielded from liability by their employee status.

There are a number of ways to control and limit liability. Among the chief of these is to carefully control the terms of the agreement when providing information. While there is a definite need to take proper care when providing information as an information broker, potential liability can also be minimized by communicating well with clients, avoiding work where one lacks expertise, and behaving in an ethical manner in all transactions.

ENDNOTES

[1] There are a number of books and resources that address the business aspects of information brokering. See, *e.g.*, Florence M. Mason & Chris Dobson, *Information Brokering: A How-To-Do-It Manual* (1998); Sue Rugge & Alfred Glossbrenner, *The Information Broker's Handbook* (1997).

[2] Mary Minow & Tomas A. Lipinski, *The Library's Legal Answer Book*, 246 (2003).

[3] John A. Gray, *Personal Malpractice Liability of Reference Librarians and Information Brokers*, 9 J.Lib. Admin. 71, 77 (1988).

[4] Restatement of Torts, Second § 522 (1999).

[5] *Id.*

[6] Rugge & Glossbrenner, *supra* note 1, at 454.

[7] Restatement of the Law of Contracts, Second § 1 (hereinafter, Contracts Restatement).

[8] Claude D. Rohwer & Anthony M. Skrocki, *Contracts in a Nutshell*, § 2.3 (6th ed., 2006).

[9] Uniform Commercial Code, § 2–204(3); Rowher, *supra* note 8, at § 2.3.1.

[10] See, Restatement, *supra* note 4, § 552; Dan B. Dobbs, *The Law of Torts*, § 472 (2001).

[11] Edward J. Kionka, *Torts*, 471 (4th ed. 2005).

[12] Restatement, *supra* note 3, § 552(1).

[13] *Id.*, § 552, comment a.

[14] Restatement, *supra* note 4, § 552, comment e.

[15] Restatement, *supra* note 4, § 552(1).

[16] Rugge and Glossbrenner, *supra* note 1, at 457.

▶Nine

SPECIFIC PROFESSIONAL LIABILITY ISSUES FOR ARCHIVISTS AND CURATORS

IN THIS CHAPTER

This chapter looks at the potential for liability for archivists and curators. The points covered include:

▶ Acquisitions and deaccessions, including issues of title, provenance, and restricted gifts

▶ Loans, including liability for loaned items

▶ Privacy torts and right to publicity

1. OVERVIEW OF LEGAL ISSUES

Archivists and curators face potential legal issues that are different from those of other information professionals. Where the rest of the information professions are concerned with liability that might arise from how information is used, for curators and archivists the concern shifts toward problems arising from how information and/or collected items are acquired, displayed, maintained, or deaccessioned.

This distinction is important. Rather than looking at the issue of liability arising from an end-user of the collection, archivists and curators must concern themselves with the interests—and potential liability arising from—donors of items, creators of items, and those who are depicted or described in materials in the collection.

As with other areas of the profession, the risk of personal liability for professional activities appears to be slight. However, it will be worthwhile to explore the legal issues faced by museums and archives with an eye toward possible liability for the archivist or curator.

2. CASE STUDY: LOOKING A GIFT HORSE IN THE MOUTH

Richard Doritt is the curator of the Yorken County History Museum. The museum houses many unique items from the history of the city, county, and state, and also serves as the historical archives for the area. On a typical Thursday morning, Richard is dealing with two fairly common issues for his line of work. At 9:00 he is meeting with a potential donor, who has an item of interest to the museum. At 11:00, he will meet with members of a local service club, the Skylark City Boosters, who would like to borrow archive items for a display they plan at City Hall.

The potential donor is Darren Bronfman, a local business owner. He is an amateur history buff, and a big supporter of the museum. On a recent visit to Chicago, his eye was caught by a small statue of a horse that he found in an antiques store. The pose of the horse, including the way it was holding its mouth open, was unique. The only other place that Bronfman had seen a horse in that pose was on the Yorken City crest. As a local history buff, Bronfman knew that the horse on the crest had been a favorite image of Emile Yorken, the city's founder. He had also heard that Yorken had possessed a statue of a horse on which the drawing on the crest was based.

When Bronfman first saw the statue, he thought it was a coincidence, and the asking price was too high for his taste, so he moved on. But before he left the antiques store he decided to ask the owner about the statue. The owner consulted his records and told Bronfman that he had bought it from a man who had purchased the statue at an estate sale. The estate, as it turned out, was that of one of Emile Yorken's great-grandchildren. Excited by this news, Bronfman purchased the statue, and was now offering it to the museum. He assumed it was Yorken's long-lost original statue.

Doritt was excited as well. If true, this would be a significant piece of Yorken history. He thanked Bronfman effusively for the gift. He then explained that the museum would need to investigate the provenance of the piece. This would verify its origins, and in the process help establish the value of the piece, which would be useful to Bronfman for tax purposes. Bronfman agreed, and both men left the meeting happy.

Doritt gave the statue, and the information about it, to his assistant, Stacy, and asked her to begin investigating the statue. He suggested she call the antiques dealer and, if possible, the company that held the estate sale. Doritt then went to tell the museum director the good news.

By this time it was 11:00, and Doritt hurried to his meeting with the Skylark City Boosters. He met with three members of the group, who were planning a display at City Hall on Cyril Aspen, Mayor of Yorken City during the 1980s. They wanted to profile Aspen using correspondence and other papers from the time. Aspen had died two years before, and left his papers to the museum. The group already had copies of correspondence from the files at City Hall. Doritt was hesitant, but said he thought he could accommodate the request. Aspen's papers occupied eight large boxes in storage. An assistant had gone through them and done basic identifying and cataloging of the papers, but Doritt had not had the chance yet to examine them himself. However, there were no restrictions on the papers from Aspen's bequest, so Doritt assumed anything in them could be shown to the public.

Doritt took the men to the archives section, and had the assistant there provide them with a workspace and the boxes of Aspen's papers. He explained that they could not take any of the papers out of the museum, but that the assistant would make copies of anything they identified as being of interest. He then left them to their work.

Six weeks later, when Doritt arrived at the office in the morning, he found Stacy, his assistant, waiting for him, looking concerned. He immediately asked her what was wrong. She had the provenance report on the horse statue, and she had both good news and bad. The good news was that the statue was genuine. It was of the right age and design, and matched the horse statue that appeared in several photographs of Yorken in his office. The original had a unique carver's mark inside the open mouth of the horse. That mark was visible when the gift from Bronfman was examined. The bad news was that although the statue that Emile Yorken's great-grandson had possessed was the original, it was not sold at his estate sale. In fact, it had been stolen in a burglary some years before. The man from whom the antiques dealer had bought the statue could not be found, so it was hard to say where he had gotten it. In the meantime Yorken's descendents, informed that the statue had turned up at the museum, were asking for it back.

This was bad news indeed. While he was still mulling it over, Stacy asked him if he had seen the morning paper. He hadn't. The main article on the front page was about the City Hall exhibit of Cyril Aspen's papers. The exhibit had made the front page because the people putting it together had, apparently intentionally, selected papers from the archives in a manner calculated to make Aspen look bad. Of particular note was a series of friendly letters between Aspen and a local Eagle Scout who had been doing volunteer work for the city. The exhibitors had arranged and captioned the letters in such a way as to imply that there had been an improper relationship between the two. According the paper, Aspen's widow was outraged. She said that not only was the implication of the exhibit wrong, but that the papers involved were private and shouldn't have been released. She was now planning to sue the museum and Doritt personally.

3. POSSIBILITIES FOR PROFESSIONAL LIABILITY

The scenario above illustrates two of the possible legal entanglements that can befall museums and archives, and potentially curators and archivists as well. In exploring the legal risk for curators and archivists, the issues must be examined on two levels. This first is the risk of legal action against the museum or archive as an institution. The second is the risk of legal action against a professional working for or on behalf of the institution. Most of the legal issues raised below, although very real for museums and archives, have been brought as claims against the institution, and not personally against the personnel of the institution.[1]

In order to be clear on these issues, it is helpful to look some of the activities of museums and archives with an eye toward where liability could arise. Within that context we can then examine the issues for any possible sources of professional liability for a curator or archivist. In exploring this issue we will look only at legal risks associated with the professional activities of curators and archivists. We will not look at other potential areas of institutional liability, such as personal injuries suffered by visitors, discrimination claims, and so forth. The following is not intended to be a comprehensive look at the legal issues faced by museums and archives. Such an overview is beyond our scope, but there are excellent books on the topic available.[2]

3.1 Employment Status and Potential Liability

Because archivists and curators normally are employees and act on behalf of their institution, most actions they take in the course of their work would be fully covered by the doctrine of vicarious liability. This means that any claim that could lead to liability would be against the institution, and not against the archivist or curator. This concept has been explored earlier in this book.

For now we can reiterate that employees are generally protected by the doctrine so long as their activities occur within the scope of their employment. Employees can be liable for damages resulting from harm incurred at work if the activities of the employees are outside of the scope of their employment, and the employer had no knowledge of the activity. In the context of museums and archives, it would be plausible that a curator or archivist could, without the employer's knowledge, take some action such as buying or selling an item on behalf of the institution without the authority to do so. In such a situation the archivist or curator could conceivably be held personally liable for any damages that might result. While this should serve as a warning to curators and archivists to be clear as to what authority they have to take various professional actions, we will restrict our analysis below to situations in which the employee is acting within the scope of their duties.

4. POTENTIAL AREAS OF LIABILITY

Because information professionals such as librarians and information brokers deal extensively with users of information, the focus of professional liability concerns for such professionals is on harm occurring to the user in relation to providing information. For archivists and curators, such concerns are rare or nonexistent. Instead, curators and archivists are much more concerned with harm arising out of how materials were acquired, how they are used or displayed while in the collection, and how they are removed from the collection.

Acquisition issues arise with concerns over provenance, acquiring full title to a work, and dealing with restricted or conditional gifts. Use and display issues include copyright concerns, right of privacy and right of publicity, and liability arising from the handling of loans. Deaccessioning issues include dealing with restricted donations, public interest concerns, and providing full title and copyright.

4.1 Acquisitions

Acquiring materials for a museum or archive is often a delicate business. Issues arise concerning the actual provenance of items, the nature and quality of the title, copyright ownership, and conditions on a gift or bequest.

4.1.1 Provenance Issues

Provenance concerns the chain of ownership of an item from its creation or discovery to the present day. Provenance issues can arise whether the item is being purchased by the museum or archive, or is being offered as a gift. Tracing provenance is important, because only by doing so can the museum or archive be sure that the seller or donor has full and clear title to the item. If the owner does not have clear title, the museum may be subject to an ownership challenge at a later date.

Provenance problems can arise from a number of sources. One such is when the seller or donor turns out not to have the right to sell or give the item. This could be because the item was at one time stolen from its rightful owner. Other provenance issues can raise doubts as to the authenticity of the item. While authenticity issues might not interfere with the ability of the owner to sell or give the item, it would affect its value to the institution.

Provenance issues can even arise at the international level. Antiquities and artworks have been sold around the world for hundreds of years, and many museums possess items that were found or created in foreign lands. Recently some of the originating countries of these items have begun to ask for their return. A museum possessing such an item could find itself in a very difficult position.

4.1.2 Title Defects

Title defects are problems with the ownership rights of a seller or donor of an item. While we often think of ownership as a single concept, in many cases it can be more complicated than that, and ownership rights can often have a number of parts or aspects. A number of things can interfere with having full or clear title to an item.

As an example, suppose a donor offers to give a museum a painting. The painting was purchased by the donor in good faith from an established gallery. On the surface of things, it appears that the donor has clear title to the painting, and can give the painting to the museum. However, an investigation of the painting's provenance indicates that the painting once belonged to someone who was killed in a war, and whose property was stolen by invading soldiers. Because of this defect in the title to the painting, it would be possible for a descendent of the earlier owner to demand the return of the painting as stolen property. This is true in spite of the fact that the donor bought the painting from a legitimate dealer.

Although the donor had purchased the item in good faith, and indeed the gallery he bought it from may have done so as well, the fact that the item was once stolen means that the title is defective. Owners can only pass on the property rights they actually possess, so if the museum accepted the gift it would not have clear title to the item. If a legitimate owner were to appear, the museum could be forced to give up the item or pay money to the legitimate owner for the right to keep it.

This is the case with the Yorken horse statue in the case study above. Bronfman bought the statue in good faith from a legitimate dealer. He though he had bought clear title to the piece. The dealer, apparently, had also bought the item in good faith, although he may have been deceived in the process. However, because the item was in fact stolen, the title had defects, and Yorken's family has a potential claim to get the statue back.

Another example would be a donor who offers the museum a painting she has inherited. While she legitimately inherited the painting, in this case the ownership rights she inherited were limited to something called a life estate. In a life estate, the beneficiary has the right to possess the item as long as she is alive, but it is not actually her property. Under a life estate, the donor cannot sell or dispose of the painting, and she cannot leave it to someone in her will. Upon her death, the painting will pass to someone else under the terms of the original will that left the painting to her. In this case, were the museum to accept the painting, the subsequent inheritors of the painting could successfully demand that it be returned after the donor's death.

The bottom line is that it is up to the museum or archive to be sure that they are obtaining clear title to any item they acquire. Obviously, when dealing with a donor, this can be a delicate process at best, and writers on the topic have discussed at length the problems of requiring clear title from donors.[3] Unfortunately, dealing in good faith with a seller or donor, and their good faith in turn, are not enough to protect against claims arising because of a defective title.

4.1.3 Copyright Issues

Although museums and archives often acquire items in order to preserve them, they also will want to display, lend, and sometimes reproduce the item. In order to do so, the institution must deal with copyright issues.[4] Unless the item is in the public domain, someone owns the copyright to the item. Copyright is something entirely different from ownership or title, and it is possible to acquire an item with a clear title and yet not acquire its copyright.

If the item is under copyright, it cannot be reproduced, or even in some cases displayed, without the permission of the copyright holder. Permission would be required in order to make direct copies of the item for almost any purpose, or, in the case of artwork and other objects, to use pictures or other depictions of the item in signs, brochures, books, or other displays.[5]

When considering an item for acquisition, an institution should determine if the item is in the public domain, and if not, who holds the copyright. Unless the copyright can be obtained with the item, or permanent and flexible permission from the copyright holder can be obtained for the institution to use the item as it wishes, the acquisition should be considered subject to conditions, and might be inadvisable.

4.1.4 Conditions on Gifts and Bequests

Conditions on gifts or bequests arise when a donor wishes to control how the donated items are to be used or displayed. Conditions can vary, but can include such things as requiring that the institution always display the items, never display them, display them as a group, never lend them to other institutions, never deaccession them, and many others.[6] Most experts on the topic urge museums and archives to avoid conditional gifts and bequests because of the troubles they cause.[7]

It can be difficult to decline any kind of a gift. Doing so involves not only forgoing the chance to add a valuable item to the collection, but also risks offending a donor who might have other items or resources to donate at a later date. The decision to accept or reject a gift laden with conditions can be as much a political one as a practical one.

In our case study, it is unclear whether Aspen's widow had a right to keep the papers private. In order to be effective, such a condition would need to be in writing as part of the bequest. Without such a written condition, it is unlikely that Doritt will be found to have done anything wrong in allowing access to Aspen's papers.

4.1.4.1 Estate Challenges

When an item is left to an institution in someone's will, the bequest can be the subject of a challenge by the heirs of the testator. Heirs of the donor may challenge the sufficiency of the will itself, or may claim that the donor lacked the mental capacity to make the gift. Such a challenge can arise long after the donor's estate has been settled, especially when the bequest contained conditions, and the institution cannot or will not follow them. In such a situation the heirs can argue that the fact that the institution did not follow the conditions of the bequest should result in the property being returned to the estate.

4.2 Loans

It is very common for museums and archives to lend items to other institutions for study or display. In such situations, the receiving institution is subject to the law of bailment.[8] Bailment is a legal doctrine that applies when someone has the right to the possession of property even though they don't hold title to the property.[9] This is the case when a museum or archives possesses or displays a loaned item. The person or institution holding the property is referred to as the bailee, while the person or institution lending the item is the bailor.

Bailment creates certain responsibilities for the bailee as the entity holding the item, and can lead to specific forms of liability if loss or damage occurs. If, for instance, the loan is made for the benefit of the bailee, as it usually is with museums and archives, then the bailee is required by law to exercise due care in relation to the item, and can be held liable if damage or loss occurs.[10] Indeed, under traditional interpretations of bailment law, if the bailment is for the bailee's benefit, the bailee can be liable for even slight negligence.[11]

There is some controversy about whether bailment comes under property law or contract law, a distinction that can be important for technical reasons.[12] However, if an expressed contract or agreement governs the conditions of the loan, then the terms of the contract will prevail.[13] Thus, loan agreements allow museums and archives to determine the duties and standard of care to be exercised during the loan.

Given the legal risks and responsibilities inherent in accepting loans, there are a number of steps that should be taken to control liability. For the museum, it is critical to only accept loans based on a written agreement. The agreement should specify the level of care that the museum will use to deal with the loaned item, and specify what risks and obligations remain with the lending institution.

4.3 Deaccessions

Deacessions have often been contentious issues for museums and archives. Provided that the museum or archive owns an item outright, there are generally no legal restrictions on when and how it can be deaccessioned. As a general rule, the decision to deaccession an item is actionable only if the disposal violates the terms of a trust, or is a breach of fiduciary duty.[14]

Violation of a trust would occur if the original gift of the item was made on the condition that the museum or archive retains ownership of the item forever. In such a case, if the donated item is deaccessioned, it is possible that the donors of the item, or their heirs, might sue to get the item or its value returned to them because of the violation of the trust. Breach of fiduciary duty reflects a claim that the act of deaccessioning violates the mission of the institution, or harms the financial status of the museum or archive.[15] Claims have been brought because the deaccessioning created a change in the focus of the museum, or that the item disposed of was of such value that the museum's value was harmed by disposing of it.[16]

5. POTENTIAL LIABILITY FOR VIOLATING THE RIGHTS OF OTHERS

In addition to the legal risks inherent in acquiring, borrowing, and deaccessioning items, potential legal problems can arise when possession or display of the items affects the rights of others. The two most common of these are the right of privacy and the right of publicity. Although discussed already in Chapter 3 in the context of general legal issues, these topics are repeated here because they are specific concerns for both museums and archives.

5.1 Right of Privacy

Although many people assume that we all have a basic right of privacy, the law in this area is actually quite complex. The U.S. Supreme Court has identified an implied right to privacy in the U.S. Constitution, but it is not explicitly listed in the text of the document, and its derivation and use remain controversial.[17] The bulk of privacy law in America is state law, and can be either legislative or common law in form.[18] As a result, the right of privacy varies from state to state.[19]

In spite of the variability of this area of law, there are a few basic concepts that can be addressed generally as they relate to museums and archives. There are generally four grounds for a claim that privacy rights have been violated. They are: (1) intrusion into seclusion, (2) public disclosure of private facts, (3) false light, and (4) appropriation.

5.1.1 Intrusion into Seclusion

Intrusion into seclusion involves activity that pries or intrudes into an area in which a person is entitled to privacy.[20] The act of intrusion must be such that it would be offensive to a reasonable person. As an example, spying on someone in the privacy of their home and then revealing graphic details of their sexual activities would be an example of intrusion into seclusion. People have a reasonable expectation of privacy in their homes, and spying on someone and revealing what was found would be offensive to a reasonable person. It is important to note, however, that liability for intrusion into seclusion rests with the person or entity who has performed the intrusion. A museum or archive that possesses the fruits of the intrusion would not be liable, unless the museum or its personnel had participated in the act of intrusion itself.[21]

Intrusion into seclusion can be claimed by anyone who is affected, regardless of whether the claimant is a private person or a celebrity. Although some aspects of a celebrity's activities are considered public in ways that they would not be for a private person, intrusion into seclusion involves intrusive acts that would offend a reasonable person, and celebrities are as protected by the law as anyone else.

It is important to emphasize that the tort of intrusion provides liability for the person or entity who acts to intrude, and not for those who merely possess the fruits of such an intrusion. When such items come into the possession of a museum or archive they do not create liability on the basis of the intrusion tort alone.

5.1.2 Public Disclosure of Private Facts

Public disclosure of private facts involves disclosure of embarrassing private facts in a manner that would be objectionable to the average person.[22] It is not enough to simply disclose the private facts. In order to be liable, a person or institution must actively publicize or promote the private information.[23] For this reason, if a museum or archive possesses embarrassing private information about an individual, the mere fact of possessing the information would not, in itself, be actionable. Indeed, it is entirely possible that the museum or archive could make the information available to the public, for example by making files available to researchers, without incurring liability. On the other hand, if the information is made part of a display or exhibit, or otherwise publicized or promoted by the museum or archive, liability is possible.

In the case study, the fact that the museum had papers with private facts about Aspen (if indeed it did) and made those available to the public would not constitute public disclosure. The question would be how involved the museum was in publicizing the materials. Since it did not create or mount the display, it does not appear that it would be liable for public disclosure.

5.1.3 False Light

False light is similar to public disclosure of private facts in that it requires a highly public disclosure of private information, but it also requires that the public disclosure mislead the public by placing someone in a false light.[24] Thus, false light requires that the publicized information either be false itself, or be information that creates a false implication. In the case study above, the fact that the people creating the display sought to imply an inappropriate relationship where none existed could be an example of creating a false light. Keep in mind, however, that the cause of action for a false light tort varies in its requirements from state to state, and some states have refused to adopt it as a tort.[25]

In the case study, it certainly appears that someone worked to create a false impression about Aspen, and since the false light was part of a highly public display, it would almost certainly be actionable. However, the involvement of the museum and Doritt in creating the false light appears to be minimal. It would appear that Widow Aspen's action would be against the Skylark City Boosters as the perpetrators of the false light.

5.1.4 Appropriation

Appropriation is the use of a person's likeness or name without permission, in order to create profit.[26] It is similar to the right of publicity, discussed below, but is a separate tort. Thus, if a museum or archive were to take a picture of a member of the public and then, without permission, use that person's likeness in advertising and other promotional materials, the institution could be liable for appropriation. An important distinction between appropriation and the right of publicity is that a claim of appropriation can be made by any person whose likeness or name is used for profit without their permission. Unlike with the right of publicity, it is not necessary that the person already be profiting from their name or likeness in order for them to have a claim.

5.2 Right of Publicity

Right of publicity essentially protects the right of a celebrity or famous person to profit from their identity. The right of publicity creates an enforceable property right in one's name, likeness, or other personal attribute, and prevents the unauthorized commercial use of the attribute.[27] The right is specifically intended for people who derive economic benefit from their name, likeness, or other personal attribute. A personal attribute can be any identifying skill or feature that is uniquely associated with the person, such as voice quality or special physical ability.[28] As such it prevents others from unjustly enriching themselves by using a famous person's name or likeness without permission. It differs from the tort of appropriation in that it is only available to those who already benefit economically from their identity. In addition, its function is to protect a celebrity's public image, as opposed to protecting them from violations of their privacy rights.[29]

Violation of the right of publicity requires unauthorized use of the name, likeness, or attribute, along with commercial harm. Thus, the unauthorized use must detract from the economic benefit the originator enjoys from use of the name, likeness, or attribute.[30] In many states the right of publicity extends to the celebrity's estate, and thus can continue after death. This means that items in a collection that depict a deceased celebrity might still be subject to the right of publicity.

6. ANALYSIS OF POTENTIAL PROFESSIONAL LIABILITY

The basic approach to limiting the possibility of personal professional liability for the activities of a curator or archivist is twofold: First, do everything possible to limit liability in general, whether of the institution or the individual. Second, make sure that the curator or archivist is always acting within the scope of his employment, and has authority for any actions he takes.

For museums, limiting liability involves, very briefly, such things as:

▶ being careful about provenance and clear title for items being purchased or donated;

▶ carefully assessing the status and ownership of any copyrights on items in the collection;

▶ dealing carefully with conditions placed on donations, including refusing donations when conditions are too onerous;

▶ limiting liability for loaned items by only accepting loans under the terms of a written loan agreement;

▶ making sure that the museum has authority to deaccession any items it wants to dispose of;

▶ carefully assessing any private information in the collection, and avoiding use of the information that would lead to invasion of privacy or appropriation claims; and

▶ being aware of any potential right of publicity attached to items in the collection, and carefully accounting for those rights in the use and display of the items.

For curators and archivists, the most straightforward ways to limit personal liability for professional activities is to carefully make sure that their work is covered by the doctrine of vicarious liability. This means that they should be very careful to make sure that they are always acting within the scope of their employment, and that they have authority for the actions they take. As a practical matter, some of the steps curators and archivists can take to ensure this include the following:

▶ When dealing with donors, sellers, and members of the public, always make it clear that you are a representative of your institution, and are not acting on your own behalf.

▶ Permission or concordance should be sought from appropriate managers in the institution for major decisions or commitments. Again, it should be made clear that the decision or commitment is being made on behalf of the institution, not as an individual.

▶ Ask for and obtain a clear job description that lists those activities that are within the scope of employment. Avoid any activities not on the list.

▶ Ask for and obtain clear grants of authority for any decisions or commitments to be made as part of the job. If in doubt, do not make a decision or enter into a commitment without clearing it first with the institution's leaders or board.

As with so many legal issues, practical prevention of liability comes down to several basic work habits that will always serve the professional well. Worth mentioning here are communication, documentation, and decision verification.

One can never communicate too much when decisions are being made, commitments entered into, or obligations are being undertaken. Even when a curator or archivist has the authority to take an action or make a decision, it is best to communicate the action or decision up the chain of command. Similarly, if there is any doubt about the action, communicating about it will involve the leadership of the institution and remove the possibility of the archivist or curator being solely responsible.

Good communication informs appropriate persons in the institution about what is happening, and serves as an early warning system when things go wrong. From the perspective of personal liability, good communication lessens the possibility that the curator or archivist will be seen as acting on their own, outside the scope of their employment, or without appropriate authority.

Documentation plays a similar, related role. Carefully documenting both actions taken and job roles and authority can help establish that the activities of the curator or archivist are on behalf of the institution, within the scope of employment, and under appropriate authority. Documenting activities should become a habit as part of the archivist's or curator's work. E-mail in particular has made this easy. With e-mail, a quick memo concerning a decision or action is easy to disseminate to appropriate parties, and serves as both communication and documentation.

Although museums and archives will always face legal issues when dealing with their collections, it should be relatively easy for archivists and curators to avoid personal liability for their professional activities. The key is to act within the scope of employment, to establish authority for any actions taken, and to always act as a representative of the institution rather than as an individual acting on one's own behalf.

ENDNOTES

[1] The exception to this has been actions against museum trustees for mismanaging a collection, but the legal issues of trustees are beyond the scope of this work.

[2] See, *e.g.*, Tomas A. Lipinski, ed., *Libraries, Museums, and Archives: Legal Issues and Ethical Challenges in the New Information Era* (2002); Marie C. Malaro, *A Legal Primer on Managing Museum Collections* (1998).

[3] Leonard D. Duboff, *Art Law, Domestic and International,* 272 (1975).

[4] Marie C. Malaro, *A Legal Primer on Managing Museum Collections* 115 (1985).

[5] *Id.,* at 121.

[6] Duboff, *supra* note 3, at 273.

[7] Malaro, *supra* note 4, at 103.

[8] *Id.,* at 157; Duboff, *supra* note 3, at 274.

[9] Barlow Burke, *Personal Property in a Nutshell* 182 (2003).

[10] Malaro, *supra* note 4, at 157.

[11] Duboff, *supra* note 3, at 274.

[12] See, *e.g.*, Burke, *supra* note 9, at 274; Ray Andrews Brown, *The Law of Personal Property,* 209 (3rd. ed. 1975).

[13] Malaro, *supra* note 4, at 157.

[14] Duboff, *supra* note 3, at 279.

[15] Malaro, *supra* note 4, at 141.

[16] *Id.*

[17] John E. Nowak, Ronald D. Rotunda, *Constitutional Law,* § 11.7 (5th ed., 1995).

[18] Dan Dobbs, *The Law of Torts,* 1197 (2001).

[19] Tomas A. Lipinski, *Tort Theory in Library, Museum and Archival Collections, Materials, Exhibits, and Displays: Rights of Privacy and Publicity in Personal Information and Person,* in *Libraries, Museums, and Archives: Legal Issues and Ethical Challenges in the New Information Era, 47,* 48 (Tomas A. Lipinski, ed., 2002).

[20] *Id.*

[21] *Id.*

[22] Lipinski, *supra* note 19, at 49.

[23] *Id.*

[24] Lipinski, *supra* note 19, at 50.

[25] *Id.*

[26] Lipinski, *supra* note 19, at 51.

[27] Lipinski, *supra* note 19, at 52.

[28] *Id.*

[29] *Id.,* at 53.

[30] Lipinski, *supra* note 19, at 52.

▶Part III

AVOIDING LIABILITY CLAIMS: PROACTIVE APPROACHES AND TOOLS

►Ten

PROACTIVE APPROACHES TO LIABILITY ISSUES

IN THIS CHAPTER

This chapter brings together all of the information provided so far in the form of basic suggestions and ideas to help you manage the risk of liability as you go about your professional activities. Among other things, we will discuss:

► The hidden costs of liability fears.
► Ways to approach general liability issues.

1. THE HIDDEN COSTS OF LIABILITY FEARS

We live in a litigious society, and it is only natural to be concerned about the risk of liability in our professional lives. Fears of liability are commonly expressed in the library literature, but it is safe to say that the fears of liability have largely been overstated. At the same time, liability is not an absolute impossibility.

One of the possible motivations some authors may have had for overstating the possibility of liability is the feeling that it is better to be safe than sorry. Under this theory it is better to warn of the possibility of liability, even if unlikely, than run the risk of becoming liable without warning. While this position may be well intentioned, it is also misguided. In fact, fears of liability can have a significant impact on the services provided by information professionals. They can also exact a cost. Erring excessively on the side of avoiding liability can cause services to be limited, information to be withheld, and users to go unserved. These are not trivial matters.

Instead, the goal should be a properly nuanced understanding of the risk of liability that leads to an appropriately balanced approach to providing information services. Liability should be controlled and avoided where necessary, but users should not suffer as a result of unnecessary liability fears.

2. CONTROLLING LIABILITY: GENERAL IDEAS

In the areas where liability is theoretically possible, there are some reasonable steps that can be taken to minimize that possibility. Apart from working to ensure basic competence on the part of information professionals, the most important measures are those that reinforce the lack of duty of care in information transactions, and minimize the possibility of reasonable reliance. In most cases this means taking steps to leave the customer or user in control of, and responsible for, their information need.

2.1 Avoiding a Duty of Care

Information professionals do not have an identified duty of care in information transactions, but it would be possible for one to be defined if the proper circumstances were to develop. This is best avoided. The most sensible and straightforward way to avoid creating a duty of care would be to assiduously stick to a consultative rather than a fiduciary role during information transactions. In practice, this means taking an approach to information interactions that seeks to assist users with their information need, but does not take responsibility for that need.

This approach can be accomplished in a number of ways. For example, allowing users to choose from a variety of sources, or pursue part of the search on their own, would reinforce the consultative nature of the assistance being provided. Similarly, by not providing a complete answer to any question, but rather by leaving users with sources to consult, the information professional steps away from being an authority on the information in question and assumes the role of an expert on finding information. Even in a ready reference situation, in which a user requests a simple fact ascertained from a standard source, the information professional should emphasize that the answer being provided is from the source in question.

The idea, metaphorically speaking, is to stand beside the users, exposing them to the possible sources of information that they can select and use to meet their information needs. This is as opposed to standing between the users and information sources, and in the process taking full responsibility for selecting the information that might meet their needs. The difference between these two roles can be subtle, but the key point is that the users always remain in control of their needs, and responsible for selecting what information they choose.

2.2 Avoiding Reasonable Reliance

The most effective way to reduce reasonable reliance is to make clear to the user the limitations of the services offered and of the sources used. While doing so might seem like an exercise in low self-esteem—not to mention tedious—in fact, it can be done fairly quickly and easily. For instance, in a reference interaction, the librarian might say, "This is information on X from our collection. You might find it useful, but you should satisfy yourself that it contains the information you need. There might also be other information available that you could check. I'd be happy to help you find such information, but only you can determine if it is what you need."

A statement like this has two beneficial effects for the librarian. The first is that it makes reasonable reliance much less plausible. It would be hard for a user to assume that he is turning his problem over to the librarian when he is being addressed in this way. The second beneficial effect of this approach is that it reinforces the purely consultative role of the librarian in the user's information gathering process. Users who have been left with the responsibility for their own information needs would be hard-pressed to assert that they felt that they had been given a complete answer on which they could reasonably rely, or that the librarian had in any way guaranteed that their information needs had been satisfied.

Another approach is to make clear the limitations of any materials that are consulted. Such an approach might go so far as to explain that the library cannot evaluate and verify the information in every book in the collection, but can also be as simple as pointing out the date that the book was printed, or the existence of other similar publications that might have different or more extensive information.

Once again, the purpose here is to state what is, in fact, a reality. Users remain in full control of their information needs and need to satisfy themselves that they have found what they are seeking. In reducing the possibility of reasonable reliance, information professionals are not limiting their services or avoiding their responsibilities, but rather are stating more clearly what those appropriate services and responsibilities are.

2.3 Promoting Competence

Without a duty of care, and in the absence or reasonable reliance, competence is really an irrelevant issue. But should a case arise in which a duty of care is defined, or reliance is found to be reasonable, the issue of competence could become crucial. Given the relative risks and rewards, there seems to be little disadvantage for information professionals to seek to be as competent as possible. Competence, of course, is hard to define. That said, it behooves information professionals to seek to improve their knowledge and skills, both of their professional tasks and of knowledge sources. Continuing education is a must, as is self-directed reading and exploring.

While competence is no absolute guarantee against a claim, incompetence would by definition constitute a violation of a duty of care, if the incompetence were the proximate cause of a user's harm. Careful development of competence is not only good practice, but could be good insurance against a claim.

2.4 Controlling Resource Errors

While it is impossible to know whether every piece of information in a given collection is accurate and up to date, information professionals should still take a "due diligence" approach to caring for the resources they use. This approach can be pursued in a number of ways. As always, materials being added to the collection should be assessed for accuracy and authority. Out-of-date materials should be labeled as such, or perhaps removed from the collection.

To a certain extent, resource errors are impossible to avoid. Some information acquired by the institution may be wrong from its inception. Information can become out of date, or wrong, over time. Many libraries will continue to hold materials even after they are out of date, superseded, or replaced. All of these occurrences can lead to information in the collection that is, at least theoretically in error. The challenge, then, is in how the information is presented and used. The key concept would be to avoid implying in any way that the library is guaranteeing the quality of the information that a user may encounter.

2.5 Avoiding Service Errors

Avoiding service errors is largely a matter of training. Avoiding service errors requires both promoting and maintaining basic competence at information tasks and positing services and interactions so that a duty of care or reasonable reliance does not arise.

To that end, the following items should be emphasized to avoid service errors:

- ▶ Those responding to user questions should understand the resources being used, including their limitations.
- ▶ A careful reference interview should be done to fully understand the user's request. Follow-up questions and feedback should be sought as appropriate.
- ▶ Users should be made aware of limitations of resources, including such things as how often the source is updated.
- ▶ For major projects and important interactions, it would be advisable to set up system of reviewing or double checking work product before it is delivered to the user or customer.

2.5.1 Guarantees

While it may seem counter to some of our professional standards, librarians should always avoid making guarantees about their services. This includes not trying to guarantee having found the right information, or all the information, or guaranteeing that the information is necessarily correct, complete, or appropriate for the user's purpose. The purpose of this stance is to reinforce the simple fact that the librarian is acting in a consulting capacity, and that the users remain responsible for their information needs.

In many ways, and in spite of how "wrong" it may feel from a professional standpoint, refusing to make guarantees is only logical. Precisely because a librarian fills a consulting role, most of the things she might have the urge to guarantee are outside of her control. Thus, while a librarian might have provided the best possible information from the collection in a manner that seems to fully address the expressed information need, there is no way to actually know whether the information is adequate or appropriate, if it actually meets the user's real need, or how it will be used. The only guarantee that a librarian should ever give is to exert her best effort to find information that will meet the user's information need.

2.5.2 Avoiding the Promotion of Expertise

Expertise takes many forms. We know that librarians can and should promote themselves as experts in the task of finding information for users. The problem, which in many ways is a compliment to the profession, is that librarians are often seen by users as highly educated and capable of being an expert on the topics of user information needs, as well as experts on finding information. Some users see these two things as synonymous.

In some cases a librarian might have actual expertise in the topic of the information request. A librarian might have an advanced degree in a particular subject, or substantial personal or work experience. Sometimes simpler personal experience can feel like expertise. For example, someone who has been through a divorce might feel that the experience left her with expertise about that process. Similar to providing guarantees, librarians should not promote their own expertise on the topic of an information request. Once again, this is in order to retain the consultant role and further avoid reasonable reliance. Even if a librarian has expertise on a particular topic, to be present in the interaction as anything but an expert on finding information is to change roles in a substantial way.

There are two approaches that librarians should take in relation to their own expertise on a topic. The first is not to express their expertise in response to a user's request. This means that even if the librarian knows a direct answer to the user's request, she should still refer the user to a source that contains the information. She should also not hold herself out as an expert on the topic, regardless of whether or not she provides a direct answer.

The second approach to take is to proactively assert to the user the limitations of reference work and the necessity that they satisfy themselves about the adequacy and accuracy of the information they've been provided. This can be done simply and efficiently by making it a habit to say such things as "you should satisfy yourself that this is what you need."

3. SUGGESTIONS

Having considered general approaches to avoiding liability that apply to all branches of the information professions, we can now turn to specific ideas for librarians (including law and medical librarians), curators, archivists, and information brokers. These ideas come in four forms. First are suggestions that apply to each particular branch. These are laid out in this section, divided by branch of the profession. Second is suggested training, both for interaction with users and, as appropriate, other aspects of operations. These are provided in Chapter Eleven. Next are suggested policies for avoiding liability, provided in Chapter Twelve. Finally, Chapter 13 provides a sample basic liability audit for each branch of the profession.

3.1 Librarians

For librarians, the focus of liability prevention and control takes place in interactions with users, particularly reference interactions. Our suggestions here are intended to help reference librarians control possible liability by avoiding the creation of a standard of care, or reasonable reliance, in interactions with users. Please note that law and medical reference questions are dealt with separately in section 3.2.

Basic suggestions include:

- ► Present yourself as an expert on finding information, but not as an expert on any given topic.
- ► Always reaffirm users' responsibility for their own information needs.
- ► When providing answers to direct questions, always refer to the source you consulted for the information.
- ► Always remind users that there may be other information that will be useful to them.
- ► Where possible, provide users with an array of options for information. Let the users decide which source to use.
- ► Do not hold yourself out as an expert on a given topic. Do not relate personal experiences or provide an opinion about the user's situation.

3.2 Law and Medicine

The suggestions below apply not just to legal and medical librarians, but to any librarians who provide legal or medical information as part of their reference services. In all such situations, certain basic concepts should be mastered and followed.

▶ Do not hold yourself out as having knowledge or expertise on law or medicine.

▶ Always remind users that you cannot give legal advice or provide a medical opinion or diagnosis.

▶ Do not provide direct answers to medical or legal questions. Instead, provide users with sources they can use to explore the topic themselves.

▶ Avoid letting users give a lengthy explanation of their problem or condition. Refer them to materials as soon as appropriate ones can be ascertained.

▶ Do not relate personal experiences or opinions about the user's problem or condition.

▶ Refer the user to professionals as appropriate. You may wish to keep a list of local legal and medical referral agencies and services handy for this purpose.

3.3 Information Brokers

Information brokers are unique in the information professions in that they provide a service for a direct fee. This changes the liability landscape considerably, in both negative and positive ways. The negative aspect of performing a service for a fee is that it makes the possibility of liability much more realistic, both through tort and contract law. The positive aspect is that creative use of contracts in information broker transactions allows for considerable control over the risk of liability.

▶ Training and competence are paramount issues for information brokers, because there are clear cases in which a standard of care could exist. It is very important that an information broker's work performance not violate any such standard.

▶ Always use written agreements for any information service, even if the job is quick, minor, or for a regular client.

▶ Use the written agreement to define your standard of care, the limitations of your services, and the responsibility of the customers to satisfy themselves that their information need has been met.

▶ Keep information sources as up to date as possible.

▶ Always let customers know what sources you consulted and, if relevant, what sources you did not consult.

3.4 Archivists and Curators

Because archivists and curators are almost always employees of institutions, the possibility of personal liability for professional actions seems slight. The biggest risk is that of taking an action that is outside the scope of one authority. In such a situation, if the museum or archive were to disavow the action or decision, personal liability is possible. For this reason, most of the suggestions here relate to affirming the employee status of a curator or archivist, and making clear what positions have what authority.

► Have a clear job description which includes what authority you have to take action on behalf of the institution.
► Communicate with management as necessary in order to obtain permission for actions taken and for support of decisions.
► Carefully scrutinize gifts and bequests for conditions.
► When acquiring items, take care to explore provenance, title issues, and copyrights.
► Any loans to the institution should be covered by a written agreement that outlines the standard of care to be exercised in relation to borrowed items.

4. CONCLUSION

The suggestions in this chapter are only a starting point for controlling liability. The smartest thing that you can do is use the information in this book as a beginning point for consulting with your legal counsel about appropriate steps to take to limit liability for your professional activities.

►Eleven

TRAINING SUGGESTIONS

IN THIS CHAPTER

Training is a complex issue that involves time, expertise, and resources. It would be impossible to provide complete training ideas in a book like this. The best that we can do at this point is to suggest topics that should be covered in staff training to limit the possibility of liability. Here we provide such topics for each branch of the information professions.

1. LIBRARIANS

Training should focus on having staff understand the library's policies on interactions with users. This should include referring users to appropriate staff members, and using certain types of language when assisting users.

When dealing with information requests, certain ways of phrasing answers and other interactions can be very useful. Complete training would include such language. Examples of language to reduce potential liability follow:

1. Setting the tone for interactions:
   - ► "I am not an expert on this topic, but I can help you find information on it."
   - ► "I can show you what we have in our collection so that you can decide what you'd like to use."
   - ► "You know more about what you are looking for than I do, but here are some sources that might be useful."
2. Presenting results:
   - ► "Here is some information I was able to find. You should look it over to see if it is what you had in mind."
   - ► "You should satisfy yourself that this is what you need."
   - ► "This is what is in our collection, but I don't know if it will answer your question."
   - ► "There may be other information or sources that you will want to consult."

3. Terminating the interview:
   ▶ "I have given you what information that I can find. Please let me know if this does not turn out to be what you need."
   ▶ "I can't guarantee that this is everything you need, but I would be happy to do further searching for you if you feel that you need more."
   ▶ "You should satisfy yourself that this information is what you are looking for. If not, I would be happy to help you further."

2. LAW AND MEDICINE

Training for legal and medical questions should primarily focus on the need to avoid expressing a legal or medical opinion. Some suggestions for training topics include:

   ▶ Here, as much or more than anywhere else, it is important to restrict the librarian's role to that of finding information rather than having knowledge of the topic.
   ▶ Staff should be trained to point users to sources, but not provide direct answers to legal and medical questions.
   ▶ Staff should be trained not to allow users to tell too much about their personal situations.
   ▶ Staff should be trained to never express a personal opinion on the user's problem or situation, and to avoid claiming any legal or medical expertise.

3. INFORMATION BROKERS

Training for information brokers should, as mentioned, emphasize competence in searching and information work. This is to avoid the possibility of violating a duty of care in the event one exists. The rest of information broker training should emphasize business practices, including the use of written agreements for all transactions, and appropriate communication with customers. In addition, as a business, such habits as honesty, punctuality, and fair dealing should be emphasized.

4. ARCHIVISTS AND CURATORS

Training should assure that all staff understand such issues as copyright, privacy rights, loan issues, and other potential sources of liability for the institution. In addition, training should emphasize the lines of communication of authority within the institution so that all employees understand who can make what decisions, and who should be notified of particular problems or issues.

▶Twelve
POLICY SUGGESTIONS

IN THIS CHAPTER

Policies can help direct staff toward appropriate actions and away from inappropriate ones, and can also inform users and customers about what the institution can and can't do. While actual policies need to be specific to the institution, this chapter provides some suggestions for policies to consider.

1. LIBRARIANS

Policies can have many benefits when dealing with potential liability. Policies provide guidance to employees, both before and after the fact, and can be used to back up employee actions when users are dissatisfied. Policies can be reviewed by the institution's attorneys to be sure that they conform to appropriate state and local law. Although specific policies will vary, depending on local and institutional needs, some basic concepts should be included in policies relating to liability:

- ▶ Policies should emphasize that the proper role of a librarian is consultative, not fiduciary. Policies should emphasize that users remain responsible for their information needs.
- ▶ Reference policies should emphasize:
  - Relying on sources, not personal knowledge, in answering user questions
  - Showing users sources and allowing the user to search for answers
  - Not holding out as an expert on any topic
  - Reminding users of the need to verify if the information received is adequate for their needs
- ▶ Collection policies should provide for review and weeding of time-sensitive information and for confirming the appropriateness of materials being selected.

2. LAW AND MEDICINE

Every library that serves the public and has legal or medical information in its collection should have both staff and public policies on legal and medical reference service. Staff policies should be based on the suggestions above. Public policies should express to the public the limitations of legal or medical reference service, and make it clear that librarians cannot give legal or medical advice or render legal opinions or medical diagnoses.

Suggested internal policies:

▶ Collection policies should provide for keeping legal and medical materials as current as possible, and for labeling out-of-date materials as such if they remain in the collection.

▶ The library should develop a carefully thought out policy on responding to medical and legal questions. This policy should be:

• carefully communicated to library staff, along with or as part of training, and

• communicated to the public through signs, notices, Web pages, and wherever else appropriate.

▶ Lists of possible medical and legal referral sites should be maintained and offered to users.

An example of a public reference policy might look like one of these suggestions:

▶ Reference librarians may suggest sources where particular information or publications might be found in and outside of the library, and will explain how to use the catalog and other finding tools in the library. Reference assistance does not include giving legal advice or opinions, or providing interpretations of statutes, court decisions or other primary or secondary authority.

▶ Reference librarians can assist library users with finding and using legal sources. Reference librarians cannot act as attorneys or practice law. Reference librarians cannot interpret legal materials, suggest topics, define terms, or speculate about legal actions or strategies.

3. INFORMATION BROKERS

Policies for information brokering should include how to deal with customers, expectations for levels of performance and responsiveness, and policies for basic business operations. In addition, an information broker is strongly urged to use a written agreement for all transactions.

3.1 The Agreement Letter

One of the key techniques for controlling liability for information brokers involves the use of a written agreement for every transaction. This agreement forms a contract, the terms of which would govern in any dispute about the work done. This, in turn, allows the standard of care and other major issues to be decided by agreement.

You might think that using a written agreement would require that all of the parties gather for a formal signing ceremony before work can proceed. Nothing could be farther from the truth. The only requirement for an enforceable agreement is that both parties agree to its terms. Thus, an oral agreement can be enforceable. A written agreement can simply memorialize those terms. It does not need to be signed.

There are a number of basic elements to include in an agreement:

- ▶ Define the product, including when and how it will be delivered to the customer.
- ▶ Describe payment terms, including when payment is expected and in what form.
- ▶ Define the duty of care in providing the information.
- ▶ Define limitations of the services and the information.
- ▶ Address any warranties or guarantees.

In addition, an agreement might include any or all of the following, as appropriate:

- ▶ That the information is provided based on the description of the information need from the customer and is subject to the limitations of that description
- ▶ The limitations, if any, on your ability to find information in the area requested
- ▶ Potential limitations of the timeliness or completeness of the information provided
- ▶ The need for the customers to satisfy themselves as to the adequacy and usefulness of the information provided

In practice, working with a written agreement might be easier than you think. The first step is to draft a standard agreement to be used with all customers. It would be advisable to have the agreement reviewed by legal counsel. One the agreement is drafted and approved, it can be put to use. If there is time, it would be ideal to share the standard agreement with a potential customer prior to agreeing to do work for them. Similarly, if there is time, it would be preferable to sit down together and sign the agreement prior to beginning work.

If it is impractical to share the agreement in advance or to meet to sign it, it can still be used. When discussing a potential project with a client, you should make them aware that you have a standard agreement, and briefly describe the terms of that agreement. Make it clear that you will do the work only if they agree to the terms of the agreement. After such agreement is reached, you should supply them with a copy of the agreement, personalized with the details of the project, deadlines, and so forth, as a memo of the already agreed to terms. The document can be delivered in almost any form, from e-mail, to fax, to paper copy. When sending a memo version of the agreement, include language that indicates that this is your view of the agreement, and that they should contact you immediately if they disagree with any of the terms presented. Your legal counsel can advise you on how to best go about that process.

4. ARCHIVISTS AND CURATORS

For museums and archives, policies should be aimed at limiting potential liability through such things as:

- ▶ being careful about provenance and clear title for items being purchased or donated;
- ▶ carefully assessing the status and ownership of any copyrights on items in the collection;
- ▶ dealing carefully with conditions placed on donations, including refusing donations when conditions are too onerous;
- ▶ limiting liability for loaned items by only accepting loans under the terms of a written loan agreement;
- ▶ making sure that the museum has authority to deaccession any items it wants to dispose of;
- ▶ carefully assessing any private information in the collection, and avoiding use of the information that would lead to invasion of privacy or appropriation claims; and
- ▶ being aware of any potential right of publicity attached to items in the collection, and carefully accounting for those rights in the use and display of the items.

►Thirteen

LIABILITY AUDITS

IN THIS CHAPTER

A liability audit is a list of questions intended to identify any potential areas or issues in your work environment that raise the potential for liability. Once again, we are concerned here solely with issues of professional liability. Similar audits could be performed for such areas as premises liability and other tort issues, but they are beyond the scope of this book.

The audits presented here are by necessity incomplete. Should you wish to perform a liability audit, the questions below can serve as a starting point, but you should add to and modify them to fit your particular situation. You will want to consider particular aspects of your work environment in order to conduct the audit properly. You should consult appropriate legal counsel about any issues or questions raised by the audit, and you may wish to perform the audit in collaboration with your legal counsel.

1. LIBRARIANS

The audit below is divided into four areas: (1) general issues, (2) resources, (3) policies, and (4) training. As mentioned, this should serve only as a starting point for your examination of potential liability in your institution.

1. General issues
   a. Does the library have a relationship with legal counsel from whom advice can be sought?
   b. Are there procedures for communication between the staff and management about potential liability issues?
   c. Has the library, either on its own or with legal counsel, explored what laws in your jurisdiction might have an impact on potential professional liability issues? These can include laws on:
      i. Sovereign or statutory tort immunity
      ii. Confidentiality
      iii. Any laws or cases that create or imply the presence of a duty of care

2. Resources
   a. Does the library have procedures for dealing with errata and recalls issued by publishers?
   b. Does the library have a procedure for identifying out-of-date materials in the collection?
   c. Does the library have a policy about weeding out dated materials, or, if they are retained in the collection, marking them as out of date?
3. Policies
   a. Does the library have reference policies that set out appropriate behavior in reference interactions?
   b. Do your policies impress on all library staff not to:
      i. Become personally involved in a user's information need?
      ii. Express or imply subject matter expertise, as opposed to expertise on finding information?
      iii. Provide guarantees about any information supplied to users?
   c. Does the library have a policy that requires all staff members to consult with their supervisor or management about any incident or issue that raises the potential for liability?
   d. Does the library have policies that take into account any laws in your jurisdiction that create a duty of care or provide immunity?
4. Training
   a. Have all staff members been trained on all library policies concerning interactions with users?
   b. Have reference staff members been trained on avoiding a standard of care and reasonable reliance, including not making guarantees about information and not presenting as a subject expert on any topic?
   c. Have all staff members been trained in dealing with users?
   d. Have staff members been trained to consult with supervisors or management about any incident that raises a concern of liability?

2. LAW AND MEDICINE

In order to construct a law or medicine liability audit for your library, you will need to consider the particular aspects of your work environment, including the type of library and users, and the nature and extent of your legal or medical collection. You should consult appropriate legal counsel about any issues or questions raised by the audit, and you may wish to perform the audit in collaboration with your legal counsel.

The audit below is divided into four areas: (1) general issues, (2) resources, (3) policies, and (4) training. As mentioned, this should serve only as a starting point for your examination of potential liability in your institution.

1. General issues
   a. Does the library have a relationship with legal counsel from whom advice can be sought?
   b. Are there procedures for communication between the staff and management about potential liability issues?
   c. Has the library, either on its own or with legal counsel, explored what laws in your jurisdiction might have an impact on potential professional liability issues? These can include laws on:
      i. Sovereign or statutory tort immunity
      ii. Confidentiality
      iii. The definition of unauthorized practice of law or medicine within your jurisdiction
2. Resources
   a. Does the library have procedures for keeping medical and legal materials up to date?
   b. Does the library have a procedure for identifying out-of-date legal or medical materials in the collection?
   c. Does the library have a policy about weeding out dated materials, or, if they are retained in the collection, marking them as out of date?
3. Policies
   a. Does the library have reference policies that set out appropriate behavior in legal or medical reference interactions?
   b. Do your policies impress on all library staff members the need not to:
      i. Become personally involved in a user's information need?
      ii. Provide any kind of legal opinion or conclusion, or interpret any legal material for a user?
      iii. Provide direct answers to any legal or medical question, rather than providing resources for the user to explore themselves?
      iv. Provide guarantees about any information supplied to users?
   c. Does the library have a policy that requires all staff members to consult with their supervisor or management about any incident or issue that raises the potential for liability or unauthorized practice of law or medicine?
   d. Does the library have policies that take into account any laws in your jurisdiction about unauthorized practice of law or medicine, that create a duty of care, or that provide immunity?
4. Training
   a. Have all staff members been trained on all library policies concerning interactions with users?
   b. Have reference staff members been trained on handling legal or medical questions, including avoiding legal or medical opinions?

    c. Have all staff members been trained in dealing with users?

    d. Have staff members been trained to consult with supervisors or management about any incident that raises a concern of liability?

3. INFORMATION BROKERS

The audit below is divided into four areas: (1) general issues, (2) resources, (3) policies, and (4) training. As mentioned, this should serve only as a starting point for your examination of potential liability in your institution.

1. General issues
   a. Do you have a relationship with legal counsel from whom advice can be sought?
   b. If there are employees, are there procedures for communication between the staff and management about potential liability issues?
   c. Have you, either on your own or with legal counsel, explored what laws in your jurisdiction might have an impact on potential professional liability issues? These can include laws on:
      i. Particular laws governing contracts and business agreements
      ii. Confidentiality
      iii. The definition of negligent misrepresentation and other relevant tort law within your jurisdiction
2. Resources
   a. Do you have procedures for keeping resources up to date?
   b. Do you have the resources available to provide the sort of information your customers are requesting? This would include the ability to find in-depth or comprehensive information.
   c. Do you have procedures for making sure that all relevant resources are consulted in response to a request?
3. Policies
   a. Do you have an established work-flow policy for handling information requests? The policy should cover procedures for:
      i. Negotiating with customers and authority to agree to a project
      ii. Performing the research
      iii. Checking and verifying work product
      iv. Presenting work product to customers
      v. Handling unusual or problematic results, and for dealing subsequent changes in requests from customers
   b. Do you have policies for communicating with customers, including verifying and clarifying requests, and dealing with questions and complaints?
   c. Do you have a policy that requires a written agreement for each project?

4. Training
   a. Have all staff members been trained on all policies concerning interactions with users, including understanding who has authority to agree to projects?
   b. Have all personnel been trained adequately on searching and using resources?
   c. Have all staff members been trained in dealing with complaints, requested changes, and other potential problems?
   d. Have staff members been trained to consult with supervisors or management about any incident that raises a concern of liability?

4. ARCHIVISTS AND CURATORS

The audit below is divided into four areas: (1) general issues, (2) resources, (3) policies, and (4) training. As mentioned, this should serve only as a starting point for your examination of potential liability in your institution.

1. General issues
   a. Does the museum or archive have a relationship with legal counsel from whom advice can be sought?
   b. Are there procedures for communication between the staff and management about potential liability issues?
   c. Has the museum or archive, either on its own or with legal counsel, explored what laws in your jurisdiction might have an impact on potential professional liability issues? These can include laws on:
      i. Sovereign or statutory tort immunity
      ii. Confidentiality, privacy rights, and rights of publicity
      iii. Contract law that affects the terms of loaned items
2. Resources
   a. Does the museum or archive have procedures for dealing with complaints about displays or publication of materials?
   b. Does the museum or archive have a procedure for controlling access to the collection based on donor conditions?
   c. Does the museum or archive have a policy for accepting donations and making acquisitions?
3. Policies
   a. Does the museum or archive have clear-cut policies on who can make decisions about accepting donations, agreeing to acquisitions, and deciding on deaccessions?
   b. Does the museum or archive have clear job descriptions for all positions in the institution?

    c. Does the museum or archive have a policy that requires all staff members to consult with their supervisor or management about any incident or issue that raises the potential for liability?

    d. Does the museum or archive have policies that take into account any laws in your jurisdiction that create a duty of care or provide immunity?

4. Training

    a. Have all staff members been trained on all museum or archive policies concerning interactions with donors, sellers, and users?

    b. Have staff members been trained on procedures to be followed in identifying and dealing with items that may have conditions or restrictions?

    c. Have all staff members been trained in dealing with users of all types?

    d. Have staff members been trained to consult with supervisors or management about any incident that raises a concern of liability?

▶ Glossary

▶ **archivists:** Archivists establish and maintain control, both physical and intellectual, over records of enduring value. In doing so they collect, store, preserve, and disseminate archival records.

▶ **client:** A client is someone who engages the services of a professional. As used in this book, the term client implies someone who is paying a fee for information.

▶ **contract:** A contract is a legally binding agreement between two parties. In order to be valid, a contract must involve mutual agreement and an exchange of value. A contract need not be in writing in order to be valid.

▶ **contributory negligence:** An act done by the plaintiff or the person claiming harm that adds to, and becomes part of an act of negligence. Contributory negligence will often mitigate or negate the defendant's liability.

▶ **customer:** One who purchases a service or product. As used in this book, the term customer implies someone who is paying a fee for information.

▶ **deposition:** Out-of-court testimony of a witness given under oath as part of the pre-trial discovery process.

▶ **discovery:** Discovery is the pretrial process by which the parties in a lawsuit reveal the evidence they plan to submit to support their case. Discovery can include sharing documents, allowing the examination of physical objects, and the questioning of parties and witnesses either orally, in depositions, or in writing, through interrogatories.

▶ **duty of care:** A legal relationship that arises out of a standard of care, the violation of which exposes the actor to liability.

▶ **faulty information:** Information that, in the context in which it is used, is in error in some way, whether by being wrong, incomplete, out of context, or otherwise unsuited.

▶ **governmental immunity:** A government's immunity from being sued in its own courts without consent. Also called sovereign immunity.

▶ **immunity:** Exemption from a duty or liability. Immunity most commonly applies to the government, and allows it to refuse to be sued in its own courts.

▶ **inappropriate information:** Information that may be correct or timely, but is not useful or useable in the current situation.

▶ **incomplete information:** Information that lacks a critical element or fact. Incomplete information is insufficient for its intended use.

▶ **information brokers:** Information professionals who find and supply information for a fee.

▶ **information professions:** Those professions concerned with the finding, gathering, storing, and dissemination of information. In this book, the four major divisions represented are librarians, information brokers, museum curators, and archivists.

▶ **intentional misconduct:** A bad act that is entered into voluntarily and willfully. Whether or not the actor intended the results of the action, it is intentional misconduct if the actor knew the action was wrong and did it intentionally.

▶ **interrogatories:** Written questions submitted to an opposing party in a lawsuit, or to a witness in the suit. Interrogatories are part of the pre-trial discovery process.

▶ **joint and several liability:** Liability that can be apportioned to among two or more parties, or applied to just one or a select group of parties, at the discretion of the adverse party.

▶ **legal privilege:** A grant of legal freedom to do or not to do a given act. It immunizes conduct that, under ordinary circumstances, would subject the actor to liability.

▶ **liability:** The way that individuals can be held responsible by someone else or society for harm that they have caused.

▶ **librarians:** Those who organize, manage, and provide information to users of a particular institution or entity. Most commonly, librarians work in public or academic libraries, in schools, or in companies, firms, or other organizations.

▶ **malfeasance:** A wrongful or unlawful act. Malfeasance does not require that the actor intend to do the wrong thing, only that the action itself is wrong.

▶ **malpractice:** Negligence on the part of a professional. In malpractice, the standards of the profession involved determine the standard of care by which negligence is determined.

▶ **misfeasance:** Misfeasance is a lawful act performed in a wrongful manner.

▶ **museum curators:** Directors of the acquisition, storage, and exhibition of museum collections, including negotiating and authorizing the purchase, sale, exchange, or loan of items in the collections. They are also responsible for authenticating, evaluating, and categorizing the items in a collection.

▶ **negligence:** The failure to uphold a recognized standard of care. When negligence is the proximate cause of harm it can result in liability.

▶ **negligent misrepresentation:** A form of tort in which a supplier of information fails to meet a duty of care and supplies false or misleading information.

▶ **nonfeasance:** Failure to act when there is a recognized duty at law to do so.

▶ **out-of-date information:** Information that has been superseded or otherwise rendered inaccurate by the passage of time.

▶ **patron:** In this book, someone who uses a library.

▶ **private law:** Private law governs behavior between two private parties, as opposed to society at large. The most common forms of private law are contracts (legally enforceable agreements between private parties) and torts (individual liability to another for harm incurred because of a negligent act).

▶ **professional liability:** Liability that arises from the actions of a professional. Professional liability is incurred personally, as opposed to the liability of an employer for an employee's acts.

▶ **proximate cause:** An act or omission that is legally sufficient to result in liability for the actor.

▶ **public law:** Law that deals with interactions between individuals and the government or society. Public law constitutes the structure and function of government, the constitution, criminal law, and regulatory law of all kinds.

▶ **res ipsa loquitur:** Latin for "the thing speaks for itself." A legal doctrine that states, in some circumstances, the simple fact that harm occurred provides an inference of negligence.

▶ **respondeat superior:** Latin for "let the superior make answer." Legal doctrine that makes an employer liable for the wrongful actions of employees when those actions occur within the scope of employment.

▶ **scope of employment:** The range of foreseeable and reasonable activities that an employee can be expected to engage in while carrying out the employer's business.

▶ **statutory immunity:** Immunity from prosecution or liability granted by a specific statute.

▶ **strict liability:** Liability without fault. Strict liability is based on activities where an actor takes on an absolute duty to make something safe; if harm occurs, the actor will be liable regardless of negligence or intent to harm. Most commonly applied to ultrahazardous activities and products liability.

▶ **tort:** A tort is a civil wrong, other than a breach of contract, for which damages may be obtained as remedy. A tort involves the breach of a duty that one person has toward another.

▶ **tort claims act:** A statute that allows citizens to sue the government for harm incurred because of government actions, in spite of governmental immunity. Tort claims acts often provide relief for only limited forms of harm, and often have special requirements for pursuing a claim against the government.

▶ **user:** In this book, someone who uses the services of a library. Also often referred to as a patron.

▶ **vicarious liability:** Liability that a superior, such as an employer, has for the actions of a subordinate or associate, such as an employee, based on the relationship between the parties.

►Index

CASES

▶ Index

SUBJECT

►About the Author

Paul D. Healey serves as Senior Reference Librarian and Associate Professor of Library Administration at the Albert E. Jenner, Jr. Law Library at the University of Illinois Urbana-Champaign. Healey received his JD from the University of Iowa College of Law in 1987 and his Master of Arts in Library and Information Science from the University of Iowa School of Library and Information Science in 1995. In 2008 he earned a PhD in Library and Information Science from the University of Illinois Graduate School of Library and Information Science.

Healey has been an academic law librarian since 1995, prior to which he spent seven years practicing law. He has been on the law library faculty of the University of Illinois College of Law since 2000, where he performs reference duties and supervises and teaches the first-year legal research and advanced legal research courses at the law school. He also teaches courses at the University of Illinois Graduate School of Library and Information Science.

Healey is active in the American Association of Law Libraries and has been a featured speaker on librarian liability, pro se library users, and other legal- and library-related topics throughout the United States and Canada. He has written articles for the *National Law Journal*, *Law Library Journal*, and *AALL Spectrum*, among others.